ENDORSEMENTS

"Natalie Fuller is not only one of my nearest and dearest friends, she is a friend of God. She carries His heart beautifully in maturity and with humility and integrity. What you see before you now in this book is a word for this new era. It is dripping in revelation, impartation, divine wisdom and the love of God. It will challenge you, strengthen you, encourage you, build you, activate you and awaken you to what is available to you in this new era. This book is a heralding shofar from the heart of God calling you into position for such a time as this. It is time for you to arise and step into a fullness of your destiny and this book will be like a divine road map for you in many ways in helping you navigate this new era in the wisdom and vision of God. It's my incredible pleasure and honour to recommend my friend to you, Natalie Fuller."

Lana Vawser
Author of "The Prophetic Voice of God," and "I Hear the Lord Say 'New Era,'" Prophetic Voice to the Nations, Speaker, Lana Vawser ministries: lanavawser.com

"There are books being released from heaven right now that don't just reveal the season you are in and how to effectively walk it out, but books that awaken you to the very reason you are alive. They carry an anointing that sends shock waves to tired and weary hearts, revives forgotten assignments, and commissions the decommissioned. The book you are about to read is that very thing and if you position your heart to receive - it will shift you out of frustration and complacency and back into passionate conquest of your God-given destiny. You are in a unique moment of time, a window, or opportunity to partner with heaven to see everything God planned for you to do through your life come to fruition. Let the pages of this book rekindle the flame of intimacy, put a sword back in your hands, and turn on the ignition to your divine purpose!"

Nate Johnston
Co-founder of Everyday Revivalists
nateandchristy.co

"*Finding the sweet spot where ancient allegorical reading of Scripture meets contemporary prophetic declaration, Positioned for Purpose is a timely message for the Church. In her retelling of the story of Queen Esther, Natalie Fuller responds to that perennial question: What does it mean to be alive in Christ, seated in heavenly places and simultaneously seated in the discomfort, opposition and the grit of life on this earth? Avoiding the superficial 'to do lists' that seem to fill many modern answers to this question, this finely written work calls its readers to remember who they are already - already positioned, already with purpose in Christ. Calling us to partake of the daily rhythm of self-emptying and God-filling, Natalie reminds us of a God who calls us beyond the sidelines and away from slumber, passivity, fear and into the throbbing pace of life and activity in the Kingdom of God.*"

Cass Kwakye

BA (Ancient History), M Div, Grad Dip Min, Grad Cert Theology, Phd candidate. Lecturer in New Testament Studies and Spiritual Formation at Morling College, Sydney NSW

"*This book is rich! Within these pages you will discover the power of God's love released through Nat's journey and story. Nat's vulnerability invites you to discover the relationship with Jesus that you have been designed for. This book will change lives!*"

Matt Beckenham

Author of Eden's BluePrint, Three Trees, Three Floods
greaterthingsinternational.com

"*Recently, I reached out to Natalie for wisdom to understand the unusual spiritual conundrum I found myself in. She humbly and graciously forwarded me a draft of Positioned for Purpose which articulately outlined not just my own situation, but the state of the Church and the latter days that we are currently in. If you find yourself in the snowy steppe of Siberia where I am based, or on the hot drought stricken Australian plains, or anywhere in-between, you would do well to read these thoughtful, deep and prophetic Biblical insights. I guarantee that you will find yourself nodding along and well equipped with practical steps to indeed, position yourself for purpose.*"

Jo Kay

Jo serves with her husband Tim and five children as missionaries in the Siberian end of the earth with Operation Mobilisation om.org

POSITIONED FOR PURPOSE

NATALIE FULLER

POSITIONED FOR PURPOSE

A PROPHETIC INVITATION

TO PARTNER WITH GOD'S PURIFYING

PROCESS FOR THIS ESTHER ERA

© Copyright 2020 by Natalie Fuller

© Copyright 2024 by Natalie Fuller, Second Edition

Published by Mount of Olives Publishing.

mountofolivespublishing.com

All rights reserved. This book is protected by the copyright laws of Australia, Copyright Act 1968. Except as provided by the Copyright Act 1968, no part of this publication may be reproduced, communicated to the public without the prior written permission of the publisher. This book may not be copied or reprinted for commercial gain or profit. Permissions will be granted upon request for the use of short quotations or occasional page copying for personal use, group study or church use. Unless otherwise identified, Scripture quotations are taken from the Christian Standard Bible, Copyright © 2017 by Holman Bible Publishers. Scripture quotations marked CSB have been taken from the Christian Standard Bible®, Copyright © 2017 by Holman Bible Publishers. Used by permission. Christian Standard Bible® and CSB® are federally registered trademarks of Holman Bible Publishers. Scripture quotations marked (AMP) are taken from the Amplified Bible, Copyright © 1954, 1958, 1962, 1964, 1965, 1987 by The Lockman Foundation. Used by permission. Scripture quotations marked TPT are from The Passion Translation®. Copyright © 2017, 2018 by Passion & Fire Ministries, Inc. Used by permission. All rights reserved. Scripture quotations marked ESV are from The ESV® Bible (The Holy Bible, English Standard Version®), Copyright © 2001 by Crossway, a publishing ministry of Good News Publishers. Used by permission. All rights reserved. All emphasis within scripture quotations are the author's own. Spelling and grammar are written in and consistent with British English, in accordance with the Oxford Dictionary.

Cover and interior design by Gavin Fuller.

Reach us at nataliefuller.co and gavinfuller.com

ISBN: 978-0-6487576-0-3 (paper)

ISBN: 978-0-6487576-1-0 (ebook)

ISBN: 978-0-64875762-7 (audio)

DEDICATION

To my beautiful Jesus. You have chosen me, called me, empowered me, equipped me, encouraged me and positioned me for your purpose, for such a time as this. I give you this baby - this promise - and lay it on the alter. I give you all the glory. May your Kingdom come and your will be done, on earth as it is in heaven. I thank you and praise you for your overflowing love, your unending grace and your abundant power at work in my life, your Kingdom and this world. I am unbelievably excited for the future you have ahead and all you have in store for your righteous remnant and godly lovers who embrace your truth. Thank you for inviting me to partner with you in your great purpose.

May you take this humble gift and use it for your glory.
May you continue to purify and purge me; take me lower and lower as I lift you higher and higher...less of me and more of you.

I love you my great God!

ACKNOWLEDGMENTS

The biggest thank you to my husband, Gavin. I praise God for the gift of a life partner who not just believes in me and the call on my life but who purposefully creates time and space for me to do what God has called me to do. I am so blessed to have you and don't thank you enough. I love you more than you will ever realise. Thank you for all you have done to help me birth this book. You always have been an amazing midwife!

Thank you my beautiful children who I cherish so dearly - Hugo, Everly, Fleur, Ophelia and Sérephine. Although you don't fathom the impact of this now, I thank you for sacrificing and sharing your mother for the Kingdom and God's purpose. I pray that as you grow older and read these words that you enabled me to pen, that you would increase in purpose, purity and power to arise into each of your own God given identity, authority, assignments and destiny and that you would surrender all to lay your life down for Him alone. I cannot wait to witness what you and your generation achieve for the Kingdom and impart to the world around you as you grow up in these new wineskins and with the power and authority of Jesus Christ at work in your life. I love you all!

Special thanks to my beautiful friend, Lana. As iron sharpens iron, you have encouraged me for years to write and release, build and birth. We are going to see the glory and great miracles that we have been conversing about for years on end, over countless coffees!

CONTENTS

INTRODUCTION 5

REFORMATION & RESTORATION 9

NEW WINESKINS FOR THE NEW WINE 21

ENTERING THE ESTHER ERA 43

THE PROCESS OF PREPARATION 63

PRUNING, PURGING & PURIFYING 79

AN INVITATION TO PARTNER WITH THE KING 105

POSITIONED FOR PURPOSE 121

TESTING & TEMPTATION, REMEMBERING & REVERSING 139

ARISING IN IDENTITY & AUTHORITY 159

BREAKTHROUGH TO VICTORY 177

ALL FOR HIS GLORY 189

FOR SUCH A TIME AS THIS 203

INTRODUCTION

In 2019 I penned the words to the pages you are about to read. As 2020 drew near, I felt the urgency of this message to be released as soon as possible. Back then, I had no idea what was about to take place - how the entire world was about to be shaken and our individual lives tested and strengthened to determine what foundations we had built our lives upon - intimacy or idolatry, who our faith was in - God or government, who we would obey - Kingdom or culture. Little did I realise the Western Church was about to be turned upside down and tested for what it was really founded on - casual Christianity contaminated with mixture? The man-made traditions, systems and human teachings and doctrines of religion? Or the firm foundation of Jesus, the Spirit of God and the prevailing truth of His Word? 2020 was a year that we will all remember and it turned out it really was the beginning of the new era that the Spirit had been proclaiming through the prophets for so long.

Though I wanted to publish this book the traditional way, it was looking as though that could take at least 12+ months and the urgency deep inside me kept screaming louder and louder. Then the Spirit spoke to me to release it myself, but with very specific instructions - *"Make it accessible and affordable."* This was never about selling a book or promoting a product - it was about releasing the clarion call that swiftly needed to be heralded by the watchmen. The 'accessible' instruction led to publish this as an ebook so it could be easily accessed anywhere by anyone at any time all around the world, and the 'affordable' instruction led me to price it to simply cover costs of publishing.

Once we all collectively walked further into 2020 I suddenly understood the weightiness I discerned for having this book released well before March 2020, when everything changed for the entire world. Although I had a certain level of understanding of what the prophetic message in these pages carried, I in no way imagined that it would take place so quickly and in such an extreme way. Over the past four years, I have seen these pages play out in real life - far more pertinently, profoundly and powerfully than I could have ever fathomed.

Yet, the message that lays ahead on these pages here feels somehow more significant to the times we are in right now. As I sit here now in 2023, while I have been re-reading, revising, re-editing, re-polishing and releasing fresh revelation and powerful teaching to the original manuscript, I am reminded that although much of this book has already come to pass, I truly believe this is a prophetic message for this entire era, and we are going to see deeper revelations, deeper meanings and deeper understandings of what God has unveiled as we enter the next few months and years to come.

I have therefore re-released this book, in print, for such a time as this. While this is a second edition, I have kept the original prophetic message in its absolute purity, because this is the power of the prophetic! As I have edited over the past few months, I have elaborated on things I believe God is pressing His finger on in this moment, but the original message has remained pure. As you read ahead, you will be able to recognise things that have already taken place these past few years, but I believe we haven't seen anything yet. I believe we are at the precipice of another shaking that will see both the worldly systems and the Western Church establishment sifted, shifted and shaken, yet again. If we learnt anything from 2020 and the years that followed, my deepest

INTRODUCTION

prayer is that it has opened the eyes of God's people to see His truth, awoken us all to the web of lies and deceit we have lived in, increased discernment in us between good and evil, and given leaders and lay people alike the boldness to speak and proclaim God's Word, will, way and heart - no matter the cost - in the coming days. Anything built on *anything* other than Him will come toppling and crumbling down, while that which is built on the solid rock of Jesus Christ and His Word will not just remain secure, but will become the pillars of the sanctuary as He pours out His glory and reforms and restores His Church back to His original design.

> *"See that you do not refuse him who is speaking. For if they did not escape when they refused him who warned them on earth, much less will we escape if we reject him who warns from heaven. At that time his voice shook the earth, but now he has promised, "Yet once more I will shake not only the earth but also the heavens." This phrase, "Yet once more," indicates the removal of things that are shaken— that is, things that have been made - in order that the things that cannot be shaken may remain. Therefore let us be grateful for receiving a kingdom that cannot be shaken, and thus let us offer to God acceptable worship, with reverence and awe, for our God is a consuming fire."* **Hebrews 12:25-29 (ESV)**

So here it is again, *Positioned for Purpose - A Prophetic Invitation to Partner with God's Purifying Process for This Esther Era*. I pray these pages ahead bless you, encourage you, challenge you, equip, empower and strengthen you, but most of all purify you as He calls you to deeper consecration for the weighty glory ahead.

Buckle up brothers and sisters, we have been born for such a time as this!

Nat xxx

CHAPTER 1

REFORMATION & RESTORATION

My death was a beautiful thing.

I hated the process, but I loved the death itself, because that's where I found true life. The death of my flesh saw the life of His Spirit. The death of my will produced the life of His desires. The death of my ambition produced the life of His plans and purposes. The death of my personal empire produced the life of His Kingdom. The death of my ways produced the life of His righteousness. The death of my opinions produced the life of His truth. The death of my knowledge produced the life of revelation. The death of my image produced the life of identity. The death of my striving produced the life of His grace. The death of my strength produced the life of His empowerment. The death of my building produced the life of His foundations. The death of my complacency produced the life of His purpose. The death of my tolerance produced the life of holiness. The death of my life produced His life in abundance. True life.

Oh my glorious death! My beautiful, painful, marvelous, tormenting, amazing, horrendous, awe-inspiring, wondrous death! I love my death. At first

POSITIONED FOR PURPOSE

I fought it, I went down kicking and screaming, throwing punches and flailing, rebuking the enemy and warfare. But then I realised it was *Him*. Him who had led me into the wilderness, who had wooed me - His beloved Bride-to-be - into the dry and barren desert to be with Him alone, without the voices, the noise, the distraction, in order to strip me of everything I had ever striven to be. To shake me of any foundations that were not built on Him. To sift me of security in anything other than Him alone. To take my eyes off any idols in my heart that were taking His rightful place. To tear me away from protecting and preserving my own name, my own reputation, my own glory, my own accolades. To remove my identity from any roles, positions, achievements or accomplishments. To purify me of the mixture, complacency, apathy and tolerance within me. To empty me of myself so that He could truly make me His, once and for all. Then I just gave in and allowed myself to go with the flow of the beautiful deathly emptying. It was a life-giving surrender. The greatest part of my life so far has truly been my death, and my prayer is that He would continue to do His deep work within me, daily putting to death the things of this world and taking me deeper into humility, purity and maturity, in Him.

The purging was an ugly process - the things that I saw coming up and out of me disgusted me at first and tilted my eyes and heart towards condemnation, guilt and shame - a filter that the enemy had been sifting God's purifying convictions through for most of my life. But He took my chin firmly in His hand and positioned me flint faced toward Him and said *"Don't look at what's coming UP, focus on the fact that it is coming OUT. I am bringing it up and out so that it's exposed, unveiled and dealt with, once and for all. I am setting you free."* He got me to the end of myself so that I could truly be emptied and utterly surrendered. I climbed up on that alter and gave Him my ultimate offering, the sacrifice of all of my flesh. His purifying fire fell afresh and He poured Himself into me in a greater measure than I have ever encountered in my entire life.

Perhaps you too, have felt as though you have been taken through the wandering wilderness season of putting the flesh to death, in order to discover true life. The place where we are purged, purified, pruned and polished in the presence of our beautiful Jesus. A place where He holds a mirror up to our hearts and lives and we get to look with eagle eyes at what we really see reflected. This is not to condemn, but it is a holy calling to consecration. It's the journey of any true disciple into maturity, as we are initiated into the Kingdom, where our flesh cannot prevail and we cannot be led by our hearts or minds, nor influenced by culture or religion. It is an essential process that we cannot avoid, no matter how much we may try, we cannot evade the only way in, the only door through and the only entrance to the true Kingdom life.

You may have yet to walk through the fire, but please know this - it is not to consume you, it is to purify and transform you. The painful pruning is not to cut you off, it is to mature you and cause fruitfulness to multiply from your union life in Him. The dirty dross that will come forth will be ugly, unbearable, unfaceable, but it is to be purged from you and to cleanse you of all mixture, taint and defilement. The battle will not conquer you, but it will deepen, solidify and polish you. The warfare will not weaken you, but will strengthen you.

While in the wilderness, led in by the Spirit, the enemy will come and find you weak, open, vulnerable, exhausted, and just like He waited for Jesus Himself to get to that very point, so too will he sneak in and whisper his worldly words into your weary heart. At your weakest, the enemy will come and attempt to kill, steal and destroy. His goal is complete assassination of your call, purpose, assignment, mission and alliance. But what he doesn't realise is that death is a beautiful, life-giving gift. Oh the beauty and glory of His death on the cross! The enemy thought he had won but His death paid the price and His death defeated him once and for all! His death is where life began. His death was our life. I don't know why the enemy continues to kill. Surely he has learnt in the past 2000+ years that only the very best things burst forth from complete and utter death. Only when our man-made life falls to the ground as a seed can we finally die to ourselves, to our will, to our ways, to our flesh, to this carnal world, and burst forth - from death to life - born of the Spirit, born into and unto the Kingdom, transformed by the power of the cross, His blood and our great King's death and resurrection and multiply in fruitfulness for His glory and name!

> *"As you yield freely and fully to the dynamic life and power of the Holy Spirit, you will abandon the cravings of your self-life. For your self-life craves the things that offend the Holy Spirit and hinder him from living free within you! And the Holy Spirit's intense cravings hinder your old self-life from dominating you! So then, the two incompatible and conflicting forces within you are your self-life of the flesh and the new creation life of the Spirit. But when you are brought into the full freedom of the Spirit of grace, you will no longer be living under the domination of the law, but soaring above it!"*
>
> **Galatians 5:16-18 (TPT)**

INTRODUCING ESTHER

The story of Esther has been a favourite of mine since I was a child. Even as a teenage girl I remember being so enthralled by her story that I would write out the poignant scriptures and stick them on the back of my bedroom door, reading and praying over them for my life and future as I would get ready for school each morning. As a grown woman I'm still inspired by the ravishing, courageous, bold queen. It's safe to say I've read the book of Esther countless times throughout my life and I have been immensely impacted by it every single time.

But in 2018 I had an even deeper encounter as I read through the ten chapters in what felt like a revolutionary way. A story I was so familiar with, so in love with, so touched by throughout my life was set on fire as the Spirit unveiled my eyes and mind to perceive with a deeper level of revelation the ancient truths that have always been contained within, but with a prophetic invitation for the era we were about to enter. Over the course of the next few hours I sat on my bed scribbling down words and thoughts into an old exercise book so fast that my hand couldn't keep up with the outpouring of the Spirit's flow within me.

I love how timeless the Scriptures are and how perfectly God uses the exact same words that we have held preciously bound in our brown leather bundles for thousands of years to speak to us afresh and anew every single time, again and again - the same meal, but fresh manner, the same meat, but fresh revelation. I encourage you to read the book of Esther in its entirety before you move on to Chapter One. It's not essential, but I believe it will enable you to hear what He is speaking a little bit louder if you familiarise (or re-familiarise, no matter how many times you've read it before) yourself with the Word.

What lays ahead on these pages is what I believe the Holy Spirit is doing in the Body, the Western Church, the Kingdom, the remnant, right now - this moment, this hour, this season, this era. A classic favourite story with a prominent message that has been pertinent throughout the ages, but as of now, I believe we have entered an era where Esther's and Mordecai's will arise and reform the Western Church back to its original design; the ancient way. The Four Winds are stirring as He gathers His devoted and devout sons and daughters who have said yes to the call, His remnant who have remained pure in a time of compromise with culture, who have been crying out in anticipation and expectation for so long, *"Whatever the cost Jesus, I just want you!"* Those of us who know that there is so much more ahead, that our stories are not finished yet, in fact, life has barely even begun. We have each been placed on this earth for His purpose and we are finding that our daily grind is increasingly grinding up against the healthy and holy discontent and desperation of the hungry cry, *"Maranatha - Come, Jesus, Come!"*

Assignments and alignments are breaking forth around us, His glory is coming upon His surrendered and emptied vessels for His very plans and purposes. We may look around in discouragement at the state of the world, the evil at hand, the desolation of our society, the future for our children…yet He has us perfectly positioned for His Spirit to pour out in greater measure, for His power to come upon us in deeper levels and for His new wine to flow from the throne room of heaven into vessels that have been emptied of themselves, abandoned of all human-made pursuit, agenda, people-pleasing, man-fearing, conformity, complacency, religion, tradition, and who are completely and utterly yielded in full to whatever His will is, however that happens, and whatever that looks like.

POSITIONED FOR PURPOSE

HE HAS SAVED THE BEST FOR LAST

Just like the wedding at Cana, He saves His best wine for last. He is pouring Himself out right now on an end time generation that is being purified, prepared and positioned. He is coming back for a pure and spotless Bride, without wrinkle or blemish. A Bride who has obeyed and surrendered to Him and made herself ready through His provision of grace, mercy and consuming fire. He is coming back for a mature and united Church, and though the days ahead will be full of persecution, tribulation and evil, His people will prevail through protection, provision and ascension, abiding in His presence. His righteous ones will overcome and will be established forever as the pillars of the sanctuary.

As the future of the fading world grows grimmer, the brightness of His glory shines brighter. As the days become more desolate with destruction and despair sweeping the headlines and news feeds, His light is shining brighter and His name is being elevated higher. As our world erupts in hate and violence, acts of terror and tragedies, wars and weaponised attacks against all people, His power is flowing profusely. As torment, trauma, disease and death increase around us, His healing, power and miracles are rising through us. The great harvest that Jesus speaks of is upon us and He is ready to send His people - purged, pruned, purified, polished and prepared in purity, maturity, humility and unity - into the harvest field to shine His light as a city on the hill. The darker the night around us, the brighter His light shines from within us. The more obvious the only answer is as its illumination pierces the darkest of ages, leading the way forth to salvation, freedom, wisdom, healing, fulfilment, wholeness and into the most intimate relationship with the Creator of the heavens and the earth.

You, my friend, have the call of your Creator on your life. He has a divine plan and purpose and is inviting you on assignment to co-labour in His Kingdom cause. The battle has not been for nothing, the battle has been over this very moment of your eternal assignment coming to light and coming to pass. All hell trembles at the potential of you embracing your identity as a son or daughter of the Most High - equipped and empowered by His Spirit, strengthened and encouraged by His great love for you overflowing onto all around, arising and walking in the victory and triumph that was claimed on the cross, stepping into His power and authority in the name of Jesus Christ, being clothed in righteousness and taking hold of the heavenly inheritance that is rightfully yours through the blood of the Lamb. The battle has not been for nothing. What a gloriously blinding dawn is arising upon us as the sun sets once and for all, on all we have ever known.

We as the Ekklesia - His called out, governing assembly here on earth, who bear His name and image - have entered a new era of His glory, power, plans and purposes like never before. This is not a season that will come and go, this is an era that will be established and continue into eternity as He eventually makes everything new, the heavens and the earth. He is aligning His people into their divine positions to release His will to every area of this world. He is taking back the high places of society, the mountain tops of prominence and dominance that have been tightly held in the hands of the enemy for far too long now. He is reforming the Western Church who have given way to culture, mixture and tolerated the very things He despises. He is dismantling the institution that has attempted to intellectualise His Word and His ways. He is emptying the establishment that has turned His temple into a den of thieves that behaves more as a commercial marketplace than a sanctuary of the Holy One. He is exposing the worldliness and compromise of hearts and lives of leaders and lay people who look more like the culture around them than the consecrated call that awaits within them. He is sinking the ships of entertainment and performance that has turned our alters into stages and our pulpits into platforms.

He is reforming His Church and leading her back to her original call and mandate. He is commissioning and permissioning His purified people to rebuild the ancient ruins, to raise up the former devastations, to repair the ruined cities of many generations. He is calling His consecrated to repair the breaches, to raise up the broken walls and fortifications, to lead the Church back to the ancient path that we have strayed so far from over the centuries and millenniums. He is calling us back from the boardrooms to the living rooms, from the board table to the dining table, from religion and man made tradition to His perfect design of family. He is drawing us together again to remember and reinstate the days of

Acts and the commission of the early Church. But more than that, He is taking us back to the mandate of Eden and placing His people in the seven spheres of influence throughout society so the darkness will no longer prevail but His people will govern in His authority and power like never before.

These pages pose an invitation for you to position yourself to partner with the God of the heavens and earth to see His divine destiny for His Kingdom in this world be made manifest. And you can be a key catalyst in your sphere of influence and your realm of measure that He has called you to. You have an invitation to be a strategic tool that He has a powerful purpose for in His perfect plans.

You are being divinely wooed right now to join Him in one of the greatest moments of the history of the world and Kingdom, since the cross, resurrection, Pentecost and establishment of His Ekklesia. Whatever your circumstances, whatever your past, whatever your age, limitations, failings, weaknesses, fears, whatever you don't have, haven't been, or just simply 'are not' - you are perfectly positioned for His powerful purpose and plans, *for such a time as this*.

BACK TO THE BEGINNING

Your story is far greater than simply your own life, and begins much further from even your point of conception, when life was first breathed into your very soul. Your story both begins and ends in the exact same place...His heart. Your destiny was determined before time began, your call curated before creation itself, your purpose planned from the beginning of time, your name written in the Book of Life before the foundation of the earth. You are loved, you are chosen, you are called and you are invited into a divine opportunity to partner with the Creator of the heavens and earth to see His will, His Kingdom and His plans fulfilled in this world. You are intimately and uniquely part of His perfect purpose. Your story is wrapped up in His story, and the story of all humanity and His people - past, present and future. His story is timeless and eternal, and your story - embedded and entwined in His heart - finds its birth at the very beginning of time.

If there is one basic purpose that we are called to as human beings - as

God's creation, as His sons and daughters, it is to find our fulfilment in Him, for Him and through Him. To love Him, live for Him, worship Him and glorify Him. That is our ultimate goal, ultimate purpose, ultimate act of sacrifice, love and worship. But how does that look in the every day? How does it differentiate between my life and yours? How do I know what I'm called to do and you know what you're called to do? How do we each individually and uniquely live out the assignments of God upon our life in a way that inter-threads together in intricate unity with the rest of the Body of Christ, while giving glory to God and displaying His love and truth to the world around us?

To understand the ultimate call of humanity and His Body here on earth, we have to go back to the very first mandate He gave us. It is so important to note that this mandate was commissioned to us before the fall - before sin entered our realm, before we fell short. This call was given to us within the context of His perfect design, His perfect world, His perfect creation, His perfect relationship with humanity, with nothing separating us from His presence. He gave mankind this command and commission in the context of His own perfection. *"It is very good"* He said of all that He had made (Gen 1:31). Though sin entered the world through our choices, Jesus rectified, reinstated, restored and redeemed that perfection, wholeness, intimacy and relationship when He died on the cross and rose again (Col 1:20-22). Every curse reversed, every chain broken, every part of us healed, every sin forgiven (Col 2:13-15), and if we choose to respond to His Spirit inviting us to a life of union with Him, we can step into Eden restored, amidst the chaos, darkness, pain, death, evil that still prevails from that one broken moment.

So now we stand this side of the cross and He is still calling us and commissioning us with that same initial commandment:

> *"Be fruitful, multiply, and fill the earth, and subjugate it [putting it under your power]; and rule over (dominate) everything that moves upon the earth"* **Genesis 1:28 (AMP)**

This is so much more than reproducing and populating the earth with people. This is about living a life in accordance to our God-given design - made in His imago

Dei, as creators, artisans, inventors, engineers, strategists and so much more. His original mandate to govern, rule and reign over His creation, to take charge and bring it under control, to be responsible for it and steward it, to cultivate it and create culture, to subdue the chaos outside of the garden, to take dominion and authority over it, to permeate every place with His transformative power, love and presence…is strikingly similar to His very commission He left us with before He ascended.

> *"And Jesus came and said to them, "All authority in heaven and on earth has been given to Me. Go therefore and make disciples of all nations, baptising them in the name of the Father and of the Son and of the Holy Spirit, teaching them to observe all that I have commanded you. And behold, I am with you always, to the end of the age.""*
> **Matthew 28:18-20 (ESV)**

He is a creator and we are called to create. We are called to be fruitful, not barren, to produce, not consume, to multiply, not decline, to mature, not regress, to be fruitful, not fruitless. We were given authority and dominion over creation to reign and rule and take ground for the Kingdom, and Jesus took back the very keys and taught us how to open and close, bind and loose, lock and release and then imparted His Spirit to empower us to do not just the things He did, *but even greater* (John 14:12-14). We as God's people are called to bring heaven to earth - to fill, cultivate, permeate, beautify, transform and bring into alignment all that is out of alignment (under the enemy's dominion - he is the prince of the powers of the air) in all the earth. We are called - no, commanded - to fill the earth, not segregate ourselves from it, to subdue it, not control it, to reign over it, not allow it to rule over us, to cultivate it, not destroy it, to create, not copy, to thrive, not survive.

Your call and assignment is wrapped up in this mandate in some way, shape or form. You have been given a measure and designed with unique gifts, skills, talents and tendencies to create and produce something of significant value and worth to this world and to the Kingdom, to those around you that reflect the image of God, the heart of the Father, the mind of Christ, the inspiration of the Holy Spirit, for His glory. You already possess within you everything you need to see this come to pass in your life. You have every heavenly resource and more importantly, you have the supernatural gateway to creativity within your very being - the Holy Spirit.

You may think, *'But I'm not a creative person.'* Well, let me first say, yes - yes you are - because you are created in His image and He is creative. We don't necessarily need to correlate creative with artistic, although I do believe there are many forms of artistry, yet we tend to limit our thinking of artistic towards fine arts like painting, drawing, photography, film, craftsmanship, music, dance etc. Creativity simply means to create - to produce something from nothing. That's what God is commanding and commissioning us to do. To create something from what He has already given us, to multiply what He has already put in our hands, to take what is already here and turn it into something greater. To go out of the Garden and subdue the chaos that surrounds us in the world around us. The way we do that is uniquely in accordance to our individual talents, skills, gifts and anointing but the overall implication of what God spoke to humanity in the Garden and to the dawning of the Church remains the same today as it did back then: Go forth and subdue - take authority over what is chaotic and reckless, take control over what has control over you, reign over what is reigning over you, take your position of authority over what currently has authority over you.

The very essence of the prophetic is to call into existence that which is not yet - to call forth and declare the will of God, *until* we see it form and manifest in our life and world -on earth, as it is in heaven. Subdue your life, your circumstances, your world, take authority and lead and reign in life and as you do, teach others to do the same! This is our journey from fatherless orphans of the world, to mature sons and daughters of faith, who know their identity and authority in Christ, and with deep purity and humility, lead, empower and equip others to do the same, through the power of the Holy Spirit. True, Kingdom discipleship!

CHAPTER 2

NEW WINESKINS FOR THE NEW WINE

Thousands of years later this very world is crying out for a people to rise up and take their position as the creative and productive children of God that we are called to be. This world is crying out for answers, for strategies, for anecdotes, for solutions, for pure entertainment, sources of joy, for examples of what it looks like to live with a flourishing family and a healthy, strong, impenetrable marriage - a model and example on display of God's very design and purpose for how this life was originally designed to live. When all else fails, go back to the manufacturers manual, right? I don't know if you've noticed lately, but we have more than just dwindled from this original design. As much as this world thinks it's embracing a future evolution, the pits of the hearts of people are simply yearning for answers, deeper meaning and more substantial significance.

It's just like the way little children behave - kids desperately desire boundaries to feel safe and secure. Without them they run wild, thinking they have freedom, but their 'freedom' is actually costing them the very thing their hearts desire. Love. Safety. Security. Acceptance. Unconditional love. Knowing they are loved, knowing they have a purpose and a place. Knowing there is something greater, bigger, superior, someone watching over them, looking after them, looking out for them. That they are protected under the wings of a mother hen and a father eagle. Accepted for who they are, not what they do or don't do, because who they truly are is purposefully designed, desired, wanted and longed for. God makes no mistakes and there is no one too far gone, too broken, too lost that He would not leave the 99 for and run after with all passion and burning desire to see set free from the grips of this world.

But it doesn't stop there. While the evil of this world is growing darker by the day and deceiving even those of God's people who are choosing to partner with the enemy's plans by tolerating and sometimes even proclaiming a tainted and dangerously diminished version of the love of Jesus - the Spirit of Truth floods in to remind us that true love transforms us. God's love speaks to our true identity - in Him, in His perfect design, according to His original creation - not in whoever we think we are or whatever we want to be or whatever makes us 'feel good.' Jesus' love chases after us in the deepest places of darkness, sin, evil, injustice, brokenness, abuse, trauma - yet even amidst the most painful and horrendous of circumstances, an undeniable, experiential encounter with His true love can cause us to repent and realign with His holiness. The Holy Spirit convicts us in love and strengthens us with His grace that empowers us to transform. The 'inclusive' and 'tolerant' love and grace that the worldly church has been preaching from the pulpits is an abuse and abomination to the true love of Jesus that possesses the power to transform anyone, anyhow, any way, anywhere.

A SET APART GENERATION

Not all love is love. True love transforms. Grace is not permission to continue living our less-than holy lifestyles, grace is the very empowerment to transform. We cannot do it ourselves! Not in our frail, human, fleshly weakness. Grace is what enables us to change, grace is God's mercy upon us to strengthen us and equip us supernaturally with what we need to repent. Grace is His power at work within us, transforming us and leading us on His path of righteousness as we renounce our old, worldly lives, habits, lifestyles, addictions, deeds, desires, passions and pursuits. No one is too far from His powerful love and no one is too broken that He cannot heal and make completely new and whole. The true love of Jesus reveals to this broken world that only in Him and through Him can we discover our true identity and be set free, delivered and released from every stronghold and then walk into abundant life, in Him.

However, a lost, confused and led astray generation cannot be taught identity from orphaned leadership. We cannot teach what we have not obtained through personal revelation, and we can not deliver others from that which we have not yet been set free from, in personal transformation. In this time, God is establishing true mothers and fathers who are arising into God anointed and appointed positions - those who already know and walk in their own sonship and daughterhood, who live in and from the Father's love and who will spiritually adopt sons and daughters of this generation and father and mother them into identity and maturity. Identity can only be released from those who already walk in their own Fathered inheritance.

When we encounter the true love of Jesus - not a watered down, powerless, lukewarm, tolerant, tainted, mixed version that is flowing from many pulpits, platforms and pastors today - we encounter the God who powerfully transforms every single part of our brokenness into His redeemed and renewed perfection that He purchased for us on the cross. The world (and the worldly church) pushes the concept of God further and further away thinking they can be 'friends' with the authority that rules this earthly realm. Yet just as a child instinctively yearns for the very boundaries they are testing, rejecting and so fiercely pushing against, so too do the lost and wandering ones deep down desire a Father to come along, embrace them in their fear, pain, confusion, questioning, loneliness, seeking for more, searching for significance and show them the way to really live. For Him to bring them back to their original design - to re-define (not 'redefine', but *re*-define by *reminding* us of the original definition) who they are, who they are created to be, whose they are and whose image they are created in. We all long to be truly free - but real freedom means the absolute permission to be our true selves, and the core of our true selves lies in the heart of our Creator, not our carnal flesh or the tainted version this world tries to offer.

If we are created, then the Creator knows how to best live this life - to not just survive and get through, but to thrive, reign and overcome. Boundaries don't restrict us, they actually release us into deeper freedom. Freedom means that we are no longer a slave to anything or anyone, including ourselves and our own desires. Nothing has a hold of us, nothing can control us, nothing masters us, but our one and only Master. Boundaries show us the designated place and space for which we are designed to live in, and when we live within the design of the Designer, we are going to thrive at our absolute potential. If I engineer a new invention and someone takes it and tries to use it outside of the context it was created to be used in, it may work to an extent, but it is never going to work as well as when it is used for what it is specifically designed for, and within the realms of what it is designed to do. Our concept of freedom in this world has become so skewed that it's led us into captivity - pure evil even - where we're chained in bondage and we can't even see the control that we are enslaved to, yet we label it as freedom.

The spirit of the world has slowly and subliminally crept into our western churches and without realising, the culture of the world has become the culture of many congregations and communities that are called to be consecrated and set apart for a holy cause. Instead, we have slithered into bed with the seductress and are sleeping with the enemy…all in the name of acceptance, inclusivity, tolerance, grace and 'love.' Yes, Jesus absolutely hung out with the worst sinners of all, yes, Jesus left the religious circles to go and be with the rejected, lonely, ostracised, banished, foreigners and forgotten. But He certainly didn't partake in their lifestyles or give them permission to continue. He set the standard higher and called them up to Him. In fact, just His very presence and the manifestation of His holiness caused even the most lost and defiled of them to repent and set a new course of direction for their life. He called out the woman at the well's sin - He named it for what it was - yet she didn't run off crying in offence, labelling it as hate speech - she ran off transformed, evangelising her entire town, not simply because Jesus called out her dark lifestyle, her sinful ways and her many mistakes, but because He called her to something greater, something she was deeply seeking, something she was longing for, a water that would quench the thirst that her parched soul was craving, and He gave her the ability to be able to do it. She was transformed.

The worldly church love to justify their 'love' and acceptance by pointing the finger at the consecrated sons and daughters of God who take His Word at its very word and obey His statutes and commands by labeling them religious and legalistic. Yes, Jesus reclined at the table of tax collectors and sinners instead of the Pharisaical hypocrites of the established, man made religious system. And we are called to do the same and to live by mercy and grace, just as He exemplified. Yet Jesus' very words in Matthew 9:12 was that He came as a great Physician to the sick, not the healthy. A physician heals. A physician restores. A physician makes whole again. A physician doesn't leave a patient sick or with brokenness or foreign disease. Jesus heals. He restores to wholeness, fullness and He turns entire lives around.

The Apostle Paul also had no reservations calling out the blatant and intolerable lifestyles and practices of those in the early Church who were living like the rest of the pagan culture around them, instead of the pure and set apart holy believers they were supposed to be. I fear we have become so easily offended, so quick to call conviction condemnation, so afraid to speak the truth of Scripture in case people feel shamed, worried we'll be hated by the world (newsflash…the Word tells us this is exactly what we will be if we are true disciples of Jesus), so seeker friendly, so set out to prepare perfect performances, so on par with the entertainment of this world, so polished on our platforms….that we have simply re-created the exact same arenas of the world within our sanctuaries. And we call it church. This, my friends, is not the Church. This is mixture. This is worldliness. This is desecration of the temple of God - not the buildings we go to, but of our very own hearts within us that house His presence and host His Spirit.

WHO ARE WE IN COVENANT WITH?

When we are sleeping with the enemy amongst the silky, sensual sheets of tolerance, acceptance and mixture, we are consummating a covenant. Read that again. Consummation is the most intimate, closest, encounter we can have in a relationship. Consummation is the uniting together of two to become one and is the agreed upon partnership, in covenant. It's as strong and secure as signing your signature at the bottom of a contract. The very word consummate means 'to complete.' Once you have consummated a relationship, you are bound to the confides of that contract. You are yoked to the other person in the partnership. You are one, in God's eyes.

The thing about covenant is that there are two sides to the promises. God promises to uphold His side of the covenant, and He is faithful. It is impossible for Him to break His promise and impossible for Him to not fulfil His Word. But if we - His people, who are supposed to be in covenant relationship with Him - are breaking our side of the covenant and walking back into lifestyles of partnership with the world and with the enemy's way - we are committing spiritual adultery and we have made that covenant null and void. His promises still remain, He is still faithful, but we have taken that marriage certificate and ripped it in two, tearing it to smithereens. We read over and over again of hundreds of years worth of the Israelites breaking their beautiful covenant with Yahweh by committing the same spiritual adultery, whoredom and idolatry and we think to ourselves *'How can they do that? Look at all God did for them, how can they possibly turn from Him and take on foreign wives and worship foreign god's?'*

Yet nothing has changed to this very day! All it takes is one little compromise and then slowly but surely those foreign wives we have opened doors to and partnered with, bring in their foreign gods and set them up in our hearts, one little idol at a time, one room at a time, one compromise at a time. Then we reproduce these compromises and bear fruit that is not pure, but a hybrid of mixture. These seeds grow up in mixture, tolerate the mixture, embrace the mixture, then celebrate the mixture. Then our diluted and polluted offspring marry other compromised and tolerant children and our grandchildren become a full blown generation who have completely abandoned and forgotten the very ways of holiness and consecration that we once held so close to our hearts.

I'm obviously not talking about physical people, physical marriages, physical spawn or physical families here (although...take note, because that's exactly how it works). But this is what we do spiritually, in our hearts, in our minds, in our homes, in our conversations, in our thoughts, in our actions, in our habits, in our behaviours, in our practices, in our lifestyles. One minute we're on fervent fire for God in purity and passion, yet the next minute (or so it feels), we realise we have slid so severely down the slippery slope of compromise that we have given birth to generations of godlessness and fruit of worldliness in our life. All because of that one little moment of idolatry and spiritual adultery.

But Nat, we aren't under Old Covenant law anymore, we are free from the legalistic letter and regulation and we are in the Covenant of Grace.' Yes. And it's that very covenant, that very grace that empowers us to live set apart, holy lives, consecrated for His glory! The beauty of the Covenant of Grace is that we don't have to be stoned to death as in the days of old, punished for even the slightest slip up (which, mind you, is all about purity and purging the mixture and compromise because a little yeast permeates the entire dough), but we have every invitation and opportunity to come back to Him, repent of our mixed lifestyles and be transformed by the very grace that we have so dangerously abused.

It's time to come back into covenant with our Creator and to consecrate ourselves afresh. Take no part in evil deeds, but expose them and set all those FREE who we have led astray in our teaching, pastoring, leading, influence, and tolerance, so we can truly be the Church that this broken, dying, lost, hurting world so desperately needs. So we can be the Church that extends the true love of Jesus that embraces, encounters and transforms. So that we can be the Church that overflows with the unconditional love of the Father that reveals our true identity and perfect design *in Him*. So that we can be the Church that empowers all with the transformative presence, grace, strength and power of the Holy Spirit.

That is the Church of Jesus Christ!

> *"Take no part in the unfruitful works of darkness, but instead expose them. For it is shameful even to speak of the things that they do in secret. But when anything is exposed by the light, it becomes visible, for anything that becomes visible is light. Therefore it says, "Awake, O sleeper, and arise from the dead, and Christ will shine on you." Look*

> *carefully then how you walk, not as unwise but as wise, making the best use of the time, because the days are evil."* **Ephesians 5:11-16 (ESV)**

EXPOSING AND EXCOMMUNICATING THE SPIRIT OF RELIGION

But there is a flip side to the worldly church too. Another extreme where the pendulum has swung way too far and love has been abused at the other end of the scale. Unfortunately, the Church - we who are meant to represent the holy God here on earth, in this world - by and large, hasn't exactly done the greatest job of the very thing that God is...love. In fact, in certain times and places, we've probably done more damage than good, more harm than care, more bashing than comforting, more turning away than turning to, more rejecting than accepting, more finger-pointing than self-reflecting, more creating of conditions than unconditional love. This is because of a power at work in the spiritual realm. This principality has influence, deep within a lot of the Western Church today - the spirit of religion.

The spirit of religion takes a truth and twists it by a millimetre. It takes the Word of God and changes it by a single letter. It takes the gospel and sets it off by one degree. It takes a promise and tweaks it by a fraction. It has a white washed exterior that looks beautiful, clean and pure to all around us, but it is filthy and decaying on the inside. It appears virtuous but is riddled with deceit and impurities. The spirit of religion dresses itself up in elegant apparel but is really clothed with dirty rags. The spirit of religion sounds wise but is foolish, sounds like truth but is a liar. The spirit of religion has the form of a sheep but is a devouring wolf, presents itself like an innocent dove but is a cunning snake. The spirit of religion takes grace and turns it into works. It takes love and turns it into conditions. It takes surrender and turns it into striving. It takes gifts and turns them into earning. It takes devotion and turns it into duty, takes pure conviction and turns it into guilt and shame.

The spirit of religion was fiercely at work within the Pharisees, Sadducees, scribes and scholars throughout the ministry of Jesus and the establishment of the early Church. Jesus was faced with it and confronted it everywhere He went.

Paul and the apostles who built the early church were persecuted not by the world around them, but by the religious of their day. Sadly the spirit of religion has continued to grow for the past 2000+ years as it has gradually been feeding on its followers and has slowly but surely devoured much of the Body of Christ in the western world. It now speaks louder to this world on behalf of God and the Church than His true, beautiful Bride. The world looks at the concept of God and the portrayal of Christianity and the picture of the Church, but what it predominantly sees and experiences is only the work of the spirit of religion. It causes God's people to be silent and to fear what others will think or say. It causes His people to remain stagnant for fear of being different or going against the grain of what has always been done. It causes the people of God to go against the very things that He is doing because it is different, unusual, unexpected or never been done before (in their lifetime, at least). It causes His people to point fingers at one another telling them each that they are wrong, instead of embracing the truths that they collectively share.

Most dangerously, it dictates that the power of God is no longer at work today, that the Father does not speak to His beloved children, that the Holy Spirit no longer heals, delivers, sets free or works mighty miracles, signs and wonders. The doctrine that the gifts, the supernatural, the five-fold offices and the voice of God has ceased is one of its greatest feats yet. Imagine a Church - commissioned by Jesus Himself to go and do greater things than He ever did, to be empowered by the fire of the Holy Spirit with the grace and strength of heaven itself to do through them, what in our own humanity we cannot ever do, to have every gift and heavenly resource needed bestowed upon us in order to build God's Church and establish His Kingdom, to force back the powers of darkness and take heavenly dominion over the evil in this world, to walk in the power and authority of Jesus Christ to do the very transformative work in and through people that we simply cannot do in our own human weakness….imagine…imagine taking every single one of these things away…what would we end up with, 2000+ years later?

A powerless church.
A church that sees no transformation.

A church that doesn't know her identity.
A church that has no authority.
A church of form but no power.
A man-made church.
A man- maintained church.
An institution, not a people.
An establishment, not a flow of spiritual freedom.
A Martha church, burnt out on service, but not to God, to man-made methods, ministries, systems, structures and leaders.
A powerless, impotent, biblically-illiterate and aliterate, unteachable, unchangeable, fruitless group of people who gather together, but build nothing of eternal value.

Hmmm, sounds vaguely familiar to another religious system who took the pure things of God and turned them into man-made rules, rituals, rights and passages and created an elite, exclusive, invitation-only club. We'll get to this soon, but nothing has changed since the days of Jesus, except that the same spirit of religion is now coming against His Holy Spirit. Same way, different time. Same spirit, different persona of God.

DIVIDE AND CONQUER

The spirit of religion has and is causing the greatest division amongst the Church of God because it knows that when God's people are truly unified with one heart and in one accord that nothing will stop His Kingdom from growing and His love and power from flowing. The spirit of religion knows exactly what it is doing, and unfortunately those who it is working through the most predominantly are those who think they are advocating for God, only to one day discover they are the very ones preventing His powerful move.

Selah.

The spirit of religion has flaunted itself as the image of the Church to the world

- because the true Church has been too silent and too blinded to its very tactics. The spirit of Jezebel has chased away the prophetic voices in fear and they have been cowering away in caves, too afraid to speak truth against the establishment. And so the world has rejected God. But really, they have simply rejected religion - the spirit of religion. And rightly so. It has no love. It doesn't possess acceptance, forgiveness, grace, mercy - everything Jesus is and offers. It is not a representative of the living God. It is not an ambassador of the Kingdom. It is not filled with power that heals, delivers and makes whole. It is not full of mercy, but ruthless. It is not full of grace, but vengeance. It is not God, yet it inadvertently represents - falsely - our God to this very world.

But not any longer.

THE TRUE BRIDE OF CHRIST

The time has come where the Bride is being unveiled throughout the earth. That is - the veil of deception is being removed from the eyes of those who look to the Church, the veil that this Bride is hiding behind is being lifted up by her Beloved, for Him to look her in the eyes and tell her how radiantly beautiful and pure she is and how much He absolutely adores her and loves her, for her to fix her eyes on Him, to be captivated by her Groom's divine glance and to rise up into her true identity, everything He calls her to be and everything He says she is - holy, pure, mature, beautiful, powerful, victorious, full of His authority - and she is finally about to take her rightful place as the city on the hill, shining her light for all to see the way to the Lord in the darkness ahead - the way to true freedom, true significance, true purpose in this life and for all eternity. The Bride is being empowered, equipped, strengthened, matured and established like never before. The Bride is being positioned to represent the Father, the Son and the Holy Spirit in the purity and perfection of the righteousness of Christ, like never before. The Bride is being positioned in places of influence to display His truth, His love, His hope, His design, His power, His goodness, His grace like never before.

POSITIONED FOR PURPOSE

The Bride...*is you.*

He is rallying the remnant in this era and He is calling out of the caves and hidden places, the pure voices who have been refined by the fire in their wilderness seasons, and those who haven't contaminated their robes, those who have come to Him and had their garments washed in His blood to make them white as snow in His eyes. These are the unknown names, the everyday people, the humble of heart, the lowly, meek, gentle, the nameless and faceless, the insignificant in the eyes of the world, but all of heaven know exactly who they are.

The world around us is going to see that the church they thought they knew was actually not the real deal at all. They will see and know that they too have been deceived by this false pretence of something that pretended to be spiritual and represent God's people, yet was so far from His truth. Because that one degree sets us off by miles once it keeps growing. That small fraction multiplies to the hundreds after a while. That one missing letter completely changes the meaning of the entire word as time goes on.

There is one simple answer to the spirit of religion that will bring the Church and the world back to the heart of the Father and our original design. Intimacy. I say simple because it really is simple. Intimacy with Jesus, with the Father and with the Spirit is what it's all about. It all comes from His love and it is all for His love. God is love, and when we abide in Him, He abides in us and when we love Him, we obey Him. No wonder intimacy is the very thing the enemy has attempted to grip onto and wrap his deceptive tentacles around, because once we take intimacy out of relationship, we are left with empty religion.

It's taken more than 2000+ years to realise that the world isn't drawn to God by Bible bashing, imposing strict rules and regulations, enforcing traditions and forms upon everyone around us. Likewise, the world isn't (ironically enough) drawn to the seeker-sensitive, tolerant, mixed-with-the-culture-of-society, 'inclusive' worldly church with all of its passive preaching, watered-down Word, performance mentality.

But now, the world is going to see the real God - because He is about to be made known for His holiness, His intimate love and His life transforming power.

Who He truly is. An accurate representation of His real nature and character. Who He has been this entire time.

> *"Afterward the sons of Israel will return [in deep repentance] and seek the Lord their God and [seek from the line of] David their king [the King of kings - the Messiah]; and they will come trembling to the Lord and to His goodness and blessing in the last days."* **Hosea 3:5 (AMP)**

IT'S TIME FOR REVIVAL

We are on the cusp of the greatest harvest that history has ever seen through the magnificent move of God as He overflows in power and glory. The very thing that is going to initiate revival, reformation and transformation to this world isn't fire and brimstone, isn't religion, isn't a list of rules and regulations, isn't form without power. It also isn't flashy lights, polished Grammy-worthy music, performances, worshipped worship-leader idols, profiting prophets or TED talk sermons. It's not compromising our preaching, teaching, prophesying, Bible studies, social-media posts, opinions, beliefs or mindsets to comply to the culture around us.

While there are so many prophetic words (and rightly so), concerning revival, I just want to make one thing very clear: revival isn't defined as a mass of salvations like we so often mean when we say the word. Revival means to RE-VIVE - to come back to life! It means RE-AWAKENING. The Merriam-Webster Dictionary defines it as *"to return or restore to consciousness or life; to become active or flourishing again; to restore to consciousness; to restore from a depressed, inactive, or unused state; to bring back; to renew in the mind or memory."* [1] The origins of the word in Latin literally mean 'back to life.' [2] If something is dead or dying...it needs REVIVING. The western church herself is in dire need of REVIVAL. We ourselves must first be revived. Our hearts must be revived, our holiness must be revived, our lives must be revived, our marriages must be revived, our homes must be revived, our families must be revived, our love for Him must be revived and restored back to our first love. We aren't going to see a wave of souls flooding into the Kingdom while His very house itself is dead and dying. Revival is coming to the church FIRST, and *once* we His people are healed, healthy, whole and restored, then we will see the harvest come to pass. The world is so ripe right now, the harvest is plentiful but the workers are few! Pray to the Lord of the harvest to send out labourers! (Mat 9:37-38)

Revival isn't coming to the world through a church who looks no different to them...it's going to come from deep intimacy with Jesus. His love, in truth. As simple yet eternally profound as that. It is going to be the perfect holiness of God. It's going to be the fear of the Lord returning to the Church. It's going to be intimate, personal relationship with the Creator of the heavens and the earth and Author of life. It's going to be unknown secrets and revelation and mysteries unveiled by the Spirit. It's going to be His answers and solutions through divine intelligence, flooding into impossible situations to turn them around for His glory. People will know they are loved by the living God, know they are pursued by Jesus himself, know they have a good, good Father who cares about every little detail of their life.

It's time to get real. It's time to get personal. It's time to get powerful. Because the truth of the love of God is the most powerful. It changes lives. It transforms minds. It reforms cities and births nations. It drives the darkness away and causes hells gates to tremble. True love, in intimacy, builds the Kingdom of God because our King is love and truth Himself.

THE NEW WINESKIN

The only way we as the Church can do this and display His love to the world is to partner with the very gift that Jesus imparted to us when He ascended to His position of power and authority in the heavenly places - the Holy Spirit. And in order to do this we have to exchange old methods for new mindsets. Old wineskins for new ways. Old systems for new strategies. Old practices for new processes. Old duties for new displays. Old traditions for new realms. Old structures for new capacities. Old experiences for new expectations. Old pursuits for new paradigms. Old forms for new openness. The old wine is expired and the old wineskin burst a long time ago. He is pouring out His new wine! Something we have never seen before, something we have never done before, something we have never imagined before. He is doing something new. And He is inviting you to be a part of it.

It is not new to Him, it's not new to heaven or the Kingdom, but it is new to us, this generation. The new that He is calling us to in these days is actually the old. So old that it is ancient. The reformation is us coming back into alignment with what He originally designed and the wine He originally poured out, both in Eden and when Christ's body burst on the cross and His blood spilled out for us. Heaven opened at Pentecost and His New Wine poured forth without measure for everyone to drink from and be filled with and overflow. The battle between the spirit of religion and the new wineskin Bride is going on right now. Many will reject this new move and era of God's glory manifesting through the flooding in of His love, truth and power to this world. They will use Scripture to justify their views that are based in captivity and control that is nothing but fear. But hey, so did the devil when he attempted to conquer Jesus in the wilderness. Like I said, it just has to be one degree off - the enemy is an expert at taking Scripture and changing it by a fraction. It's in the Bible, after all, but its context, application and truth are twisted to his evil motives.

> *"Remember not the former things, nor consider the things of old. Behold, I am doing a new thing; now it springs forth, do you not perceive it?"* **Isaiah 43:18-19a (ESV)**

LET IT GO

Why are we so afraid of God's love, truth and power? Why are we so afraid to love the way Jesus loves, that calls people out of their lifestyles of the worldly ways and into something that will transform them into the likeness of Jesus? What are we so afraid of? Why would the power of God manifest be so big and scary?

Because there is freedom in love.

And if there is freedom, it means we don't have control. Or should I say, the spirit of religion and Jezebel no longer have control. The spirit of religion is afraid of God's love, of His children discovering and living in intimacy with Him, because real relationship releases truth *and* power. In and of ourselves, we crave it. True love doesn't control, it sets free. True love accepts everything and everyone exactly where we are at, no strings attached, no agenda, no 'ifs or buts.' True love doesn't condemn, but it certainly doesn't condone either - it just loves. Love is what sets us free into the pure truth and uncontrollable power. Why is it so hard, so scary to love, in truth, the way Jesus did? Why do we think we need to be God and put definitions, limitations, conditions and boundaries on love itself?

The spirit of religion is being cast out of the beautiful Bride and the intimate love of Christ, our Beloved, is filling that void. The Spirit of unity is flooding in and binding the Church together as one Body with one head - Christ Jesus, the Anointed One. I recently had a dream where I saw this working so perfectly together - I was in a new building with a whole heap of God's people and we were all from different denominations, styles of worship, themes of belief - there were Charismatics, Anglicans, Pentecostals, Evangelicals, Baptists, Jews, Catholics, Presbyterians, Orthodox, you name it they were all there. And love emanated from everyone around, so much so that we were laughing and joyfully joking at one another's differences but with such honour that it only made us feel more and more unified and connected together as brothers and sisters. The building we were in was called the Centre Point Tower and we were on top of a hill overlooking a large city at night that had all of its lights on, twinkling and shining like innumerable stars in the sky. Hundreds and hundreds of boats and ships were landing on the wharf in front of us and the sons and daughters of the world were rushing to get off, some even jumping the gap to the wharf because they were so eager to get to the ground and climb the mountain to be with us in the true Church. It really was a prophetic picture of these days ahead and holds so much significance of what the Church can look like and what impact we will have when we unify in oneness - both to Him in intimacy, and then to one another in love - and then overflow from that unity with God's love to the world.

ICHABOD: THE GLORY DEPARTING

With that picture in mind, this may come as a shock…I don't believe the churches and denominations of today are all going to join together in one accord and unify as one church. In fact, I see the opposite. Many today are making a deliberate choice of who they will worship. Perhaps the spirit of religion, by partnering with cessationism and other man-made doctrines and idolatries, or perhaps digging their heels in and continuing to live compromised, mixed and tainted because they want to look like the world. I believe those churches and people may continue to 'minister.' Perhaps their lamp stand will be snuffed out as God floods in to deal with evil, but this may not necessarily look how we expect. Sure, some of them may shut down, close or even lose clergy, leaders, elders and pastors, but by and large, what I see happening is much worse than that.

I believe God is giving every leader, every pastor, every elder, every movement, every ministry, every single person a window of grace in which to thoroughly look at ourselves and all that we have built. As we have spoken about the purging (and we will delve much deeper into this purifying process in coming chapters), He is giving every single one of us an opportunity to make ourselves ready, to fill up our oil lamps, to be washed in His grace and mercy, to allow His illuminating light to shine deep into our hearts, minds, lives and homes and to clean house. Every single one of us have this opportunity and many will repent and do full 180 degree turns. But there is a heavier weight on the leaders of the Church at this time, a deeper calling to heed and respond to the voice of the Lord at this very moment in time. Perhaps the snuffing out of the lamp stands in this era to come may not look like full blown closure or pastors, prophets, leaders etc being removed from their posts, but perhaps, something I personally fear far greater… the glory will simply depart. Let that sink in for a minute.

Hear me out - God's will is for everyone to partner with His purpose and Kingdom plans in this era. His invitation is for the entire family, not a select few. But it's exactly that…an invitation. His grace is the open window, His messengers are the prophets, He is giving full and fair warning to all who have ears to hear and hearts to heed. He is not a God who leaves anyone behind, or cuts anyone off, but it is His pure love and grace that gives us every opportunity to join with Him. Today is the day of salvation, *today* is the day of grace.

> *"'If the people of the land take one man from among them and make him their watchman, and he sees the sword coming on the land, and he blows the trumpet and warns the people, then whoever hears the sound of the trumpet and does not take warning, and a sword comes and takes him away, his blood will be on his [own] head. He heard the sound of the trumpet but did not take warning; his blood shall be on himself. But if he had taken warning, he would have saved his life. But if the watchman sees the sword coming and does not blow the trumpet and the people are not warned, and the sword comes and takes any one of them, he is taken away because of his corruption and sin; but I will require his blood from the watchman's hand.'"Now as for you, son of man, I have made you a watchman for the house of Israel; so you shall hear a message from My mouth and give them a warning from Me. When I say to the wicked, 'O wicked man, you will certainly die,' and you do not speak to warn the wicked from his way, that wicked man will die because of his sin; but I will require his blood from your hand. But if you on your part warn the wicked man to turn from his [evil] way and he does not turn from his [evil] way, he will die in his sin; but you have saved your life. "Now as for you, son of man, say to the house of Israel, 'Thus you have said, "Truly our transgressions and our sins are on us, and we are rotting away because of them; how then can we live?"'Say to them, 'As I live,' says the Lord God, 'I take no pleasure in the death of the wicked, but rather that the wicked turn from his way and live. Turn back (change your way of thinking), turn back [in repentance] from your evil ways! For why should you die, O house of Israel?'"*
>
> **Ezekiel 33:2-11 (AMP)**

I believe the united church of this era is not the leaders and movements and denominations coming together, but a gathering of the remnant from the ground up. God always has a remnant. Throughout every wave of disobedience and rejection of the Israelites in the Old Testament, throughout every period of time in Church history, He always, ALWAYS, preserves a remnant. A remnant of those who have not soiled their garments with the ways of the world. A remnant of those who have not rejected His presence or power by handing control over to religious ways. A remnant who have maintained the purity of His Scripture and who obey His words and commands at whatever the cost. There is always a remnant. And I believe in this era, we will begin to see, all across the earth, these people gathering, these people coming together, these people finding one another, through divine means and through relational connections that look like a net cast over the whole earth. It won't be top down from the religious institutions or the hierarchies or the established movements and denominations. It will be a new thing. It will be a grassroots, ground up, everyday lay people who walk in deep intimacy with Jesus, who constantly abide in Him and who haven't sold out to either religion or the world, who have kept themselves pure and not defiled with mixture, who have remained steadfast to the Word of God and who walk in the power and presence of the Holy Spirit.

And from these people, revival will break forth. From these homes and hubs, the harvest will be hosted. From these barns and farms the pure worship and discipleship will take place. From these communities, equipping and commissioning will go forth. From these living rooms and dinner tables, discipleship will happen. From these families and generations, legacy will be built. From these places of purity, the Kingdom of God will quickly accelerate and advance, like we have never seen before.

THE HARVEST IS RIPE

His people are being made pure and mature, for such a time as this. His Bride is being perfected in the fullness of His intimacy and the consecration of holiness in order to go forth and enter into the greatest harvest of history. The spirit of religion will 100% buck up against this move - but that's because the control is being handed back to the rightful priesthood. That's because the influence is going to be displayed to the world from the right temple. That's because power is going to be the proof of His truth, and that truth is going to be reinstated where both impotence and tolerance has tainted.

The interesting thing about the term 'the harvest is ripe' is that it doesn't just pertain to salvations, as we often refer to it as. Absolutely the harvest is about salvations, but this is just one side of the coin. As we see in Joel 3:13 as well as Revelation 14:14-20 'the harvest is ripe' refers to the spiritual judgment of harvest time.

> *"Put in the sickle [of judgment], for the harvest is ripe; Come, tread [the grapes], for the wine press is full; The vats overflow, for the wickedness [of the people] is great."* **Joel 3:13 (AMP)**

Recently I had a dream where I was at a great conference. The conference was birthed out of a church called 'The Harvest is Ripe' and the conference itself was called 'The Harvest is Ripe.' As I was sitting in my seat watching the screen, the Holy Spirit manifested as a man of fire behind the speaker and He grew so tall that He outgrew the screen and the entire auditorium we were in. As soon as this happened revival exploded and in my dream, the revival was called 'The Harvest is Ripe.' I was so excited that it was finally here, but there was such a fear of God knowing that it wasn't just about the nets of harvest for the salvations, but also a time of great holy judgment for the Church and the world. Please hear God's heart here and heed the real warning - this isn't about judging people, this is about judging evil - within us, amongst us, through us, from us. Revival cannot exist without repentance. The worldly church has reduced repentance to complete obsoletion, because it preaches salvation without sin, and offers spirituality without Scripture. The religious church has no need for repentance, because they believe they are above sin, like the Pharisees, and therefore preach holiness without the Holy Spirit and consecration without conviction. But the harvest that is coming is ripe for judgment, so that it can lead to revival, salvation, transformation and discipleship into maturity.

THE GREAT FALLING AWAY

Despite the words of Jesus that talks about the great harvest at hand, the New Testament has more verses depicting the great falling away, through deception, tribulation and compromise. It contains more warnings about being on guard to the great deception than the many salvations that will occur. That doesn't mean it's going to be more prevalent or larger in number and quantity, it means it's a sincere, genuine and very, very urgent warning to us. Paul talks about the last days, that those who once believed the truth will be able to be deceived and then God will hand them over to their choices. This is serious, pertinent stuff. I know for certain that the great harvest is at hand, because I am witnessing all around me in my own life and own circle of friends and relationships, within 'Christianity' the great falling away. Deception is rife right now and the majority of the Western Church doesn't even realise it.

It's getting real folks. Our faith is truly being tested in this time. The fire is coming and consuming the chaff and only that which is true, solid and eternal will remain. All that can be shaken will be shaken and only that which is built on the firm foundations of the Rock and truth will remain. Get ready to get stripped naked. Get ready to get exposed, but pray for humility first - because God will expose to you alone, your own heart first, and if we are humble enough to accept and repent, then His grace, love and mercy will empower us to turn it all around. But I believe there is a greater exposing coming that will shake the Western Church first and then the rest of the world. If we don't humbly walk in complete unity with the Holy Spirit through our own exposing (between Him and us), then I fear the exposing will be made public, and we will begin to see the truth all around us, for what it is. Remember, the exposing is for His purifying. The exposing is for His justice. The exposing is for His righteousness. We have an invitation to work with Him, or we may find ourselves unintentionally working against Him. Humility, or humiliation, either way, the shaking is bringing a plumb line back to the purity of His truth and the holiness of His people, here on earth.

Life isn't a little game, there's no practice runs, everything is at stake! Will the fire of purification solidify our foundations and purify our faith, proving us strong, established and victorious? Or will it cause us to crumble and give up the very beliefs we have lived by for so long? If you are at this place in your journey right now let me encourage you - or exhort and admonish you with such passionate love, grace, concern and zeal - don't give in now. Don't give up now. There is a line being drawn in the sand and the chaff is being blown away.

Where will you be found standing?

NOTES

1. Merriam-Webster. (n.d.). *Revive*. In *Merriam-Webster.com dictionary*. Accessed September 14, 2023, from https://www.merriam-webster.com/dictionary/revive

2. Ibid

CHAPTER 3

ENTERING THE ESTHER ERA

SETTING THE SCENE FOR THIS SEASON

In this chapter I want to unveil to you the prophetic symbolism in the story of Esther, and throughout the remainder of this book we will refer to the significance of the interpretation in light of todays times and our own personal journeys and lives. If you haven't already, I encourage you to read the first chapter of the book of Esther right now. The setting for chapter one is the same scene that we are in today throughout the Kingdom of God. Our King has called us to abide in His fortress - safe and secure in His domain, close to Him, in His presence - and He has placed before us an abundant feast to gorge ourselves on - every spiritual resource in the heavenly realms. Everything paid for on the cross by His blood. No expense is spared, nothing is held back from those who are closest to the King. He has invited everyone, from His own personal royalty, to His workers, to those abiding in the city, in order to display the glorious abundance, inheritance and victory of His Kingdom and the magnificent splendour of His greatness. This banquet also takes place in a royal garden - our garden of intimacy where we come into His presence and meet with Him. Our secret place with God.

> *"He who dwells in the shelter of the Most High will remain secure and rest in the shadow of the Almighty. I will say of the Lord "He is my refuge and my fortress, My God in whom I trust.""*
> **Psalm 91:1-2 (AMP)**

Our King has poured out the best wine and He has told us each to drink according to our fill. This wine is the precious Holy Spirit. He is poured out freely, as a gift, according to the King's unlimited bounty. He has created each and every one of us as a unique goblet to hold the wine. We are all distinctly individual with a special design and purpose, and we as these vessels are called to hold the Wine. There are no restrictions on this imbibing! The wine being poured out is unlimited. It is also intoxicating in the very best of ways, but God, as a gentle Father, places the onus on us, and allows us to be consumed by the Holy Spirit as much as we welcome Him in to our lives and as much as we choose to surrender to Him (Es 1:8).

> *"You prepare a table before me in the presence of my enemies. You have anointed and refreshed my head with oil; My cup overflows. Surely goodness and mercy and unfailing love shall follow me all the days of my life, And I shall dwell forever [throughout all my days] in the house and in the presence of the Lord."* **Psalm 23:5-6 (AMP)**

Right now, in this era, God is wanting to put his beautiful Bride on display to the world. He has a wedding feast prepared and He has invited all. He is calling the world to Him in these end days, and He is doing it through His goodness, greatness, power, provision, protection, love and grace. God is flaunting Himself to the world and He wants to flaunt His beautiful Bride on display, with her royal crown on her head for all to gaze upon her beauty. It is time for the Church to arise in her identity and authority and be seen for who she truly is.

SAYING NO TO THE KING

Queen Vashti was originally chosen for this royal position of queen, but she refused the king. She said no to his invitation. For so long her character in this story has been admired for standing up to a chauvinistic drunk who wanted to show off his wife's good form, but there is actually a deeper prophetic connotation of this act of disobedience and rejection of saying no to the King of Kings. In the past God's chosen people refused His call and they instead put to death their awaited Messiah. Before we point the finger at them we need to look around at the current situation and recognise that today, God's chosen people who have the seal of the Holy Spirit are also at a pivotal point where we are refusing the King's edict by refusing to display His goodness and greatness, His power and authority, His love and magnificence, His truth and justice to the world and putting the beauty of His Bride on display.

When we decline this royal invitation we are saying no the to the King. We are saying no to His plans and purposes for this time, this season, this divine moment, when He wants to display His goodness, love and power through us, His chosen ones. Right now, there is an invitation to be on display for the Kingdom in this era, but many will say no because they think it's inappropriate, unexpected, not how it's always been done, or even evil and ungodly. Religion loves to tell us what's apparently ungodly. Queen Vashti said no to the King, but Queen Esther said yes to the call. Religion says no to the opportunity, but the Spirit says yes to the summons. What will your RSVP to the banquet be?

THE KING'S INNER CIRCLE

God loves to speak to me in the middle of the night by waking me up with a single word or sentence. It's actually when I hear His voice the clearest, probably because it's when everything is at its quietest - both my external environment and also my own mind and heart. And because of the quietness, His voice in these times is therefore the loudest, so I know it is His powerful voice! Just a few weeks ago He woke me up saying *"Who will ascend the mountain of the Lord?"* I immediately knew the scripture He was referring to (Ps 24:3-4), and I intrinsically knew that He was asking who would be willing to lay it all down, to purify themselves, to be purged of all contamination, who would be willing to take the narrow and difficult path up to the highest peak? I knew that not everyone would do this - many would love the idea, but when it comes down to it, they wouldn't be able to make it to the top, because many are unwilling to let go of heavy baggage, to leave friends and family and the familiar behind, to go somewhere that doesn't have their usual comforts. The cost is simply too much. But He was asking me, as though He was seeking and searching the earth for someone to simply say yes - *Who will ascend the mountain of the Lord?*

In this era God is doing His work through those closest to Him. These are those who occupy the highest positions in the Kingdom - not in the form of titles, platforms, positions or ministries, but those who have personal access to Him. Those who live the ascended lifestyle - who dwell in the throne room, the bridal chamber, the secret garden, the upper room of prayer and intercession, those who abide in His presence, those who circle the mountain peak like eagles, carried on the wind, high above the chaos of the natural realm surrounding us. God isn't doing His work through those who possess worldly positions or powerful public platforms, but those who have positioned themselves in places of intimacy with Him, in His presence, those who walk with Him (Ps 27, Ps 91). When we have access to Jesus we have access to the power and authority of heaven. When we have access to the Father we have access to His heart and will, His love and grace. When we have access to the Holy Spirit we have access to every heavenly resource. How does God want to display His goodness, greatness and the beauty of His Bride in this season? Through the manifestation of the magnificence of the Kingdom realm at work in the world today. And these are the people God is using to do this - those who are His intimate friends, who know their royal position, who understand their identity as children of God, who know God intimately and know His goodness, holiness, truth, love and grace. This is the message God wants to take to the world in this season and these are the messengers He is using.

> *"Here's the one thing I crave from God, the one thing I seek above all else: I want the privilege of living with him every moment in his house, finding the sweet loveliness of his face, filled with awe, delighting in his glory and grace. I want to live my life so close to him that he takes pleasure in my every prayer."* **Psalm 27:4 (TPT)**

He is using those closest to Him, who have their ears resting on His chest, reclining in His presence, those who linger in the tabernacle of intimacy, those who pursue Him for His face and His heart more than His hand, because it is only through this connected relationship that He imparts His wisdom, understanding and strategy. And He only reveals through His Holy Spirit. Human knowledge falls short, if we try to study and understand God in order to box Him and His ways into neat little packages of religious doctrines, we are denying the very revelation He desires to impart to us through His Spirit - our teacher, guide, counsellor. He gave us this Helper for a reason, because human knowledge falls ridiculously short of the wisdom and ways of heaven. While we in the Church may think we are immune to the worldly ways of thinking, we create our own foolishness by eliciting form without power. Newsflash: we can still believe in Jesus today, we can still have the seal of the Holy Spirit, but unless we are drunk on His intoxicating presence, revelation and love we are barely better off than the very religion that mocked, persecuted and crucified the prophets, John the Baptist, Jesus Christ and the apostles and martyrs of the early Church. Wake up slumbering souls! Awaken to see the times we are in, see the season that is around us now! God doesn't want our sacrifices, He wants our hearts, our love, our affection, our focus, our surrender, our lives laid down on the alter!

DISCERNING THE TIMES

> *"...The tribe of Issachar [were] men who understood the times, with knowledge of what Israel should do..."* **1 Chronicles 12:32 (AMP)**

POSITIONED FOR PURPOSE

The key to accepting the invitation from the King is about recognising, interpreting and understanding - through discernment - the times we are in. And the only way we can do this is through the Holy Spirit. This is why Jesus sent Him to us after His ascension into heaven, and this is why He told the disciples to wait until they were baptised in His power before they obeyed His command to take the gospel message to the ends of the earth. He is the only source of discernment, wisdom and revelation - only He gives us the eyes to see, the ears to hear and the knowledge to understand from a heavenly perspective, not the foolishness of humanity or the piousness of religion. Just as these guests in king Ahasuerus' feast would have been completely intoxicated with wine, so must we be intoxicated with the Spirit in order to perceive and receive what the Father is saying from the throne. It won't look how we want it to look. It won't make sense. It won't fit into our boxes, it won't be how it has been done in the generations leading up to us, but God is doing a new thing (The old thing! The true thing! The original thing!) He is writing a new story, there is a new breakthrough and new path that no one is expecting because we have our minds set on how we 'think' it should look. We cannot box God! If we can't recognise what He is doing and say yes to His invitation, then we will miss out. We will be left behind. We will remain in our comfortable religious cliques that point the finger in judgment both at the world around us and the brothers and sisters who are drunk on the royal Wine. This is not a good place to be. Only those in the King's inner circle, His closest friends, overflowing with the Spirit and His revelation will recognise the times, the season, the moment, what God is doing...now.

KNOWING THE VOICE OF YOUR SHEPHERD

Perhaps the greatest fruit of the sons of Issachar wasn't so much that they could discern the times...but that they knew what to do with that understanding. They didn't just interpret, they applied God's wisdom, will and ways, so that all of Israel would succeed in God's plans and purposes. Living a lifestyle of intimacy with Jesus, abiding in Him continually and living a life of intercession causes us to receive the heart of the Father and the mind of Christ, through the Holy Spirit. As we abide in Him and transform into His likeness, we begin to see what He doing and hear what He is saying and know exactly what His will is for the Kingdom of God here on earth. We become like the sons of Issachar when know - through intimacy and divine intel - how to apply discernment of the times we are in, and what God's people, here on earth today, need to do.

Please hear me when I say this, the Word of God is absolutely pivotal and pertinent to hearing His voice. God is not going to speak outside of His Word, but He will bring deeper revelation from *within* His Word. We cannot possibly think that we understand the Word of God in its fullness. We must come every day in humility, with a teachable heart. His Word is our continual feast. His Word is what we are to meditate on day and night. His Word is the truth in our life. His Word directs our ways, our choices, our values, our desires. His Word is the ultimate truth. His Word is our plumb line. His Word is the gift and guide He has given us to traverse this life on earth. But it's not just a book. It's not just words on a page. It is life itself because it is Jesus Himself (1 John 1:1). The funny thing is that those who accuse God's devoted people of 'adding' to the Word through prophetic insight, words of knowledge, wisdom etc, are the very ones who claim to have a monopoly on the interpretation of the Word. Yet the Bible itself says that the only way to truly receive truth from Scripture is through the Holy Spirit Himself who will illuminate, reveal and unveil the mysteries, wisdom, and divine knowledge from within. No true prophetic voice would ever say that what we 'hear' today is on par with Scripture.

There have been few and far between who claim such ludicrous extremes and they are quickly extinguished because it is so blatantly obvious that they are coming against the Word of God. Prophecy today never adds to Scripture. Not a single prophet would believe their words, albeit from God, are held in as high esteem as the Bible. But the words we hear from God absolutely have to align with the Bible. If it goes against it, even in the slightest way, it's clearly not God's word.

Personally, I have more fear of God regarding taking away from His Word. It's ironic that those who claim prophets are adding to the Word (which we've clarified, they are not, nor do they think they are), are actually the ones detracting from it. The entire cessation doctrine does exactly this. Teaching God's people that they cannot hear the voice of their Father, Creator, Saviour, Counsellor is not just ridiculous, but it is completely unscriptural! I could write an entire book on how many New Testament verses teach us about prophecy and the many gifts that require we hear God's voice! Denying that God speaks today is one of the biggest downfalls of the religious church, but we are coming into a time where it is going to be so obvious who the Spirit of God is on and who He is not, that this won't even be a question anymore. Of course, many will continue in their religious ways with their fingers in their ears and their pride in their hearts, but the Spirit will lead and move, provide and protect, anoint and cover, and work so powerfully through His surrendered people that it will only be possible for God to get the glory.

The Word of God is unlike any other book in all of the world. This book comes to life because it was penned with life and only when we have the Life-giver leading us as we read it, can we truly encounter the life-giving life within it.

> *"Now we have received, not the spirit of the world, but the [Holy] Spirit who is from God, so that we may know and understand the [wonderful] things freely given to us by God. We also speak of these things, not in words taught or supplied by human wisdom, but in those taught by the Spirit, combining and interpreting spiritual thoughts with spiritual words [for those being guided by the Holy Spirit]. But the natural [unbelieving] man does not accept the things [the teachings and revelations] of the Spirit of God, for they are foolishness [absurd and illogical] to him; and he is incapable of understanding them, because they are spiritually discerned and appreciated, [and he is unqualified to judge spiritual matters]. But the spiritual man [the spiritually mature Christian] judges all things [questions, examines and applies what the Holy Spirit reveals], yet is himself judged by no one [the unbeliever cannot judge and understand the believer's spiritual nature]. For who has known the mind and purposes of the Lord, so as to instruct Him? But we have the mind of Christ [to be guided by His thoughts and purposes]."* **1 Corinthians 2:12-16 (AMP)**

The ongoing conflict between those who are self-proclaimed 'Word based' Christians and those who are so-called 'Spirit-led' believers is abruptly coming to an end as the true breed of God's beloved are arising who are both 100% Word based and 100% Spirit led. That's the only way it can be. There is no Word without the Spirit, and there is no Spirit without the Word. They are both a gift from God and they are the two most powerful things we have been left with here on earth. If you are not deeply in love with the Word and nourishing yourself multiple times a day like you would sustain your natural body with food, then I encourage you - no, I adamantly urge you - to dust off your Bible and ask the Holy Spirit to open your eyes as you read, to unveil His truth to you, to reveal His mysteries as you read and to speak to you profoundly through His written Word. And if you have been afraid to 'hear from God' or simply don't know how, I encourage you to open yourself to the Spirit of Truth when you bask in His Word and ask Him to meet you there, to touch you, to impact you and speak profoundly to your spirit and soul. He longs to speak to you more than you desire to hear Him. Abandon your fears, renounce false doctrine, repent of being deceived by the spirit of religion, and open yourself up to the Author, Poet and Storyteller of Scripture itself.

REMOVING RELIGION

Just as Jesus was opposed by the spirit of religion, so now the Holy Spirit is opposed by the same accuser. It's taken over 2000 years, but because it's been so gradual, it's been seemingly unnoticeable. That is, until we pull our heads out from underneath its influence and actually see it for the abhorrent, ghastly, seductive, subtle, deceitful force that it really is. It's here. Let's finally face it and accuse it and call it out for what it is. Biblical truths are being silenced by theologies and doctrines that declare God's power no longer exists, that His voice no longer speaks, that signs and wonders are from the devil himself. It sounds so ridiculous when we hold it up to the truth of Scripture and Jesus' very words that tell us the complete opposite - Jesus Himself who said we shall do greater works than He did (John 14:12), who said we would hear and know the Fathers voice if we are really His children (John 10:3- 4), who said we should live off every word that continually proceeds from the Father's mouth (Matt 4:4). Paul warns us of those who claim to be for God but condemn His power at work (2 Tim 3:5). Why are we so afraid of surrendering to a God who is full of love, who is full of power, who performs miracles, who heals the sick, who sets the captives free from bondage and torment, who raises the dead? What are we so afraid of?

> "...having the appearance of godliness, but denying its power. Avoid such people." **2 Timothy 3:5 (ESV)**

We're afraid of being deceived. We're afraid of being on that 'wrong' side of deception and falsehood verse eternal truth. The funny thing is, the spirit of religion actually deceives by making people feel afraid of being the very ones who are deceived. Let me tell you, if you are being led by fear, then you are already deceived! We don't have a spirit of fear (yes, I'm talking about an actual spirit called the spirit of fear)but we have the Spirit of Truth who leads by hope, faith and perfect love and that results in a sound mind. The Kingdom of God is peace, joy and righteousness. I know so many Christians who are so afraid of being deceived. If you worry you might get it wrong, if you fear you could be led astray by falsehoods, if you experience anxiety about whether or not you've got it right - that is the spirit of deception at work.

The Word tells us to stay on guard and be sober-minded, awake and alert, it doesn't say be afraid, anxious and look for a demon behind every door. It means asking God for wisdom and discernment as we are instructed to do and not out of fear - being tossed to and fro by double-mindedness (James 1:5-8). The Word tells us that true maturity is the ability to discern good and evil (Heb 5:13-14). We don't need to fear being deceived, we need to be confident in God's truth and the only way we can do that is if we have the Spirit of Truth living and working within us, leading and maturing us and rightly dividing the whole of Scripture as we surrender to His Spirit in humility.

There is a very simple strategy to see if you are deceived - submit to the Holy Spirit. Out loud. Right now. Speak it out - say *'I surrender to no spirit but the*

Holy Spirit.' Renounce every other spirit you can possibly think of that you have partnered with, aligned yourself to, been taught falsely by, opened doors to, come into agreement with, opened yourself up to, anything in your family history, heritage or generational bloodlines. Ask the Spirit to illuminate your heart and soul and to expose anything and everything. If you've never renounced anything before there's probably an entire history of generations you will need prayer ministry and deliverance for with someone much more mature and advanced in this gift. But right now, do deliverance on yourself! Surrender, submit, reveal, renounce, repent, sever ties, bind and cast out! Day by day, surrender and submit to the Spirit of Truth. Seek the seven fold Spirit of Isaiah 11:2 - the Spirit of the Lord, the Spirit of wisdom and understanding, the Spirit of counsel and might, the Spirit of knowledge and the fear of the Lord.

So many in the church today are deceived by the spirit of religion, deceived by fear, deceived by complacency, deceived by experience over the Word. The funny thing is that the spirit of religion points its finger at the people who are doing the very things that Jesus commanded us to do - signs, wonders, miracles, healing, deliverance, walking in power and authority - and tells its followers that these people are deceived. Instilling fear! Fear of the unknown. Fear because it can't control. We aren't called to be in control, we are called to obey. We are called to have faith. We are called to surrender. We are called to trust even when it goes against the natural realm and how it's 'always been done.'

We are called to an audience of One. Not tirelessly pursuing the acceptance of others at all costs. We are called to please God, not people. I simply cannot accept a gospel that renders God's power and voice redundant in todays day and age. I'm sorry, but I am happy to be called a heretic and a false teacher or false prophet by those deceived by the spirit of religion, than to stand before God when He asks me why I was silent when I specifically read, over and over again, His very words that commanded me to follow the example of Jesus, to walk in greater signs and wonders than Him, that said the evidence of the gospel preached would be His power manifest. I stand in more fear of God to obey His biblical commands than to keep this message silent for fear of man.

Just as Jesus came against the religious of His day, so too is the Holy Spirit sifting and purging the religion out of the modern day Church, because what God has in store for this world in the coming days and from this era forth cannot be boxed, cannot be indoctrinated, cannot be held back by human understanding. We have to be so open to absolutely anything happening, so abandoned to His leading that we obey anything He tells us, so intoxicated with His Wine that we receive the fresh impartation of heavenly revelation, that we will go wherever His Spirit leads as He displays His goodness, greatness and beauty in whatever way He wants. And it's not going to be how we expect.

> *"Not everyone who says to me, 'Lord, Lord,' will enter the kingdom of heaven, but the one who does the will of my Father who is in heaven. On that day many will say to me, 'Lord, Lord, did we not prophesy in your name, and cast out demons in your name, and do many mighty works in your name?' And then will I declare to them, 'I never knew you; depart from me, you workers of lawlessness."*
> **Matthew 7:21-23 (ESV)**

We can't just 'know of' Jesus, we have to truly *know Him*, on an intimate level. In a culture that uplifts celebrities, coupled with the technologies of social media to peer inside the intimate details of peoples lives, this verse could be compared to such a thing. I may know of a particular celebrity. I may be obsessed with them even, their biggest fan who knows every detail of their lives. I may watch every Instagram story, every tweet, every TikTok, I may know them better than any other fan in the world…but if I ran up to them on the street expecting a welcoming embrace in return… they're going to say the exact same words to me! *"Get away from me! I don't even know you."* Knowing of Jesus and knowing Him are two very different things. Even the devil knows of Jesus. He believes in His existence, He is aware of His power and authority, I'd say more than most believers. But the devil doesn't *know* Him, or love Him, or have a connection or relationship with Him. This is why intimacy is everything. Intimacy is what we are called to, and on a continually deepening level. The key to this verse in Matthew is that it links 'knowing Him' to 'doing the will of the Father.' We get deeper into this later when we delve into John 14 & 15, but it's not about the external 'ministry' we do, but our internal intimacy with Jesus.

At this particular feast and celebration in Esther 1, King Ahasuerus had his closest, most trusted people, who met with him regularly. I would demise that these people went beyond being his typical workers and were his trusted friends and advisers. These were the people he turned to when Queen Vashti denied him. We aren't called to serve God as mere servants and little workers like religion will tell us to do. He calls us friends and He invites us to partner with Him in the work of the Kingdom, to co-labour with Him (John 15:14-15). He entrusts His Kingdom to us, His Body here on earth, and it is up to us to faithfully and wisely steward the seeds He gives us. Intimacy with God is so much more than being able to recite Scripture, to write theses' or theology, even to preach how we should live as so called Christians. This lifestyle is no different than the Pharisees and religious sects that Jesus was so opposed to in the gospels. Except this time, it's the Holy Spirit being inadvertently denied and what's at risk in these days is even greater, because if we are blinded by the spirit of religion, we will not be able to see what God is doing at this time. Just as the religious thought they were being godly and holy by crucifying the prophets, Jesus and the early Church, so too are the religious of this day and age crucifying the messengers who are delivering God's fresh rhema words for these specific days that He is empowering and equipping us to navigate.

DON'T SHOOT THE MESSENGER

In King Ahasuerus' time, eunuchs were used to deliver messages to the harem so that the king could be certain they could be trusted with his women, and his queen. In the same way that Queen Vashti refused to obey the King's edict, so too did the religious because they didn't accept the messengers. They said no to the delivery and the deliverers because it didn't appear how they expected. The religious spirit continues to do this today within the Church, all through the name of Jesus, of course! Jezebel loves to castrate those around her and make impotent, seedless and fruitless, the true messengers of God.

Out of fear of false prophets, religion throws the baby out with the bath water. Not only does the spirit of religion reject the messengers, the scribes, the prophets, the fathers and mothers, the apostles today, but in order to safeguard itself and keep God's people blinded, it goes as far to say that God doesn't even work like that today. God doesn't heal. God doesn't do miracles. God doesn't speak. All of that ended with the death of the apostles and the complete canonisation of Scripture. It doesn't happen today, so anyone claiming it does is therefore a false prophet. I see Jesus weeping devastatingly into His hands as His very people deny His power, authority and the greatest gift of His Spirit that He is pouring out in abundance. Jesus taught that if people wanted to embrace the Father, they had to embrace Him. Today, if we want to embrace Jesus, we have to embrace the Holy Spirit. The Spirit has spent too long put up on the back shelf in the religious church, hidden away, squashed down and denied. We have come full circle in the past two thousand years and parts of the Church are back to the very roots of deception that held the Pharisaical and religious sects bound in opposition to the very thing that God was doing.

Religion says that God doesn't speak. The religious devour the messengers, making them impotent eunuchs. The spirit of religion, the spirit of legalism, the spirit of control, the politic spirit, the spirit of Jezebel, the Leviathan spirit and the Python spirit continues today to put the prophets to death. The religious say no to the King and refuse His command and invitation to come and put His beautiful Bride on display for all to see His goodness and greatness manifest in the world around us.

The King's invitation and command for these times comes through His messengers. In order to receive His message, we must recognise His messengers, and the only way we can do this is through His Holy Spirit. God speaks today, and He is speaking loudly and powerfully. If we're not open to hear through His chosen messengers what He is saying today (this season, this moment, His rhema word - fresh and continually flowing from His heart and mouth, Matt 4:4), then we will miss the move of God, and ultimately we will miss God Himself...only to be told on that day that He doesn't know us.

A LITTLE YEAST

The religious of today are not just saying no to the Holy Spirit, and therefore the King Himself, but are teaching people to do the same. Vashti as a wife denied her husband - and similarly the religious spirit encourages the Bride to say no to her betrothed Husband and deny coming into His presence, because it is here in this intimate relationship that we can actually hear His voice and His truth comes forth. When King Ahasuerus' advisers recommended he make an example of Vashti so that no other wife would deny her husband, this wasn't a chauvinistic statement about wives obeying men in a powerless and debilitating way (as religion does!), but it was a wise strategy to nip in the bud what they didn't want spread through the kingdom. It's about us saying yes to the relationship with our Groom. If the religious keep saying no to their betrothed King, and keep teaching their followers to do the same, many, many more will follow suit. But in this era, God is putting this to death in order for Him to clear a path for His magnificence to be displayed.

Just like His chosen people who were in exile in Persia in this story were facing complete and utter annihilation if someone didn't intercede for their future, so too are some of His very own children today at risk of causing spiritual separation from what He is building and doing because they simply don't recognise the time, accept the messengers, or like or agree with the message, or don't want to see His goodness, love and holiness put on display to the world. Everything is at stake here. It has to be stopped before it spreads - before too many are blinded, before too many are lost, before too many are devoured from following the example of the wrong teaching. This isn't to say they will lose their salvation completely (I'm certain many who witnessed Christ's death and the subsequent events turned very quickly from persecuting Him to giving their lives over to Him, realising He truly was the Messiah), it's to say that they will miss the move of God and come against His very will and plan in this time, leading many into error as they do. This is exactly why leaders, teachers and preachers are held at higher accountability and will be judged with higher standards, because they have the ability to influence many.

The urgency for the royal verdict to reach the ears of the wives of Persia 'before this day is over' is the same urgency required in the Church today, in order for His people to rid their minds and hearts of both religion and mixed worldliness, to have their ears opened to hear His voice, their eyes opened to see His face, their hearts opened to know and recognise their King and to choose to move deeply into an intimate relationship with Him, no matter what that looks like. The urgency is real - NOW! Because now is the time, now is the moment, now is the season, can't you see it? Can't you discern it around you? Biblical prophecy is being fulfilled right before our eyes! The signs of the times are given so that we can perceive the days we are in. We are reminded over and over again in the New Testament to 'look for the signs,' so that we can easily recognise and declare the season as clearly as we recognise the changing of winter to spring, summer to autumn. The day and the hour are in the Father's hands, but we are instructed to stay alert, awake and aware of the times so that we are not caught off guard (ie, not found ready). We are not in the dark like the world, we are children of the light! Don't be left out of the loop, don't miss out on His plan and purpose for you in this moment of the world!

> *"For you are all children of light, children of the day. We are not of the night or of the darkness. So then let us not sleep, as others do, but let us keep awake and be sober...But since we belong to the day, let us be sober..."* **1 Thessalonians 5:5-8 (ESV)**

MANY ARE CALLED, BUT FEW ARE CHOSEN

What is at stake here is what Jesus described in the parable of the wedding feast in Matthew 22: *"The kingdom of heaven may be compared to a king who gave a wedding feast for his son, and sent his servants to call those who were invited to the wedding feast, but they would not come. Again he sent other servants, saying, 'Tell those who are invited, "See, I have prepared my dinner, my oxen and my fat calves have been slaughtered, and everything is ready. Come to the wedding feast."' But they paid no attention and went off, one to his farm, another to his business, while the rest seized his servants, treated them shamefully, and killed them. The king was angry, and he sent his troops and destroyed those murderers and burned their city. Then he said to his servants, 'The wedding feast is ready, but those invited were not worthy. Go therefore to the main roads and invite to the wedding feast as many as you find.' And those servants went out into the roads and gathered all whom they found, both bad and good. So the wedding hall was filled with guests. But when the king came in to look at the guests, he saw there a man who had no wedding garment. And he said to him, 'Friend, how did you get in here without a wedding garment?' And he was speechless. Then the king said to the attendants, 'Bind him hand and foot and cast him into the outer darkness. In that place there will be weeping and gnashing of teeth.' For many are called, but few are chosen."* (Matt 22:2-14 ESV)

Jesus used this parable to show His disciples that though Israel are God's chosen people - His first choice, His cultivated olive tree - those who do not embrace Jesus in fullness will miss out on the wedding banquet. Many of His chosen said no to the invitation at the Messiah's first coming, and the good news was then offered to the Gentiles - grafting in the wild olive branches, adopting us as His sons and daughters - and now we all have an opportunity to be called to sit at the banquet table at the eternal wedding with our Beloved. He is calling many into deeper intimacy with Him and a lifestyle displaying His power, goodness and glory. He has sent His invitation out to His Church today, but His messengers have been beaten and killed and His invitation has been denied. Few have responded with excellence. Some answer the call but refuse to embrace the King with intimacy. Religion pays lip service to the external call, but ignores the internal call of relationship, presence and power.

In order to embrace what God is doing in this season, in these times, we have to have a new wineskin to be able to hold the new wine He is pouring out. Verse 12 describes a guest who did respond appropriately to the invitation, but he was not wearing the proper wedding garments and he too was banished. If we are really serious about saying yes to the call, then we have to choose to 'change into' the wedding clothes provided. This is a gift, freely given by grace, we need to not just respond, but be changed and transformed by the power of grace. Religion tells us to strive and earn, grace freely gives and enables.

The word 'chosen' in this verse is the Greek word 'eklektos.' [1] While it can be interpreted as chosen, it can also be translated 'favourite, worthy, pure, choice, excellent.' This is interesting when we come to the part of this story when Vashti is banished and the King begins to find a new queen who is *worthy*. Vashti was chosen, but she wasn't worthy. Esther was called, and proven worthy, excellent, pure and choice. She wasn't originally the first choice (as the Gentiles weren't either), but she was eventually chosen, because she responded faithfully, excellently and worthily to the call. What a prophetic picture of the people of Israel and the Church today!

Just as some of God's called ones denied the invitation and even murdered the messengers and the Groom Himself, so too are we faced today with a similar predicament - His called ones need to respond in excellence, worthy of the call, and enter His presence through the Holy Spirit. The religious didn't recognise Jesus as the Messiah and they missed the opportunity to be a part of what God was doing (just the greatest act in the existence of the world and humankind), and today religion is not recognising and is discrediting and denying the Holy Spirit, therefore missing the opportunity and invitation to be a part of what God is doing now and in this era. The spirit of religion spreads the yeast that permeates the body, teaching others to deny the presence, power and purpose of the Holy Spirit.

God has an endless supply for love, forgiveness and grace, but there is just one sin that Jesus says is unforgivable - to blaspheme the Holy Spirit (Matt 12:30-32). Blaspheming and speaking against the Holy Spirit is attributing what God Himself is doing to the devil and the kingdom of darkness. This is what Jesus was referring to in Matthew 12:22-32. The context of His words here are toward the Pharisees who claimed He cast out demons by the power of Beelzebub, the prince of demons. Today, the spirit of religion claims that the manifestations and works of the Spirit are from the devil and evil spirits. Jesus declared the exact opposite: *"If you see me casting out demons, you know that the Kingdom of God is upon you"* (Lk 11:20).

We cannot be so blind and deceived that we claim the work of God's very Kingdom is the work of the devil himself. No wonder this sin is unforgivable.

Friends, this should put the fear of God in us! Imagine spreading such deceit thinking we are being godly, when we are actually proclaiming the one unforgivable sin. This lie has to be stopped - just as Vashti was banished from the King's presence - before the spread of religion and blaspheming the Holy Spirit permeates to too many in the Church.

SIFTING AND SHAKING

In order to heal and perform miracles Jesus first had to clear out and remove religion from the temple, the house and the room. Today, He is doing the same thing in the Church and in our hearts. He is about to come in power and authority on levels we cannot imagine, and He will use those who's hearts are open and who's faith believes for the impossible. This is the divine invitation. Are we worthy of the call? Or are we too easily offended by the package it comes in, the form it moves in or the way in which it is delivered? He is not looking for people who simply know *of* Jesus or can recite the Scriptures or deliver in depth exegetical sermons, or teach tight biblical theology, but those who *know Him*, in intimacy, who abide in Him and Him in them, and who receive His revelation of the truth in His Word through the Holy Spirit.

> *"You are wrong, because you know neither the Scriptures, nor the power of God."* **Matthew 22:29 ESV**

If we don't want to be 'wrong' or deluded or deceived in these times then we need the revelation that comes through the Holy Spirit - for Him to reveal to us the truth - and the power of God. In this season God is sifting and shaking the Church of the spirit of religion, and the spirit of worldly culture, because He is coming in glory, power and wonder in greater ways than we have ever seen before. He will protect His righteous ones from coming destruction, He will multiply food in times of famine and provide overflowing resources in times of economic decay. He will be the Healer and protector as deadly plagues kill the world around us, but His righteous remnant will remain in His spiritual Goshen's of protection, provision and power. He is exposing and uprooting the source of unbelief and destroying it so that He can come swiftly and profoundly in power and love and enable His goodness and greatness to be flaunted and the beauty of His Bride put on display to the world as He calls them to Himself as a good, holy Father.

He is breaking down the powers of religion and the stronghold that the religious spirit has had over His chosen people who have been blinded and deafened by its lies. If His first choice of people don't respond to His call and invitation in obedience then He will use someone else who is surrendered, humble, obedient and worthy of His call. Let's read on to see how Esther was this very person, and how we too, can partner with what God is doing, at whatever price we have to pay.

NOTES

1. Strong's Exhaustive Concordance of the Bible. (n.d.). *Eklektos* #G1588. In *biblehub.com*. Accessed June 7, 2019 from https://biblehub.com/greek/1588.htm

CHAPTER 4

THE PROCESS OF PREPARATION

"Just as [in His love] He chose us in Christ [actually selected us for Himself as His own] before the foundation of the world, so that we would be holy [that is, consecrated, set apart for Him, purpose-driven] and blameless in His sight. In love He predestined and lovingly planned for us to be adopted to Himself as [His own] children through Jesus Christ, in accordance with the kind intention and good pleasure of His will—to the praise of His glorious grace and favour, which He so freely bestowed on us in the Beloved [His Son, Jesus Christ]."
Ephesians 1:4-6 (AMP)

Have you ever felt like you don't belong? Like you haven't found your place in life? Have the past few years, decades perhaps, been a time where you have felt surrounded by people - community even; church, the workplace, family, social networks - yet so isolated? Have you ever felt like you can't get your roots planted deep down in the place that you're in, or have no where to call home? Have you ever felt abandoned and alone? Or that you just can't find your tribe and Kingdom family that you *know* are out there? Do you ever feel like Elijah crying out to God that you're the only one, yet you feel firmly in your spirit that there's seven thousand others (or more!)?

We so often view the story of Esther from the perspective of the end of her story: a brave, conquering, victorious queen who was strategically and supernaturally used by God to deliver an entire people group from the hands of evil. But to fully understand her success, we must look at her beginnings - where she came from and who she was before she was our victorious Queen Esther. There aren't many verses describing her early life, but from the context of the first few chapters we can see exactly where her story really began. And it's not in a grand palace, an extravagant lifestyle or an opulent position. Instead, our leading lady was an exiled orphan.

As an Israelite girl who was an exile in Persia, it meant that she had a home, but she wasn't living there. She had a place of security and safety, an abode of comfort and peace, but she wasn't dwelling in that inheritance. A healthy home is a place of belonging and connectivity, a place of family, life, community and generations. But Esther didn't have either of those - she was displaced and exiled. You too may be feeling, or have felt, that you are displaced. That you're not dwelling in your real 'home', that you can't get your roots to get planted deep, down in the life you're in because you have felt so disconnected. You may feel forgotten, fatherless, motherless, even with biological parents, family members, church leaders and spiritual siblings right above you and beside you. The essence of fatherhood and that protective, secure, safe relationship of being under the eagles wings may be foreign to you. But in the same way that we can see Esther dramatically fathered and embraced, so too does God adopt us as His children, welcoming us warmly into His family and calling us His very own. You have a place. You have a Father. You have a family. And you have a home. Your past may be dripping in disappointment, displacement, despair, depression, discouragement, disownment, disdain, darkness even, but just like Esther, your future in His Fatherhood, adopted into His family, grafted into His olive tree, is nothing short of extravagant.

THE REFORMATION OF THE FAMILY FOUNDATION & FUNCTION

In this era, I believe that God is restoring and reforming His Church back to the place of family. Not simply the empty catch-phrase of the modern mainstream church, but real, true, authentic, relationship where we will gather together in homes, communing over multi-generational meals, around the dinner tables instead of pulpits and platforms, uniting together in prayer and worship in the living rooms of life, rather than the stages and screens, performances and conferences. In this time, we are coming back to Eden, back to the House of Acts, back to the simplicity of the gospel and the gathering and scattering church, and back to God's original design for community and communion - family.

For too long now we have had many leaders, teachers, instructors and guides, but very few fathers (1 Cor 4:15). Mothers and fathers lead from a place of equipping, empowering, commissioning and sending. We are about to see again what it looks like to find Kingdom family and to come under the covering of a genuine mother and an authentic father, to find spiritual sisters and brothers, to have healthy homes and covenant relationships we belong to and can go to to rest in, to be our vulnerable selves and receive what we need in that day, week, moment, to be spiritually and biblically taught and trained to be discipled, to grow, develop, deepen, strengthen and overcome, not just build some inwardly focused ministry but to build the Kingdom outside of the four walls of the established and institutionalised Western Church.

The difference between business-like leadership and family, is both relationship and reproduction. Fathers and mothers truly love. They don't care about systems and structures, programs and protocols, they care about real people and real lives. Their goal isn't to build bigger buildings and gain more followers, numbers and congregation members, their desire is to disciple and equip and empower. As this is done in healthy covenant relationship, sons and daughters are discipled into maturity. Just as a healthy mother and father prepare their physical children for adulthood, so too is the goal of spiritual parents. As sons and daughters grow up in this maturity, with strong, healthy and firm foundations, they too go on to reproduce spiritual sons and daughters who mature into mothers and fathers. And so the spiritual legacy continues.

Instead of the local church being built upon one man's vision, or one man having the burden and pressure of the entire church on his shoulders, the functionality of the five-fold offices in Ephesians 4 is specifically designed for fostering maturity and unity through equipping and empowering sons and daughters in the context of authentic family. The responsibility and accountability is spread across many, instead of one. God's design has always been family. Never hierarchy. Always intimacy, authenticity and relationship. Never CEO-style leadership or pyramid positions where illegitimate children lord it over others because of their orphan mentalities. Family is about Fatherhood, and the family of God thrives in a healthy five-fold household, because this was the original design of the Ekklesia.

Upon the re-establishment of the five-fold roles (not positions), of their offices (not titles), of their mantles (not counterfeit coverings), of their anointing (not man-made displays of conjured up 'power') and their *healthy* functioning, the five-fold will finally find its fulfilment in what a flourishing and fruitful family and household were designed to look like, act like, live like and upon this God-given design and blueprint will the true Church thrive as the Kingdom of God goes forth - equipping and empowering the saints for the work of ministry - teaching and training, disciplining and discipling into full maturity, sons and daughters of healing and wholeness, identity and authority, who spread the gospel of Jesus throughout the earth through authentic relationship, not simply systems and structures (old wineskins).

ADOPTED, NOT ABANDONED

Just as Mordecai adopted Esther, so too does God become our Father. He embraces us and grafts us into His chosen family. We have a hope in the future, we are no longer abandoned orphans, but we have an inheritance because of whose child we are. Esther's people in exile had nothing…but this promise of inheritance gave them hope for a future.

THE PROCESS OF PREPARATION

"To those [elect—both Jewish and Gentile believers] who live as exiles, scattered...who are chosen according to the foreknowledge of God the Father by the sanctifying work of the Spirit to be obedient to Jesus Christ and to be sprinkled with His blood: May grace and peace [that special sense of spiritual well-being] be yours in increasing abundance [as you walk closely with God]. Blessed [gratefully praised and adored] be the God and Father of our Lord Jesus Christ, who according to His abundant and boundless mercy has caused us to be born again [that is, to be reborn from above—spiritually transformed, renewed, and set apart for His purpose] to an ever-living hope and confident assurance through the resurrection of Jesus Christ from the dead, [born anew] into an inheritance which is imperishable [beyond the reach of change] and undefiled and unfading, reserved in heaven for you, who are being protected and shielded by the power of God through your faith for salvation that is ready to be revealed [for you] in the last time."

1 Peter 1:2-5 (AMP)

Another aspect of this story that we often don't take into too much consideration is that Esther would have been very young, a teenager. Some scholars believe she could have been as young as 12-14 years old at the time of her marriage, as this was the cultural norm of the day. Anywhere between 12-18 is the general consensus, so let's just say she was 15 years old, for the sake of example. That's 15 or so years of living in exile. Fatherless. Homeless. A slave in a foreign land. I wonder what Esther thought of her life up until this point? How did she view herself, her identity? How did she view her past? I know we will never know the answer to this as the Scripture doesn't reveal to us her inner narrative and deepest thoughts, but I do wonder what her perspective of her life was. Did she despise her life and her displacement? Did she think it would always be like this? Was she living in discouragement and hopelessness or did she dream about a different destiny, a future of freedom in so many ways? Could she ever have imagined what God had in store for her? Did He encourage and inspire her with His quiet promises and reveal a glimpse of His plans and promises to her sweet heart? I dare to surmise that her heart did not lean towards discouragement, or despise her tragic past nor present circumstances. I'm sure she was as human as all of us and she would have painfully felt and struggled with her situations at some point in her life, but judging by the level of favour and position that lay ahead of her, I truly think our courageous queen stewarded her heart, thoughts and circumstances faithfully and hopefully as she trusted her great God.

Often, coming to this place of acceptance of the circumstances around us, coming to the place of facing our past, is the very thing that catapults us into a favourable future. I don't for a minute think she played the victim. And hey, we've all been there at some point - pitying ourselves, wallowing in our woundedness, rehearsing our unfair misfortunes, wondering 'why me?' Comparing ourselves to others seemingly perfect and easy lives, holding on to unforgiveness and bitterness. But we can't be a victim when we're called to be the victor. We can't dwell in discouragement when the war is already won. We can't focus inwardly when we're called to arise outwardly. No matter our situations or circumstances, no matter our past or present, in Him and through Him we have the victory, and living anything less than that is living less than what He has already paid the price for. Lift your eyes and look to Him! Look to the hope He has in store for you! Not just in the next life, but in this, the land of the living. This is how I believe Esther lived. She positioned her heart toward Him and He was able to position her in His place of powerful influence for His purposes. In less than a year she went from being an abandoned, exiled orphan to being the favoured queen who played a remarkable role in saving her entire people.

Don't let your past or your present dictate your future. Don't think you can't be used because of what you lack, what you haven't achieved or who you're not. Transformation and turnaround can happen in an instant when God has a great and mighty plan. Your 'suddenly' moment could be right around the corner. Just imagine for a moment...what could your life look like a year from now, if God decides to breathe on you, position you and release you into *His* purpose and plans He has prepared? Everything you have walked through can be used for your good. Just like Esther, God prepares us in the darkness - the hiddenness, the hardship - and releases us in the light.

A CITY ON THE HILL

Let's take a closer look at the context of Chapter Two of the book of Esther in order to get a perspective of what God was doing in her life, but also what He is doing in ours. It's important we read this through the mindset of our new wineskins, and ask the Holy Spirit to truly reveal His truth and ask for revelation eyes to see. Without the new wineskin in our hearts and minds we may easily get offended, and when we hold offence we are open to deception, and when the enemy has a foothold into our hearts and minds, we can easily be deceived and completely miss what He is saying in this hour.

Our duty isn't to judge what the Spirit is doing, it's to obey. Likening a secular harem of a worldly king to the Church of Christ may bring a large amount of offence to some, but when we have eyes to see we can view this story not simply as a historical document but as a prophetic picture that points to both Jesus Himself, and His end times Church.

> *"Some time later, when King Ahasuerus' rage had cooled down, he remembered Vashti, what she had done, and what was decided against her. The king's personal attendants suggested, "Let a search be made for beautiful young virgins for the king. Let the king appoint commissioners in each province of his kingdom, so that they may gather all the beautiful young virgins to the harem at the fortress of Susa. Put them under the supervision of Hegai, the king's eunuch, keeper of the women, and give them the required beauty treatments. Then the young woman who pleases the king will become queen instead of Vashti." This suggestion pleased the king, and he did accordingly."* **Esther 2:1-3**

Verses 1-3 of Chapter Two provide a picture of the Church today. Those dwelling in the harem can be likened to those living in the presence of God - that is, those closest in intimacy to the King. While our biblical values and beliefs as well as the culture and modern times do not condone the promiscuity, immorality or polygamy of this worldly practice, the symbolism of this goes beyond the physical and natural. These women (young virgins - pure) were those who knew the king on a deeper level (intimacy). They had been with the king in a deeply relational way and they resided not just in his kingdom, but in his palace, and in a beautiful oasis within his palace. They had people positioned over them, around them and under them to look after them, serve them and guide them, who were appointed by the king himself.

Hegai represents the Holy Spirit in this story - appointed to Esther to watch over her, to teach her and guide her, to lead her in the ways she should go and to no doubt comfort and counsel her. We find out later that Esther valued Hegai's wisdom and leading, and listened to his voice. God has given us His Spirit to lead us and teach us his ways.

The connotation of young virgins also symbolises purity. As God's people in this world and in this era, He is calling us to deeper purity. Complete consecration. Heightened holiness. We cannot be mixed with the world, we cannot be tainted with worldly ways or blemished with worldly desires. There can be no flies in the oil. We have been washed pure and clean by the blood of our Saviour - we now stand before God and He sees us as pure and holy (Eph 1:1, 4; 4:24; 5:25-27; Col 1:22-23; Titus 3:7; Heb 3:1, 10:10; 12:23; Acts 15:9), we are the righteousness of God, through Christ (Rom 3:21-24). While we live in the world, we are not of the world (John 17:14-19; Rom 12:1-2), we are not called to live within the four walls of the church, nor to segregate ourselves from society by creating our own little sub-culture that we call Christianity, but we are called to be a city on a hill (Is 60), shining His light, illuminating the way to the hope and truth, the only answer in a world crying out for a Saviour. Our light is not to be hidden away, but to be placed and positioned on a platform of prominence (Matt 5:13-16). The more desolate the darkness we live in, the brighter His light shines. This is the moment He is calling us to live lives that are the city on the hill - individually and collectively.

Our purity is essential in this era because while we live in the world, we cannot conform to the world. We need to be consecrated - set apart for a holy use - because it is in this very darkness that God can use us most powerfully. If we are living lives the same as everyone else in the world, then there will be nothing that clearly sets us apart in the eyes of those around us. There will be no light that shines towards them and captures their attention. There will be no difference in our lives that they can recognise from their own. For too long the western church has either stood out like a sore thumb to society in ways that do not bring glory to God (for all the wrong reasons), or conformed so closely to the culture around us that there is really no difference at all, except slapping a Jesus sticker onto everything we do and say. But now He is calling His people into deeper consecration - to be truly set apart for a holy purpose - in order for us to display His glory, power, presence, love, grace and truth.

He requires purity of His people so He can use us for His purposes. This positioning is not for our gain, but for His glory. Think of our position (a city on a hill) more as being used as a tool in the beautiful call to co-labour with Him, than being elevated because of earning or striving. It's not about the promotion or the elevation, it's about God's purpose and His overall plan - but He can only position those who's hearts are truly pure. This is all about humility. The lower we go in our own perceptions of ourselves - letting go of all pride, and self-importance - the higher He is able to elevate us for His glory. This is not some religious form of false humility where we say all the right words but inwardly our heart is puffed up with our own piety, this is a complete and utter emptying of ourselves, our flesh, our desires, our name, our glory, our achievements, our accolades, our all. It's not thinking less of ourselves and belittling our worth in Jesus' eyes, but knowing our full value in Him and recognising the priceless value in others, seeing them the way He sees them, serving them the way He came down and served us in the ultimate act of humility and emptying of self.

If we are going to be used by the Lord to display His design of Kingdom life, then we have to be behaving differently to the world around us. We have to be thinking differently, speaking differently, acting differently, believing differently, living differently. We must be set apart for a holy purpose - in the world but simultaneously dwelling in the holy of holies, living a lifestyle of abiding in Him. The Lord is continually purging His people of any impurity that contaminates our hearts. To be joined to Him in holiness means that our blemishes cannot co-exist in union with His holy presence. Therefore, His holiness devours our impurities and that is how we can stand before the Lord righteous in the eyes of God, and enter into His presence, holy. What we used to tolerate in our hearts and lives He is exposing to us, where we used to conform to the culture around us, He is illuminating within us, where we used to be complacent in spiritual apathy He is igniting a fire of passion within us. The Lord is ushering in a wave of consecration and refining fire in order to increase our awareness and hunger for holiness so that we can walk in all that He has ahead for us, that when His glory falls, its weight won't destroy us, but will move powerfully through us.

I believe there are three things that Esther possessed that God is also giving us in order to be used for His purposes and display His glory and power in this world. These things set us apart for a holy purpose and as people around us see them displayed in our everyday lives, they are drawn to the light and ultimately led to the source to discover the answers, solutions, healing and wholeness they are deeply craving and crying out for.

ESTHER POSSESSED A GIFT

God always gifts us with tools and resources to use for His glory as He builds His Kingdom through us. Whatever gifts we have been given, we are to steward faithfully, unto His name.

Esther had something special going for her. I'm sure she had many more as well, but the Scripture tells us that this gift was exceptional, it was so prominent that it set her apart from everyone else. She had beauty. God had specifically and deliberately created her with extravagant, ravishing, captivating beauty. There are a few ways we could respond to this. Firstly, we could think how unfair it is that someone like her gets given good looks, while we feel like we've been dealt the rough end of the stick in the beauty department. But God isn't unfair, and He has made each one of us fearfully and wonderfully according to His perfect and unique design for our individual lives. However this isn't a book about self-acceptance, identity, security (there are plenty of powerful resources available if you struggle in this area of self worth), so the next response could be the other extreme which is to think 'how superficial' because, I mean come on, God doesn't value beauty and He certainly doesn't use extravagance in His Kingdom. Well, I hate to break it to you, but that's the lies of the religious spirit right there. God is both a lover of beauty and extravagance, because He is the creator and designer of those very things! Beauty originated within His heart and was brought to life through His fingertips and His spoken word. Beauty is defined by Him because He designed beauty itself. He is the author of extravagance and excellence because His opulent and eternal Kingdom determines those very concepts. If we think that 'beauty' is too shallow and superficial of a gift to be used by God, then we only prove that our mindsets are too shallow and superficial for His power, purposes and paradigms (did someone say new wineskins?).

When we lessen the gifts that God has endowed us or others with, we are devaluing the very creation He perfectly and purposefully design us to be. When we cannot accept our own individual make-up, we look to the left and the right, comparing ourselves with others and wanting what others have because we see that as more worthy, more valuable, more important, more purposeful, more useful than what we have been given. And when we're desiring and coveting something that is not ours, we are neglecting the very things that have been implanted and impregnated within us that God intends for us to grow and develop, steward and use for His purposes and glory. We pine after another persons life at the very cost of our own.

Ok, so chances are you may not have been bestowed with the gift of captivating beauty to the extent of Esther, but you have been created with the very gifts for the very purposes and plans that God has for you and your life. Stop brushing off aspects of yourself as unimportant, worthless, selfish or even vain. Don't allow the spirit of religion to speak lies into you that tells you those God-given gifts and traits are superficial, shallow, worldly or evil. God has a reason for designing you the way He did and His gifts in your life have a significant purpose. Embrace them as Esther did and use them for His glory!

ESTHER POSSESSED FAVOUR

Esther's God-given gift of beauty got her the gig, but God had a measure of favour that came upon her causing Hegai, the keeper of the women in the harem who supervised them, to be pleased with her, gaining his favour. When God's favour is upon us, others favour us in return. Even those in the world and with worldly positions and situations. Life isn't divided into sacred and secular - all of life is sacred when we live in and from the presence of God and when we live from an intentional and continual place of worship, surrender and sacrifice, no matter what we are doing. We magnify His presence wherever we go and as He dwells in us and rests upon us, everything we put our hand to is an act of worship if we do it unto Him. With the favour of God upon us and our gifting and positioning, things are accelerated in the natural.

We may have all the gifts we need, but without the anointing of the Spirit, we cannot open doors for ourselves, nor build His Kingdom - it would all be in our own strength and ultimately we are building the house in vain. God's favour is the anointing of Holy Spirit - His very presence - going with us, on us, in us and through us. The anointing is God Himself. It's not simply the ability or the ease or even the grace, but the grace, strength, empowerment and ease all come for the abiding anointing of the very person of the Holy Spirit. The oil doesn't get more slippery than that!

The favour and anointing of God that was upon Esther was what caused her to be accelerated through the beautification process. Not only did she receive the best treatments and nourishment but she was also assigned her own female servants and was given the best living quarters in the entire harem. When we are operating in our gift and walking in obedience to His call, His supernatural favour rests upon us and doors of opportunity open that neither we, nor any other human could open or close. When His favour rests upon us and what we are doing, natural processes are accelerated beyond not just what is normal, but beyond what is humanly possible. Opportunities become ours because they were only ever created with our name on it. We don't need to look around and wonder why these other people seem to keep getting all the chances, all the acceleration, all the opportunity, all the blessings, we just need to align ourselves with what God wants us to be doing and where He wants us to be doing that. When we are on His path and doing His will, His favour can and will pour over us to access the realm that God has created for us to be dwelling in - obedience to Him, working in our gifts, positioned for His purposes and His will to be made manifest in this earth, as it is in heaven.

I call this the *'stay in your own lane'* mandate of Paul in 2 Corinthians 10:12-18. We each have a realm, a place, a sphere, a call, an assignment a mission that we must run in and toward. If we run the race looking at others we will get out of our lane and be disqualified. If we compare or compete with anyone around us, our specific role will not be fulfilled, and God will have to raise up someone else to do it. We each have a part to play in the Kingdom, we each have a role just as the body is made up of many parts and it can only function when we each play our own specific, designated role. Stay in your own lane, don't look to the left or the right, and the oil will cause you to run your race well and finish victoriously!

When the favour of God is upon you, it's not just for one specific occasion. Not only was Esther accelerated through the process, given the best of the best, bestowed upon with gifts and servants and a dream abode, but at the end of it all - despite the countless other young girls who were also vying for the position - verse 17 says that *"the king loved Esther more than all the other women. She won more favour and approval from him than did any of the other virgins. He placed the royal crown upon her head and made her queen instead of Vashti."* This gal was snowballing in favour! The more favour she had the more she gained, it was unending and unstoppable! But before we feel jealousy rise up in our hearts for those around us who seem to be rolling in the favour of God, have a look at what the purpose of God's favour is. It's not for our own blessing. It's not for our own personal gain. It's not to build our own little empire around ourselves. It's for overflow. It's for the plans and purposes of God. It's for others. It's for His Kingdom and His glory. Esther 2:18 says *"The king held a great banquet for all of his officials and staff. It was Esther's banquet. He freed his provinces from tax payments and gave gifts worthy of the kings bounty."* Depending on where you live around the world, to have your tax payment lifted from your income could see you bringing in up to 50% more financial gain! And a king's gifts that are worthy are of the highest value, extravagance, exuberance and all the over the top, unnecessary levels of abundance that we should humbly decline as super-holy Christians (new wineskins needed!). God's favour leads to extravagance that is so abundant it cannot be contained and therefore has to overflow onto everyone around us. Every single person in the kings provinces received favour and experienced abundant blessing because of Esther's favour. Favour is oil for overflow.

Now, before we get too caught up in the worldly churches concept of 'prosperity' (or the other extreme - the religious spirit's false-humility of poverty mentality), let's have a look at what abundance actually means in the Kingdom. Paul reminds us that, though he himself had known what it is to have both a lot, and a little, God - through our obedience and allegiance to Him - will continually supply to us not just what need for life, but more than enough to overflow on to all around us (2 Cor 9:8-12). We are called to overflow! I believe we are entering the days ahead where the true Church is going to come back to the lifestyle of Acts 2:42-47. For too long now believers have become just like the world - storing up riches, hoarding for the future, focusing on ourselves, building our own empires and family dynasties instead of being the overflow we are created and called to be. This lifestyle of continually pouring out with all that God gives us requires the deepest faith we will ever know. Faith that trusts in a good Father. Faith that believes He will continue to provide for our needs and we don't need to live in fear of hoarding for the future. This is true trust, true dependence, true security in God as our Father and provider, our Jehovah Jireh. The real Church family who come alongside brothers and sisters in the faith and meets every need out of the abundance supplied to them, is a Kingdom to be reckoned with. And this is certainly not reserved just for material and monetary possessions, but is even more powerfully manifest when we break down all religious, denominational and branded movements, barriers and burdens and overflow to one another with every heavenly resource, every Kingdom inheritance, all revelation, power, authority, supernatural gifting and manifestations of the Holy Spirit Himself being poured out and overflowing amongst us all! Can you even imagine?

ESTHER POSSESSED WISDOM

Not only was she beautiful in form and face but she had the goods to go with it. Esther was a woman of wisdom. She had discernment and a humble, pure and teachable heart. She knew that she didn't just get here by her good looks, and even if she did, that wasn't going to sustain her position for life (hello aging!). When the favour of God is upon us it is most wise to seek counsel from those above us as to know how to best steward the grace we have been given. Esther was obedient to God's leading. She exercised wisdom by seeking out and heeding wise counsel from those who God had appointed around her.

God gives us authority and leadership within the Body of Christ for our own protection, safety, empowerment and ultimately our good and the collective good of the Kingdom family. Esther was accountable and remained under the influence and instruction of those who had been positioned around her. She didn't go off and do things her way, however she thought best, as a young, naive teenager, but instead listened and obeyed. God leads us in instruction and wisdom through those He places over and around us for our own benefit. When spiritual mothers and fathers are both appointed and anointed by God, we can be sure their hearts are not just focused on our good, but for the good of all those around us.

There are no lone-rangers in the Kingdom of God. We are called the Body of Christ for a reason. It is essential that we remain under the covering God gives us - to protect us and empower us. We need to surround ourselves with wise counsel. We need to seek and ask, but more importantly, we need to obey, adjust to and heed what they say. It is imperative in life and in our own spiritual growth to surround ourselves with people who are bigger than us, spiritual mothers and fathers who are more mature, wiser, stronger, who are living thriving, victorious, fruitful lives, who have more experience and most importantly who know the King better than we do. Because if they know the King intimately, then they can give us counsel and wisdom, leadership and protection based on His goodness and love and from a place of true covenant relationship.

"When her turn came to go to the king, she did not ask for anything

> *except what Hegai, the king's eunuch, keeper of the women, suggested. Esther gained favour in the eyes of everyone who saw her."* **Esther 2:15**

Esther could have had anything she asked of the king. It's interesting that verse 15 doesn't specify what exactly it was that Esther requested, but emphasises it was exactly what Hegai suggested. When we submit to the God-given anointed and appointed authority around us and heed their wisdom, we develop a habit of making the right choices, which leads to gaining favour in the eyes of everyone around us (verse 15). This reminds me so much of a few people in the Bible who all increased in favour with both God and man. The first was Samuel (1 Sam 2:26), the second was Jesus (Lk 2:52), and the third was the early Church (Acts 2:47). Wow, if Jesus himself had to grow in favour with both God and man, how much more so do we!

CHAPTER 5

PRUNING, PURGING & PURIFYING

With God's gifts, favour and wisdom upon her, Esther embarked on the year long journey of beautification in preparation for the king. Now, I know us ladies can take a long time to get ready for the men in our life, but 12 months really does seem like an exceptionally prolonged endurance for a girl to be prepared for presentation to another guy. I mean, my husband struggles to wait half an hour for me to get ready, let alone a year! But when the man at the end of the process is the king of the entire empire, it's imperative to value the seriousness and weightiness of that marathon process. The correct preparation could see you living in the palace for the rest of your days. A lack of preparation, or being presented before you are fully ready, could see you miss the mark before you even had a chance.

Preparation and process are two words our modern minds and hearts do not receive too well. We're used to everything instantly at our fingertips. If we can't have it immediately we don't want it at all and we'll just move on to the next best thing. To think that something would take an extension of our time and effort is almost despised in todays culture. But without the adequate preparation we won't make the final cut. Without the necessary process we won't be properly developed.

POSITIONED FOR PURPOSE

For God to fully and faithfully release us into our position for His purpose, He must first prepare us. We must go through the process of purification, purging, pruning and polishing before He can use us for His plans.

I know how it feels. The preparation can seem like forever. The process can feel so unnecessarily drawn out. We know our call, we're excited for our assignment, we're passionate about our mission, we're full of faith and fervour for the Kingdom and we're rearing to go. But the process of preparation is what is going to establish us to remain in the Kingdom position for the long run. It's the refining fire that fortifies us time and time again before we are finally shaped and strengthened as God's tools. It's the training, tests and trials that prove us ready for the arena in front of us, because once we're there we will either live from a place of victory or be struggling to stand because we overestimated ourselves and are under-prepared.

THE SWEET SMELL OF SUFFERING

> *"During the year before each young woman's turn to go to King Ahasuerus, the harem regulation required her to receive beauty treatments with oil of myrrh for six months and then with perfumes and cosmetics for another six months."* **Esther 2:12**

Although it is just one small verse in the whole book, I find it fascinating that the author mentions that the virgins beautification preparation required that the oil of myrrh was used for six months and then other perfumes for six months. Myrrh was used for the embalming of bodies and represents the oil of death and suffering. There is so much symbolism in the need for us to be prepared with the oil of suffering and death to ourselves, before we are prepared with the sweet smelling aromas of perfumes. Our preparation for positioning isn't easy. It is long, arduous, difficult and at times makes us want to give up. The purging and purifying is part of this process and it is painful! The emptying of ourselves is a difficult procedure, we truly feel the oil of suffering in our great preparation.

Just as Jesus was prepared for His burial by the sweet smelling perfume, it was counter balanced with the oil of myrrh. The place where Mary anointed His feet with the oil was called Bethany, which means *'house of affliction.'* [1] Jesus was prepared for the cross - His death and burial - through both the anointing of His feet with the perfume from the alabaster jar and the prophetic oil of suffering. Our preparation involves suffering. If we can't take up our cross and die to self when we're hidden away in our private life, then how are we possibly going to do it when we're surrounded by pressure? Don't for a minute think it will be any easier when you finally experience your breakthrough and you're running in your realm of assignment, mission and call. We must first endure the suffering before we endure the beautifying and polishing. We need to experience the suffering so that we smell like the fragrance of Jesus at the end of it. We can only smell like Him when we spend time with Him. Our preparation takes place in His presence, hidden away in the secret place, in our very own garden with our Groom, where we are prepared for presentation and positioning into our Promised Land.

A DEEPER LEVEL OF DEATH

Our relationship and faith-life joined in union with Jesus involves both suffering and beauty; it is both difficult and exquisite, the greatest sacrifice but for the most exceptional joy. Jesus endured the suffering of the cross for the joy set before Him (Heb 12:2). Everyone wants the good and glory but aren't willing to walk through the difficult hardships, the painful processes and the suffering situations. The reality is, we can't have the good and beautiful if we don't die with Him and take up our cross. But it is the very suffering that makes us beautiful. It is this painful process of purification that prepares us for presentation. Even the most exquisite in all the land, our Esther, was still required to go through the process of preparation.

God has to prepare us in the wilderness - the barren, dry, desert - before He can position us in our Promised Land, to make sure we can maintain the places and purposes He has planned for us to possess. Our foundations are absolutely essential if God is to build anything lasting on them. Without the right foundations, or if they are weak and flimsy, or if He allowed us to be positioned before we were fully prepared, the break-through would actually break *us*. The increase would incapacitate us. The promises would pummel us with its giants preventing us from possessing the positions of territorial, regional and governmental authority. It is by His grace and love that He takes us through a process before releasing us into His promises. He must ensure we can handle the call He has in store for us, that we will steward it faithfully and not obtain personal gain or use the favour, anointing, blessing or break-through for ourselves, but for His glory and His Kingdom. The oil of suffering we first endure in the painful purification process is to establish us, fortify our foundations and to ensure we are pure, mature and secure in identity and humility. This is what He can then build upon.

Let me stress this - absolutely every area of our own life must be put to death. Absolutely every part of our heart and idol of our affections and desires must be destroyed. Absolutely every mindset, thought, feeling, belief, opinion, alignment must die. We cannot have an ounce of flesh or an ounce of worldliness remaining. We truly are joining Him in His death - emptying our bodies of ourselves, so they He can fill up these vessels with His Spirit. Less of me and more of Him! We must climb up on that alter daily and surrender to Him every single ounce of us. There is always, always a deeper death. Even things we have died to before, He will come back again in due time and ask us to die deeper still. We never arrive, we are always being sanctified. Even when there's nothing left to purge out of us, He requires the polishing of the good within us. While the first death is by far the most profound and life transforming, we are continually being refined. We might as well set up our home on the alter, because we're never climbing down!

Purification is essential to the preparation process. Walking through the refining fire causes us to be purged of anything that is unequally mixed within us. It is the consecrating fire that purifies our hearts more and more. It sets us apart, consecrating us - He doesn't want us to be mixed with anything unholy, but more importantly, He doesn't want anything unholy mixed within our hearts, even if that is deep, deep down and almost oblivious to our conscience. In fact, these hidden agendas, weaknesses, idols, unbeliefs, insecurities, fears, strongholds, jealousies, offences, opinions, mindsets, tolerances, whatever they may be, are usually more volatile than those that we are already aware of. When we don't think we have an issue....that's an issue! Purifying digs deep down, deep within and removes the dross, the dirt, the 'works of the flesh' out of us. Again, we should not be upset about what ugly things we see coming up and out during this process, but we should be so thankful and joyful that He is purging them out of us (Rev 2:7, 3:18b-19, 9:1-2a; Eph 5:8, 13; John 8:32).

> *"You have tried my heart, you have visited me by night, you have tested me, and you will find nothing..."* **Psalm 17:3 (ESV)**

> *"Search me, O God, and know my heart! Try me and know my thoughts! And see if there be any grievous way in me, and lead me in the way everlasting!"* **Psalm 139:23-24 (ESV)**

If Esther wasn't properly prepared she wouldn't have been considered by the king. She would have missed her chance and the rest of this story would be non-existent. Even Esther, with her gorgeous God-given gifts, beauty, wisdom and heavenly favour still had to go through the process of preparation. This shows us that just like her, we too cannot simply rely on our gifts, or our anointing, or our favour. Our foundations have to be strong in order for Him to build upon. Our hearts need to be purged of anything worldly. We are after longevity in this life, not a flash in the pan promotion only to be knocked down by the first shaking that comes our way. If we gain positioning by our own doing, then *we* have to sustain that by our own strength. If God positions us when He knows we are fully prepared, then *He* will maintain our placement. Your preparation will determine your foundation and the strength of your foundation will determine your elevation.

The pruning, purging and polishing process of preparation isn't pleasant. It isn't easy. But it is absolutely necessary if we are to have any chance of not just prevailing, but remaining. The process of preparation to be completely used by God is long. It doesn't happen in magical moments, it doesn't occur in supernatural instances, it takes more than days, weeks, months even. Because it's in the hidden, quiet, unseen places of preparation that our hearts are truly purified and prepared for the positioning of His promises, plans and purposes. It's easy to read this story and in a matter of mere verses Esther is elevated from an exiled orphan to the favourite wife of the king and becomes queen.

In the same way, we can look at other people around us and think they've had sudden overnight promotion, but we haven't seen the years of preparation they have lived through to get to this point. We haven't seen the struggles, the trials, the tests, the failures, the losses, the cost, the price, the pruning, the sacrifice, the stripping, the shaking, the battle, the warfare, the assassination attempts of the enemy that they have had to endure to get to where they are before God finally released them into their divine assignment. Don't be fooled by the limited number of words in these small sentences, preparation takes time. And just like Esther, if we obey His leading and work with the Holy Spirit and what He has given us, if we apply the wisdom He is bestowing upon us through the people He has appointed around us, His favour will pour out over us and see an acceleration happen within us. Only He can do this, but we can partner with Him in the process by surrendering and yielding ourselves to Him moment by moment.

PRUNING THE FRUITFUL FOR FURTHER PRODUCE

One of my all time favourite passages is Jesus the Living Vine in John 15:1-17. I continually meditate on this and always come out with more and more depths of revelation for abiding in Christ. One thing I love most is that Jesus tells us that God prunes the branches that are *already* producing fruit. We often associate the act of spiritual pruning with cutting off dead things, but John 15:2 tells us that Jesus cuts off fruitless branches but *'prunes every fruitful branch to yield a greater harvest.'* Here is the encouragement my friend - if you are being pruned, then that means you are already fruitful. And if you are being fruitful and pruned by God, then it's for the purpose of yielding a greater harvest. I love how the Amplified version describes it - *"...and every branch that continues to bear fruit, He [repeatedly] prunes, so that it will bear more fruit [even richer and finer fruit]."* In order to continue producing fruit for God we have to be prepared to be continually pruned. God only disciplines those He loves (Heb12:6). I can only discipline my own children. Imagine I dared to discipline someone else's child! Similarly, imagine if I *never* disciplined my own children, that would be a form of neglect - abuse even - and shows a complete lack of love for their wellbeing and future. If we are feeling disciplined by God, it truly is His greatest love for us and a clear sign of His shaping and forming us into all He has called us to be.

But what exactly is the fruit that John 15 insinuates that we're expected to yield? It's the obedience to His commands and it's the fruit of the Spirit. These two go hand in hand, because we can't obey His commands without the fruit of the Spirit and we can't produce the fruit of the Spirit without obeying His commands. And the best part is that it all comes down to the one thing, as Jesus points out to us in verse 10, you guessed it - love. The fruit He is producing in us is love. The fruit of the Spirit is love in the various expressions of joy, peace, patience, kindness, goodness, gentleness and self control (Gal 5:22-23). The mark of maturity is love (Col 3:14). Love is ultimate obedience to His commands (John 15:12; Mark 12:30-31).

In this passage Jesus tells us that we are His true, intimate friends when we obey all that He commands us. What does He command of us? To love. *"Love the Lord your God with all your heart and with all your soul and with all your mind and with all your strength, and love your neighbour as you love yourself. There is no command greater than these "* (Matt 22:37 ESV). But the amazing thing is that not only are we commanded to love, but love itself is what empowers us to obey! Can you see the gracious cycle here? There is no striving or trying in human strength, there is no place for religious to-do lists, because it doesn't originate from us but it is produced *within* us by the Holy Spirit when we live in union with Jesus (John 15:5). And when we live unified with Him we can ask whatever we desire and it will be done (John 15:7). How can we be sure to ask the right thing? Because when we are mature, intimate friends, He speaks to us and reveals God's will (John 15:15) all for the purpose of going into the world to bear fruit for the Kingdom. Wow! It all comes down to intimacy and abiding in Him. He reveals His secrets and His mysteries and His ways to His closest friends. We must abide in His presence, *in Him*.

Continuing with this theme in John 16:22-24 Jesus tells us that we can ask the Father with boldness anything in His name and the Father will do it because of our relationship with Jesus. So it's crucial to know what our relationship is with Jesus. Are we a servant, or a friend (John 15:14-15)? Burdened by the heavy religious yoke, or co-labouring with Christ's easy load (Matt 11:28-30)? Acting as a Martha trying to do all the things, or sitting at His feet as a Mary? What is our relationship with God? Is He our Father, or a dictator? Are we a child - a son, a daughter - or an orphan? Our level of identity reveals our level of intimacy, but only those who live continually in union with Christ can ask anything of the Father in His name and it will be done in order to bear greater fruit. These children of God who are positioned in the heavenly places, bringing the Kingdom to earth in Jesus' authority, who are pruned and purified, are the carriers of His power here on earth releasing miracles and wonders to the world that all point to God's love, power, Lordship and all for His glory.

A CALL TO INTERCESSION

The way we can know His will and ask anything in His name and receive it, is to abide in Him. But let's take a deep dive into the New Testament understanding of intercession. The Greek word for intercession is *énteuxis*. This word is always used separately to prayer, because it's function is actually very different to simply praying, but is instead, a *way* of praying. According to Strong's Greek Concordance, intercession means *'intervention led by God, marking intersection between heaven and earth as it reflects God's specific will.'*[2] The root term is *tygxánō* which means *'to strike, hit the bullseye, spot on, to fall in line with.'*[3] So intercession means intervention between heaven and earth which literally hits the mark of God's will!

No doubt the first thing you think of when you hear that is that intercession is therefore an antonym of sin - the word *hamartánō*, which means *'to miss the mark'* and is likened to an archer's arrow missing the target.[4] As Strong's Greek Concordance points out, biblical intercession centres on waiting upon the Lord to learn what hits the mark (what is His will), therefore guiding us to act as His agents here on earth. It sure takes 'your will be done on earth as it is in heaven' (Matt 6:10) to a whole other level! If missing the mark is sinning, then how powerful is intercession for us to know the will of the Father in order to align ourselves with His very will and be able to pray knowing our prayers hit the mark!

We can't just come and simply ask Him anything we want, like we so often do in prayer when we pray from our flesh and from our human nature. I can't just pray whatever I want, whatever my will is, even if I think it's pretty good - I must first find out what *His* will is and then join my faith to His will in order for my prayers to actually *hit the mark*. But how can we know what His specific will is in order for us to pray it? Well, the word *entygxanō* means '*to meet with, to converse with, to consult, to confer with, to entreat, to encounter, to call upon and make petition and supplication.*'[5] In Greek, the preposition of 'en' in this word actually intensifies the rest of the word and means '*in the realm (sphere) of, as in the condition (state) in which something operates from the inside (within).*'[6] Can you see the beautiful picture unveiling before us that brings the whole of John 15 and 16 alive as we abide in Him and we gain His heart and therefore can ask anything in His name and it will be done? Let's continue in this revelatory treasure hunt!

So our word for intercession *énteuxis,* means Spirit-directed intervention - the petitions of believers as they fall in line with God's will - revealing how the one intervening should get involved after drawing near to God and agreeing with His revealed will. True intercession seeks to act only as the Lord directs![7] It is in the realm of abiding in Him - in the sphere of being in His throne room, in the place of dwelling in the heavenly Holy of Holies - that we are transformed, through intercession, as we discover what God's will really is (as we linger longer and wait upon Him in worship, adoration, exultation, magnification), and as we change our mere opinions, beliefs, values, understanding to align with His heart, His mind, His will, we become one with Him. We abide in Him and His Spirit abides in us, revealing the heart (will) of the Father and the mind of Christ (1 Cor 2:10-16). This is sanctification! This is purification! This is consecration! This is transformation! This is the call of the hour we are in, unto intercession!

POSITIONED FOR PURPOSE

THE FRUITLESS FIG TREE

Jesus gives us a glimpse into what our life (and churches) will look like if we pursue anything other than His Kingdom and righteousness. In Mark 11:12-14, Jesus and His disciples come across a fig tree that looked luscious and leafy from a distance, but upon closer investigation, when Jesus went to pick its fruit, they found it was completely fruitless, for it was not in season. Jesus then had the audacity to curse the fig tree! The very next day, the group passed by the same location and the disciples discovered that the tree had withered and was as good as dead (Mk 11:22-21).

Jesus expects us to bear fruit for Him, for His Kingdom. Too many believers, churches, ministries and movements look impressive from the outside. From a distance, the large leaves look luscious and lovely, the canopy of vibrant green colour captivates our senses and woos us in. The structure of the ecosystem inside looks strong and durable and plenty of other people are enjoying the plant in all its prestige. Yet there is one thing missing…fruit. The grandiose of great movements are not what God is asking for. He is expecting fruit. What fruit? The fruit that He Himself produced in His ministry time on earth (Is 61). The fruit of the Spirit (Gal 5:22-24). The fruit of the early church. The fruit - evidence of His purity, power and presence - that we have written all throughout the New Testament as a plumb line and measuring stick for a life that we will one day have to give an account for. Fruitfulness or fruitlessness that will eventually determine what we will govern over as we steward what we have been given right now, today, in this life, on earth (Lk 19:16-27).

A fruitless tree is missing three essential things: water (the infilling, indwelling and overflowing of the Holy Spirit), a deep root system (the foundation of Word of God), and pruning (the refining of the Father). In this passage in Mark, Jesus warns that He will completely uproot anything that does not bear fruit. We can produce all the luscious leaves we want, we can have the prettiest facade, the sturdiest structures, the most intellectual institutions, but without the fruitfulness of the Kingdom we will simply be uprooted, never to produce fruit again.

But Nat, the fig tree wasn't even in season, how is this fair?

We are to be prepared in season and out. When we are planted firmly, deep down in fertile soil, by the streams of living water, we will naturally produce fruit in every season of life (Ps 1:3). These verses in Mark also reveal to us that it is our inner life that God expects to be flourishing, not our outward facade. Our hearts need pruning of the things of this world, we need rich and fertile soil around us for our roots to go deep down into the timeless truth of His Word and the unshakable foundation of Jesus, and we need the continual flowing streams of living water of the Holy Spirit to be pouring out over us, in us and through us that we may produce His fruit in *every* season.

> *"He is like a tree planted by water, that sends out its roots by the stream, and does not fear when heat comes, for its leaves remain green, and is not anxious in the year of drought, for it does not cease to bear fruit."*
> **Jeremiah 17:7-8 (ESV)**

> *"And on the banks, on both sides of the river, there will grow all kinds of trees for food. Their leaves will not wither nor their fruit fail, but they will bear fresh fruit every month, because the water for them flows from the sanctuary. Their fruit will be for food, and their leaves for healing."*
> **Ezekiel 47:12 (ESV)**

THE KING CALLS YOU BY NAME

> *"The king loved Esther more than all the other women."*
> **Esther 2:17a**

God has a call and position for His purpose reserved just for you. But even more than that, He has a place in His heart just for you. He desires you and your affection, more than anything you could ever do for Him. And He chooses you, calls you and summons you by name, every single day. You don't need to earn

His affection through the heavy yoke and difficult burdens of religious duty and striving - you already have His affection. And *from* His pure affection and intimacy, you obey Him and His Word, because you too, overflow with love toward Him. *You are loved by the King!* You are sought after by the King. Your heart is pursued. This love story is not about your position, your purpose, your calling, your destiny, your assignment, your mission or anything like that. It is about your heart! It is about your affection! He is a jealous God! His heart longed for you, and He created you and conceived you and brought you into this world because He desired *you*, and He wants nothing other than your love and affection. Everything else is a byproduct, everything else is the overflow, but this love story is about the most intimate story of all, His love for you that made Him choose to leave the glory of heaven and come down to this humble earth and to endure the cross, His passion, for *you*. He desires your heart, your affection, your thoughts toward Him, like a rightfully jealous husband who watches on as His Beloved lustfully flirts with ministry, assignments, movements, programs, promotions, platforms, chasing after all 'the things.' He desires *your heart*. Your *whole heart*.

Song of Songs takes us into the most passionate journey of Jesus' love for us as His Beloved - for *you*. As we read His wooing words dripping with adoration for us, His Bride to be, our identity in Him becomes solidified as we begin to see our worth, value, and identity as pure, holy and righteous. Not just loveable, but loved. Unconditionally. It is the overwhelming encounter with His love that convicts us and causes us to turn and repent. Why wouldn't we? Why would we do anything else? Why would we stay in lifestyles and habits that grieve His Spirit so deeply? Why would we do anything that hurts or disappoints the One we love, our Beloved? When we know we are loved and live from that overwhelming love of God, when we know our worth, when we know we are favoured by the King, then He can position us in the promises that He has prepared for us, and prepared us for.

Your preparation is pivotal, because your position isn't for you - it is for God's plans, purposes, pursuits and people. This is exactly why we need the purging and purifying process to solidify His foundations in our hearts and lives. We must be able to faithfully and humbly steward the positioning into the prophetic promises for His glory and His Kingdom. And let me just say, having a false humility that is deceived by the spirit of religion that says 'positions and prophesies and promises are not to be pursued,' is just as detrimental and demonically deceiving as having eyes and agendas for our own personal gain. If His positioning of His people is for His purposes and His glory and His Kingdom, then anything less is selfish, faithless and disobedient. And that includes 'humbly' declining the positioning, thinking we are being godly.

Think about this for a moment…a people who believe they are powerless, who possess no authority (of Jesus), who don't know their identity as heirs of the Kingdom or sons and daughters, who don't believe they can hear the Father's voice, who have never experienced the overwhelming power and presence of the Spirit that releases supernatural manifestations of the gifts given to them, who then never take an ounce of dominion over the dark kingdom or the powers and principalities of the unseen realm …are not at all a threat to the enemy, are they? Selah that for a moment and think about how this doctrine of demons disempowers God's people for the very assignment and commission they are called to in His Kingdom.

Let me be crystal clear - I'm not at all talking about worldly platforms here, I'm talking about God given mission fields and ripe crops ready for harvest. We aren't talking about fame or name, we're talking about Kingdom influence that breaks conformity to the culture around us and sets us apart as His holy people. We aren't talking about public platforms or preachy pulpits coveted by the flesh (because who else knows that Christian celebrity culture is just as real and rampant as the carnal world?), we're talking about the foundations upon which God will build. We're not talking about 'successful' ministries led by single people and sole names, we're talking about movements of the Holy Spirit that include the everyday remnant from all over the earth. We aren't talking about individual empires, we're talking about the collective Kingdom. We aren't talking about mega churches, we're talking about homes and hubs that host the atmosphere of heaven. We aren't talking about denominations, we're talking about families. We're not talking about the selfish fulfilment of fleshly promises and prophesies, we're talking about His sovereign hand coming down in justice and judgment -

breaking His people away from the bondage and oppression of the world's systems and the evil that prevails and taking them back to their God-given Promised Land - the spiritual territory and inheritance where we take dominion over the darkness through our God-given authority to reign over in His power and by His presence (Ps 2).

HEARING THE ENEMY'S PLANS

> *"When the virgins were gathered a second time, Mordecai was sitting at the King's Gate. (Esther had not revealed her family background or her ethnicity, as Mordecai had directed. She obeyed Mordecai's orders, as she always had while he raised her.) During those days while Mordecai was sitting at the King's Gate, Bigthan and Teresh, two of the king's eunuchs who guarded the entrance, became infuriated and planned to assassinate King Ahasuerus. When Mordecai learned of the plot, he reported it to Queen Esther, and she told the king on Mordecai's behalf. When the report was investigated and verified, both men were hanged on the gallows. This event was recorded in the Historical Record in the king's presence."* **Esther 2:19-23**

Suddenly in the story we have been snuck into a side-scene regarding Esther's uncle, turned adoptive father, Mordecai. As we read through this story we must realise that Mordecai is a prophetic picture of the coming Christ and all He was to accomplish. And today, as we read this, we see Mordecai representing Jesus in the time we are in right now. Exiled from heaven to earth, He took on the form of a foreigner from His own home. Just as orphaned Esther was rescued by her next of kin, so too have we been saved by our Kinsman Redeemer. Just as she was adopted into His family, so too have we been adopted as sons and daughters of the living God.

Mordecai was waiting at the city gate when he overheard a private conversation regarding the assassination attempt of King Ahasuerus. He told Queen Esther, who passed on this pivotal piece of information to the king and

PRUNING, PURGING & PURIFYING

these two scoundrels were executed; the kings life saved. Jesus doesn't just wait for us at the gates, HE IS THE GATE! (John 10:9) And as we offer our thanksgiving we enter His gates and as we praise, we enter into His courts (Ps 100:4). When we live in His presence we grow deeper in relationship with Him and He whispers to our souls and speaks revelation mysteries (Dan 2:22; Jer 33:3). As we grow in our gifts of supernatural discernment, hearing the voice of our Father, Shepherd and Friend, He reveals secrets of heaven, strategies, solutions, blueprints, ideas, innovations, wisdom, understanding and insight. He also reveals to us through words of knowledge and revelation the schemes of the enemy planning to bring us down. Through the Holy Spirit we can learn of the strategies of the enemy to attempt to assassinate us, others, God's people and the plans against His Kingdom. A great example of this is the story of Elisha hearing the kings battle plans and thwarting them before they occurred (2 Kings 6:8-14).

As I have personally grown in my prophetic gifting and pressed in to hearing the sounds of the spiritual atmosphere more and more, I have experienced this phenomenon on many occasions. If you are in any way prophetic you will most likely be familiar with the 'chatter' that seems to come part and parcel with the gift of the prophetic. This chatter can often feel like a swirling around our minds of all the words, curses, slander, witchcraft, divination, judgment, jealousy sometimes even thoughts and feelings against us from other people (the source being the enemy and the demonic spirits behind them, not people themselves). As I have grown in these giftings and discernment, I have learned to be able to sift through what is intended by the enemy to confuse and torment me, and what is allowed by God to graciously reveal to me behind the scenes information that will help me to pray and intercede, if not completely come against an attack of the enemy before it even happens. Proactivity is greater than reactivity!

There have been times where I have been shown scenes in my mind of people reacting to me or my words or a particular situation. There have been times I have overheard conversations (in the spirit, not in real life) amongst others who were talking about me and against me. God has downloaded plans against me and empowered me with solutions and strategies to come against these attacks before they even happen. I have even been taken into 'board meetings' and 'crisis meetings' of leaders and institutions that God opened my eyes and ears to see in the spirit and hear what was being said and to be able to prepare for and prevail over in prayer and intercession, the very plans against me (which ultimately, are against God and His plans). God has even revealed to me personal stalkers on social media (not serious crime stalkers who are actually a danger…just people on the outskirts of my life who are surveilling my every move and who are 'watching' and 'tracking' because of their own insecurities, woundedness and brokenness), through hilarious yet supernatural means, so I know who's watching and when, and can even pray against the attacks of their flippant words and conversations/ curses against me. There is nothing too small or insignificant, if we believe He can do it, He will!

Imagine we all grew in this gift that is available to all of us (as Paul urges us to earnestly desire the greater gifts, especially prophesy: 1 Cor 14:39). Imagine how the Kingdom of God would advance and overpower the prince of this world and the spirit of the air, if God's people stood up into their rightful positions and embraced the gifts He is freely giving us to govern with Him on this earth. What secrets of the enemy would we hear and be able to overcome in an instant? What plans of attack would we be able to thwart before they even have a chance to come to fruition? What injustices and blatant evils would we be able to completely prevent and obliterate if we had access to supernatural intel? My friends, WE DO! We DO have all of this, AND MORE!

In His kindness and compassion the Holy Spirit reveals the plans of the enemy and his tactics so that we can defeat him before he even attempts the attack upon us (Eph 6:10- 18; 2 Cor 2:11; 2 Tim 2:23-26; 1 Pet 5:8). That's how we can fight from victory. But it requires us to be so intimate with Jesus in order to hear His voice. And it requires us to have all our armour on, ready for battle, and be mature soldiers, not easily swayed or knocked down. It requires us to be on guard and aware of the enemy who prowls around like a lion looking for people to devour.

PRUNING, PURGING & PURIFYING

LIVING FROM A PLACE OF DEEP INTIMACY

Why do we need this ability? Because as we are purposefully and strategically placed into our position in the Kingdom, there will always be attacks of the enemy to bring us down or better yet, to prevent us from even taking our place in the first instant. But words of knowledge, wisdom and prophecy, words of encouragement, exhortation, admonition, warnings and simply hearing Jesus' loving voice over us and the heart of God for us is enough to break down these schemes and everything that rises against us.

Jesus used these very things to lead people to Himself. Love. Words of knowledge. Words of prophecy. The woman at the well in John 4, Zacchaeus in Luke 19:1-10. Hearing the voice of God through means of prophetic words or words of knowledge for others takes us (and them) deep into the heart of the person. Religion cannot do that. End of story. The enemy does have a counterfeit that is working profusely within the world, but it doesn't come from and lead to the love of God. Its fruit is not lasting. Although its immediate satisfaction may appear promising, it is deceitful and ultimately unfulfilling. This is the real definition of a false prophet. The New Age, astrology, psychics, mediums and everything else that goes with all of this is absolutely one of the biggest false prophets in the world today. While the religious point their finger at the real prophets (and call them false, simply because they don't believe God speaks today - but in reality, if there are false prophets then there obviously has to be real prophets), the *actual* false prophets in the world are gaining influence, because the Church is too busy bickering within to align in unity and point the finger outwardly and to rise up in authority and power and to call down and destroy the *real* deception!

We have to be positioned in His presence with our ear on His chest, listening to the beat of His heart to know the rhythms of grace that are overflowing from Him to captivate those He is passionately pursuing. Intimacy. It all comes from intimacy and all comes back to intimacy. It is all about His love. He speaks, because He loves. He woos because He loves. He pursues because He loves. He heals because He loves. He reveals intimate, unknown, individual details, because

He loves. He sent His Son, because He loves.

There's a reason why the greatest verses of love are smack bang in the middle of the chapters on spiritual gifts and prophecy (1 Cor 12-14), because all of our giftings and anointings have to come from and return to and be filtered through love. Love remains and love is the greatest. Prophecy has to come from love and draw people to His love. All the gifts we work in are for the purpose of connecting people to the heart of God. Prophesying can only come from a place of love, giving words of knowledge can only come from God's heart of love, healings and miracles can only come from His love (Jesus was moved by compassion every time He healed = LOVE!). Love is intimate. Love is individual. Love is where it begins and ends. Knowing the God of the heavens and earth knows them, sees them, understands them, has a heart for them, has time for them, has a plan and purpose for them...*this* will set the captives free.

And love is where it ties in to the family of God in this era. It is possible for people and churches to manifest the gifts of the Spirit, whilst also walking in worldliness and lifestyles of sin, because the gifts that God gives us are irrevocable (Rom 11:29). However, it is essential that we grow in the fruit of the Spirit while we simultaneously grow in the gifts of the Spirit, in order to produce the greatest fruitfulness for this Kingdom. On one hand we have the religious church who renders the gifts of the Spirit redundant, therefore never moving in any power, never walking in any authority or dominion over any of the enemy's domain, but on the other hand we have the extreme opposite where we see many individual names moving in the manifested power of the gifts but absolutely void of any fruit of the Spirit. When we don't have the level of character and purity to match the level of gifting we are working in, we create the perfect conditions for a personal fall. And sadly, when this is a public ministry, a world renowned mega church, or someone who has a large influence, this personal fall can take many down with them. Our character must match our gifting. In fact, character must be the foundation upon which our gifts flow from. A healthy, internal heart will produce healthy external fruit.

THE GREAT EXPOSING

We are entering a season of exposing and cleaning house, and while I fully believe that this means God Himself will unveil all the evil and blatant injustice that has been running and ruling our world for centuries (millennia even, right back to Genesis 6 & 11). But before the truth is exposed in the world, I believe the exposing is going to begin in God's house first (1 Pet 4:7). When we speak of things such as revival and the great harvest, we have to be prepared for our own personal shaking first and foremost, to prepare the way as He creates a firm foundation from which to build His Church upon. This is nothing to fear, but the necessary purging, pruning and purifying that we have been speaking of. If done well and with the leading of the Holy Spirit, this can be somewhat private - assuming we are quick to accept what the Lord is exposing within us and to us, and that we are quick to genuinely repent and turn from our ways. This requires true humility. But as we are *all* being purified, there is going to be an exposing within the Church herself. Not all will be able to so easily let go of their platforms and prestige, their names and fame, their self-built empires or man-made glory, nor their lifestyles of hidden sin and carnal bondage. I believe the Church will be deeply shaken with the exposing of shocking and devastating truths coming to light. But, if we have our faith firmly in Jesus alone, we ourselves will not be shaken by the exposing of such devastating darkness in people we thought held the light. All of this exposing, both personal and corporate, is essential to precede the greater exposing that is coming to the world and those that we know are truly corrupt. If God is to deliver many blinded by the deception, then He also must first clean house so that He can deliver them *into* a Church that is pure, consecrated, set apart and holy. He must first set His people free. It is His mercy and goodness, His grace and love that He gives us an opportunity to cleanse us deeper and deeper, so that He may build on firm foundations and establish His true Church in the times to come.

The true Church that is arising in this era moves in the gifts granted to us by the Spirit which is for the building of the Kingdom of God, but simultaneously - and I would say, foundationally - grows in the fruit of the Spirit first and foremost. Again, imagine an army of sons and daughters equipped with the power and authority of heaven who possess the purified character and internal foundation of the purist virtues of the Lord, fully alive and thriving in their life and world, set free from all demonic strongholds, addictions, lifestyles, secret sins, and delivered from the generational bondage of their forefathers that is lying dormant as it's passed on in bloodlines because it has never been confronted and cast out. The enemy could not stand against it! This is the great commission, this is the call of the Kingdom.

GOD IS THWARTING THE ENEMY'S PLANS

When you are called you are automatically on the enemy's radar. When you begin to walk towards the paths, plans and purposes God has for you, you are on his hit-list. When you start stepping into the very assignments God has designed you for, he calls in the heavy arsenal. And when you are on the brink of break-through, he brings out the big guns. Just as God has a plan of purpose for you, so too does the enemy have a plan of destruction, disruption, distraction and ultimately, assassination of your assignment and destiny.

Here in chapter three of Esther we are introduced to the villain of the story. Haman was promoted to a position of power by the reigning ruler of the earthly world. And once in this place, demanded to be worshiped. The world around him would bow down to him. He wanted glory and his corrupt heart desired to be worshiped. He represents our real enemy - the same principality who saw God's glory and coveted it for himself, who pursued being worshipped over being the worshipper he was actually created to be (Ez 28, Is 14). As the fall of Lucifer saw him banished from God's presence, he set out to deceive and destroy humanity. Still hungry for worship and the glory that was God's, he thought he had won the eternal battle when Jesus took His final breath on the cross. But he was crushed under His heel when three days later the power of God resurrected Jesus from the dead and He took back the keys to death, ascended to the heavens at the right hand of God and commanded us to walk in the authority and power that is rightfully His. Now our enemy roams the earth like a lion, looking for souls to devour (1 pet 5:8).

Satan didn't just want to destroy Jesus, he wants to destroy all of God's people. Because destroying us destroys God's Kingdom...or so he thinks. The enemy's goal is to steal, kill and destroy (John 10:10). He is the power at work in this world, but God's people have been given the keys of the Kingdom, and all authority in heaven and on earth has been given to Jesus Christ, who has commanded us to go forth and use it (Matt 28:18-20).

We share in His power and authority as we are united as one with Him (Eph 1:19-23; Phil 3:10; Acts 2:33), sitting with Him in heavenly places at the victorious right hand of God (Eph 2:5-6), and we are called to co-reign in this world - not over people, but over the powers and principalities of the spiritual realm (Eph 6:10-18). Our positioning is for a purpose - God's Kingdom - for the Kings dominion to be extended and strengthened, for His domain to be deepened throughout this earth like the great commission commands us to do, until the very day He comes back as the Lion of Judah, and treads both feet on the Mount of Olives, defeating the enemy of Israel and He establishes in fulfilment, His Kingdom on this earth as we His people, reign in righteousness with Him (Zech 14).

If the enemy can't completely take us out, then he will do all he can to weaken and lessen our purpose here on earth. He knows Jesus won that battle on the cross, but he's not giving up in his pursuit to devour and destroy any and all he can. He is not a happy loser. If he cannot get us to worship him the way the world inadvertently does, then he will do all he can to prevent us from walking in God's will and diving into our Kingdom call here on earth.

Just as Mordecai refused to bow down to Haman because it went against his beliefs and values, so too will we have to make a stand that shows everyone around us that we will not compromise, we will not go with the flow, we will question what we are expected to do and we will not bow down to the god's of this world. We will stand out like a sore thumb. We will stand out like someone who is standing upright while everyone else has their face on the ground bowing down to the beast system. And once we have taken our stand, our true identity will be made known. Calling ourselves 'believers' cannot look like living the same way as the rest of the world. Modern day Christianity in the western church has become so complacent and the term so loosely used to simply having some kind of distant belief in God but not actually worshipping Him as Lord of our life. It means calling upon Him in desperation in times of dire circumstances as a very last resort, but not living in His presence everyday and growing in loving relationship with Him as our Lord. Knowing Him as our Saviour is the entrance, knowing Him as our Lord is the ultimate. Casual Christianity cannot cut it in this era we have entered. Saying a prayer and hoping to get into heaven one day while living whatever lifestyle our lewd hearts desire is not placing Jesus as Lord over our life. He must be the centre upon which our hearts, minds, souls and will turn.

A line is being drawn in the sand. If we are for Him then we must start living that way, acting that way. It's time to get serious in our faith, in our beliefs, in our convictions, in our values, in our obedience. It is pivotal that we are prepared to be put on display in the most powerful way, but that requires taking a stand and obviously living differently to everyone around us. Are you really up for that? Are you prepared to pay the price, even if (when) that means persecution and suffering?

Because when you truly do, the world will want to devour you. The enemy will come after you. God's people are destined for persecution. Christianity is the only 'religion' in this world that is not tolerated, because we are not willing to tolerate what our God does not tolerate. We are called to care more about what He cares for, than our own life. Are you *really* up for that? Mordecai's bold and faithful stand saw the enemy's target instantly aimed at him. But not just him, his entire people. We may want to keep our real identity as Jesus lovers hidden and quietly subdued, but there is going to come a time when we simply cannot keep silent if we are genuinely serious about our faith in the one true God. We cannot go along with the status quo and the practices of our culture. If we genuinely live by different values, then it must show. It must be obvious. It must be revealed by the way we live. Although it may cause many around us to despise and ridicule us, if done in the leading of the Holy Spirit and walking in our identity in Christ, then it will be the bright shining beacon of light to all, pointing the way to something greater from within us.

THE ENEMY'S PLAN FOR OUR DESTRUCTION

> *"Then Haman informed King Ahasuerus, "There is one ethnic group, scattered throughout the peoples in every province of your kingdom, keeping themselves separate. Their laws are different from everyone else's and they do not obey the king's laws. It is not in the king's best interest to tolerate them. If the king approves, let an order be drawn up authorising their destruction....Letters were sent by couriers to each of the royal provinces telling the officials to destroy, kill, and annihilate all the Jewish people - young and old, women and children - and plunder their possessions on a single day, the thirteenth day of Adar, the twelfth month."* **Esther 3:8-9, 13**

In this story, Haman is the enemy's weapon to destroy God's people. If He can't win he'll bring everyone else down, too. There is a letter sent out with your name on it with orders to destroy, kill and annihilate you, because you are God's. There is an army sent out to conquer you. The enemy has a plan for your destruction because he sees you as a threat. Mordecai threatened the power, position and plans of Haman. *You* threaten the power, position and plans of the principalities of this world. The enemy has free rein of this world we live in, but God has given all authority and power to Jesus, and - united with Jesus - through us too. But if we don't know we have authority, how can we walk in it? If we don't believe we possess the power of the name and blood of Jesus, how can we possibly wield it?

Just as God has sent forth messengers and an invitation to the world, so too does the enemy make it his aim to get to every soul who poses a threat to his kingdom and ruling power here on earth. If you pose a threat, you're on the list. We are born into a fallen world, but we are reborn into a Kingdom, a family that resides in - yet lives above - this natural realm. We have all power and authority that Jesus has given us and empowers us to use. The apostle Paul speaks of the three heavens throughout his epistles. The first heaven is earth, the natural realm, where we physically reside. Ephesians 2:5-6 says that we are seated in the heavenly realms with Christ, that which Paul was taken up to the heavens in his great encounter in 2 Corinthians 12:2, which he calls the third heaven. The second heaven is in between and this is the spiritual realm is where Satan and his principalities and powers are at battle with the angelic armies of heaven (Eph 6 10-18). Therefore, if we are seated in the third heaven, united with Jesus, then we have power and authority over the second and first heavens - both the spiritual realm and the natural realm here on earth. We are called to co-reign with Jesus, in accordance with God's will, with the empowerment of the Holy Spirit. Of course you are a threat to the enemy. And the more you are awakened to this revelatory truth and begin to step into this identity, the more targeted you will become.

Oh my Friends. My weary, exhausted, battered and bruised brothers and sisters. This is why the battle has been so fierce. This is why the torment has been relentless. This is why the days have felt like decades and why the disappointment and discouragement knocks on the door of your heart and mind, beckoning to be let in. Your call is so pertinent and powerful to the Kingdom of God that the enemy will do anything he possible can to prevent you from stepping into it. You are the greatest threat to the kingdom of darkness when you arise in your identity, when your eyes are unveiled to the falsehood and tactics of the spirit of religion and the complacent, compliant, compromised, tolerant, mixed spirit of deception in this world, and take up your position of power and authority, unified with Jesus, sitting at the right hand of God, ruling from the heavens, embarking on the ripe harvest field of the great commission. All for His glory!

Please know that we aren't trying to focus on the enemy, but it is ignorant to think we don't have one and foolish to not become aware of his schemes, strategies and tactics. We cannot be a passive, ignorant, oblivious Church. Being unaware of him is just as destructive as putting too much focus upon him. The passive church doesn't pose a threat to him. But the wise, faithful, bold warrior Bride certainly does.

WHO WILL YOU USE YOUR POSITION FOR?

Haman used his power and position for his own personal purposes, unlike Esther who used it for the greater good. Where are our hearts at? This again, is why the purging and purifying is so important - it is maturing, strengthening and developing humility within us so that God can trust us with positions, purposes, assignments and spheres of influence.

We are called to live like Mordecai - to be in the very midst of this dark, lost world, but to live in such a way that is so obviously different, even when it means persecution. God is doing a mighty move and He is calling us to partner with Him in purpose to see His rule and reign established in its fullness here on earth. The enemy's plan is to steal, kill and destroy, but God's plan is to protect you and set you up in positions to be used for His glory and to extend His Kingdom.

NOTES

1. Strong's Exhaustive Concordance of the Bible. (n.d.). *Béthania* #G963. In *biblehub.com*. Accessed July 5, 2019 from *https://biblehub.com/greek/963.htm*
2. Strong's Exhaustive Concordance of the Bible. (n.d.). *Énteuxis* #G1783. In *biblehub.com*. Accessed October 11, 2023 from *https://biblehub.com/greek/1783.htm*
3. Ibid *tygxanō* (#G5177)
4. Ibid *hamartánō* (#G264)
5. Ibid *entygxanō* (#G1793)
6. Ibid *en* (#G1722)
7. Ibid *énteuxis* (#G1783)

CHAPTER 6

AN INVITATION TO PARTNER WITH THE KING

"When Mordecai learned of all that had been done, he tore his clothes, put on sackcloth and ashes, and went out into the city, wailing loudly and bitterly. But he went only as far as the king's gate, because no one clothed in sackcloth was allowed to enter it. In every province to which the edict and order of the king came, there was great mourning among the Jews, with fasting, weeping and wailing. Many lay in sackcloth and ashes. Esther's female servants and her eunuchs came and reported the news to her, and the queen was overcome with fear." **Esther 4:1-4a**

Do you ever hear bad news and become overcome with fear? Do you lay awake at night worrying about your impossible circumstances or find yourself wracked with anxiety about problems you have no answers for? Do you ever sit back and dwell on the condition of the world that we are in now, or the circumstances surrounding you that you are feeling so suffocated by and end up feeling unbelievably overwhelmed with terror, crippled with confusion or devastated with despair? Yes, we know God can use all things for good, but when we focus on all the evil in the world, all the destruction happening around us and the future state of our children and generations to come, it's so easy to end up in a pit of depression, uselessness, powerlessness and hopelessness. So don't.

My greatest encouragement is to look for the Kingdom shining brightly amidst the darkness of this world today. Look for the places where faith is rising and His glory overpowering the darkness. Seek out the testimonies of healing, miracles, breakthrough and impossibilities being manifest in peoples lives and stories. I sadly hear so many believers despondently regurgitating all the horrible headlines they hear, all the evil they are seeing in the world, how far short we have fallen as the human race, how utterly hopeless not just the future, but even the present is for us as people. They say seemingly holy sentences like *'If only Jesus would come back now and save us from all of this'* or *'If only we could all just go to heaven and let this world lead itself into the doomed destruction it is destined for.'* Wow. Just...wow. Where is the hope in this? Where is our faith in God? Most importantly, where does the Word and His faithful promises and prophetic timeline come into play with these kinds of mindsets?

It sounds holy and humble but it's actually selfish and unscriptural. Furthermore, it's wrapped in religion. The answer to the evil, destruction, doom and gloom in the world we live in today isn't Jesus coming and taking us all away...it's Jesus coming out of us and His love and power overflowing into the world around us. It's us partnering with the plans and purposes that He has already predestined His people to do. When we wait around apathetically for the rapture to simply capture us away, we ignore the very real and imminent assignment of the hour we are in. We begin to focus inwardly, selfishly and lazily, instead of partnering with what God is doing in preparation for His great and powerful second coming. We aren't called to live in the little Christian bubble - only concerned for ourselves and separated from the real world around us. That real world couldn't get any more real - that real world is your children, your parents, your brothers and sisters, your family, your friends, your co-workers, your community, your city, your nation, your people. Just like Esther had a people, these are your people who's souls and eternities are on the line, and just like Esther, you have an opportunity to partner with the Creator of heaven and earth to see His sovereign will come to pass.

Too often we quote scriptures that rightly talk about how dark and dismal the end times will be. It's true, this world in and of itself is dark, evil and hopeless, and in the natural, it is only ever getting worse. It's true, suffering and persecution are destined for those of us who love the living God (John 16:33). But what so many believers fail to focus on, is the answer. Jesus. The majority of the western church are going to have an incredibly rude shock when they realise that the Bible's idea of being protected from the fiery wrath of the Lord that is undoubtedly coming against the wickedness of this world isn't Him giving us an early escape, but the very strength to endure to the end. He isn't removing us *from*, but preparing us to remain amongst and amidst the very world He is so desperate to save so that we can be the light we are called to shine bright in the darkest of times. A believer who thinks they're going to get whisked away prematurely is an unprepared person who is going to suddenly realise they've always been conscripted into an end days army and instead of using this time we have been given to strengthen, deepen, grow and learn to prevail, conquer and overcome in the victory of the cross and the blood of the Lamb, they have been sitting back waiting for a free ticket out that isn't coming until AFTER we prevail! God will absolutely protect His people in the times of His great wrath, but it will be like the Israelites in the land of Goshen, it will be like Noah who took shelter in the ark, it will be those who have the blood of the Lamb across the lintels of their hearts and the mark of the Bride on their forehead.

That is what Scripture promises and prophesies. A mature Bride who embraces her identity in Christ and all that the cross and resurrection have purchased, who has made herself ready and walks in purity, separated for a holy cause. An end times Bride who sits in her rightful place with her beautiful Beloved at the right hand of God in the throne room of heaven and who co-labours with Jesus (Eph 2:5-6), who wields His authority and power as He instructs us to do (Matt 28:18-20) in order to bring heaven to earth (Matt 6:10) and to see His will come to pass and His plans and purposes fulfilled in this world. A world where Christ reigns and He uses His people here on earth (that's why we are called the BODY of Christ!) to subdue and overpower the chaos, evil and plans of the enemy and usher in the goodness, glory, majesty and love of God.

WE ARE CALLED TO CONSECRATION, NOT SEGREGATION

> *"Arise, shine, for your light has come, and the glory of the Lord shines over you. For look, darkness will cover the earth, and total darkness the peoples; but the Lord will shine over you, and his glory will appear over you. Nations will come to your light, and kings to your shining brightness."* **Isaiah 60:1-3**

As the Israelite people were exiled in the land of Persia, so too are we living in a place that is not truly our home. But while here, we are not called to segregate ourselves and to build up walls of protection and privacy around us, we are explicitly called to be in the world. *"How can your light shine if it is hidden under a bowl?"* (Matt 5:13-16). We are called to be a city on the hill that shines the light of God and points the way to Him (Acts 13:47; Is 49:6). Our positioning in culture is about being placed on the top of the mountains of society in order for us to reign and govern over our own lives in a way that points to a holy God. The darker the night around us the brighter our light shines in the midst of it all. The more evil this world becomes the more separated we will appear. Our call is consecration, not segregation. Separation of values, character, integrity, truth, pursuits, desires - not physical boundaries and walls built up, with our precautionary moat and drawbridge pulled up nice and high for our own personal preservation and protection.

When we live as pure and holy separated people in the world, we stand out and shine brightly like the city on the hill that we are called to be. We point to the only answer this world has, we hold the only hope that is available. To ask to be removed from this horrendous home is self-serving and unbiblical. Our life is not about us, we are here for His kingdom and His glory. It's time we work with Him and look out to the great harvest that is upon us, we are fishers of men! No wonder the workers are few when we're only ever focusing on how bad the

AN INVITATION TO PARTNER WITH THE KING

world around us is He requires a people emptied of the desires and values of the world and filled with His eternal purposes and promises, walking in power and authority. Yet again, we come back to humility. Is this about us, or is this about Him? He desires many, many more to be saved, and it is only by His grace that He makes this time available - and make no mistake, He sees every heart that either has their own preservation and comfort and security as their main agenda, or those who have the Kingdom and His purposes and plans, no matter the cost (even our own lives), at the forefront of their hearts and mind.

The powerless believer cries out for an end of their personal suffering in this evil world, but it's at the very expense of the great call and commission, at the cost of making disciples of all nations. The believer who also suffers in this evil and dark world for the sake of His name, at the hand of the atrocities that we face each day of the enemy at play, but who knows their true identity as a child of God, who has a real revelation of the Kingdom realm, their inheritance, their place of position in the heavenlies, the mandate of authority and dominion that God commissioned to mankind in Eden and that Jesus passed on to us before His ascension, who nourishes themselves day and night on feasts of Scripture, who pray and intercede continually to discover and align with His will, who strengthen and deepen their intimacy with Jesus daily, and who know the Father's voice and that of their Shepherd and Counsellor...that believer...*that* believer does not fear! That believe does not sit back in apathy or hopelessness, because *that* believer is an overcomer, more than a conquerer, a victor, a pillar of the sanctuary (Rev 3:12), *that* believer walks in the power of the Spirit and sees and knows that Jesus transforms, Jesus sets free, Jesus heals, Jesus delivers, Jesus makes whole, Jesus has a mighty plan and a purpose, Jesus has given us biblical insight and foresight into the times and seasons to come, and we are not living in the dark like those without Him or those who are asleep, but we are living in the light where all things are revealed and made known (1 Thess 5:5), and Jesus has equipped us with every heavenly resource for such a time as this (Eph 1:3-6). We have no fear!

> *"But you, believers, are not in spiritual darkness [nor held by its power], that the day [of judgment] would overtake you [by surprise] like a*

> *thief; for you are all sons of light and sons of day. We do not belong to the night nor to darkness. So then let us not sleep [in spiritual indifference] as the rest [of the world does], but let us keep wide awake [alert and cautious] and let us be sober [self-controlled, calm, and wise]."*
>
> **1 Thessalonians 5:4-6**

So many believers are scared of words like 'position,' 'promises,' 'call,' 'assignment,' 'commission.' When we're not looking through the filters of Jesus' heart (nor have embraced the new wineskin), we think we're being so holy saying how selfish, prideful, wrong and ungodly these are. But when our hearts are truly purged of worldly ways, values and desires - through the fiery purifying process - it is then that God can lift us up into positions and places of His power, because He knows He can trust us. He can trust that we aren't going to use our positions, placement or influence for selfish gain. He can trust us that we will build His Kingdom and not our own. He can trust us because He knows we trust Him. Well meaning believers quote scriptures like *"live a humble, quiet, gentle life"* (1 Thes 4:11) in order to justify their passive existence and to vilify any other brothers or sisters who have any kind of position, platform or influence. But what is the point of possessing the Light of the World if we then go and cover it under a basket?

We are called to let our light shine and God Himself will position us in places that He has a specific plan and purpose for. *As* we live such humble, quiet, gentle lives. This description is not about the external, outward appearance of our lifestyle that is visible to everyone around us, it's describing our HEARTS! The position of our heart should be humble, gentle and quiet which will also be the fruit we bear in our life! This is the everyday army that God is polishing and preparing for these times we are in. Not the big shots, not the famous, not those with huge platforms and prominence, or followers and fans, but the humble, everyday, simple people who have been hidden in the caves, wandering in the wilderness and being prepared through their devotion, abandonment, worship, interceding in their war-rooms, and paying the cost of the expensive oil.

IS YOUR OIL FULL?

The timeless tale of the ten virgins has never been more pertinent than the days we are entering in this era. We cannot find ourselves without oil. We cannot come to a place where we suddenly realise we have been caught out, and now it is too late to 'purchase' the anointing we need. This oil will not be able to be purchased in a last minute realisation of the moment we are suddenly in. It must be purchased *now*. It must be collected and stored up *now*. It must be cultivated *now*. In the quiet. In the hidden. In the secret and secluded. In the every day. Oil certainly has a price. A costly price. It cannot be quickly rummaged up in an instant, we cannot borrow others oil, or pay someone to impart to us what can only be developed within us over time and through experience. Years of intellectual study cannot create it. Decades of service to the system cannot earn it. Selling ourselves out to lifetimes of ministry at the cost of our marriages, children and family cannot develop even an ounce of it.

Our oil is produced only through our intimacy with Him. The only way we can store up our oil is by pouring it out in abandoned worship to Him. We ourselves are the alabaster jar, shattered at His feet, anointing Him with our acts of worship and intimacy that breaks all the boxes of religion. The more time we spend with the Holy Spirit, the more time we are deep in the Word, the more time we are in the prayer closet interceding and communing with the Father, the more time we bask in the bridal chamber enjoying the presence of our beautiful Jesus, the more we worship and glorify and bless and honour Him in praise and thanksgiving, the more we develop this consecrated oil that will keep us burning at the crucial moment we need it most.

In Leviticus 24:1 we see that the Lord told Moses to command the people to bring pure oil from beaten olives that the lamps of the tabernacle may be kept burning at all times. This is the very oil He is calling us to have full. Our oil is produced through the pressing, crushing, beating, whatever you want to call it, you know it when you feel it. Just as an olive is beaten and put under intense pressure, the pressing determines what comes forth - will we be crushed and destroyed when the pressing occurs? Or will we surrender to the Spirit and allow the pressing to pour fourth the pure oil from within. This is how we produce pure oil for Him. This is how we keep our lamps full. This is how we pour out our oil at His feet. We are to keep the flame burning at all times and to let the fire of the alter never go out (Lev 6:12).

It is going to become very clear in the coming days who has lived a lifestyle of keeping their oil lamps full, in comparison to those who have been living off the whiff of the flames of the fiery ones. Those working out of their own strength, building their own empires, forging their family's dynasty and forgotten the true ointment of intimacy that will keep us awake, alert prepared and ready for the arrival of our great Groom. The Martha's and Mary's will be made known. We cannot look at the surface level of big names, big ministries, mega churches or movements, because the worldly way of weighing 'success' is not the measuring stick God uses for His people. Performances, prestige, buildings, campuses, followers, numbers, all of this means nothing in the end when we find ourselves without oil in our lamps, with nothing left to burn because we're burnt out, with no fuel for the fire and unable to endure when we need it the most.

But those who are truly lowly, humble, desperately-in-love and adoration with sweet Jesus, filled with the fear of the Lord and continually crying out in worship and groaning in love are going to be the ones leading the charge in the days to come when we all realise the religious and worldly church machine has run out of its man-made, synthetic oil, and doesn't possess the anointing of the Lord. The cogs are getting clogged, the engines burnt out and only a move of the Spirit, fueled by His power, fire, oil, ointment and anointing can continue to build the real Church and His true Kingdom.

SHINING HIS LIGHT FOR HIS GLORY

When people are truly positioned into places and positions of influence, it is because they are humble and pure. God only exalts the humble and only the humble can be promoted because they possess a purity of heart (Prov 15:33; 1 Pet 5:6; James 4:10). God exalts the humble because He can trust those lives, not to take the glory. We are called to be co-labourers with Christ, not co-stars.

AN INVITATION TO PARTNER WITH THE KING

If our hidden, ulterior motive and agenda is to be glorified in this world, we will only ever be humbled (interpretation...humiliated!). But if we are truly purged of these selfish and worldly desires and aspirations, no matter how subtle, subliminal or secretive they may be (even from our own conscious awareness) through the illumination of the Holy Spirit, then, and only then will God lift us high for His holy purpose.

My friend the world is getting darker, but have hope for He has already overcome the world and He has a humbling invitation for you to be a part of His perfect plan to bring the only Hope to this hopelessness. We can choose to remain in sackcloth and moan and grumble, wail and whine or we can allow the Father to replace our garments for praise and joy (Is 61:1-3). Then we are allowed into the King's presence (Esther 4:3), because when we are in His presence we can see from His perspective - and His perspective is hope and victory, because Jesus has already paid the price for our beautiful exchange.

Jesus mourned the destruction of this world and the relational separation from His Father's children so much that He gave up His position in the ultimate palace and humbly came to earth to pay our price, in our place and took our punishment. He too could have remained in the comfort of heaven, but He too said yes to His Father's perfect plan and partnered with Him to see His people - His chosen ones, His sons and daughters, brothers and sisters, His Body and Bride - rescued from eternal extinction and annihilation. Let that sink in in light of this story of Esther. You too are called to partner with the greatest plan of our holy God. Will you remain in the comfort of your seeming 'security' or will you say yes to an invitation to leave a mark on this world, to make a dent in the devil's dominion and to violently take hold of the Kingdom of God bringing heaven to earth in the realm that He has perfectly and purposefully positioned you in?

AN ETERNAL INVITATION

We can look at the condition of the world we live in and either choose to partner with fear of the future, or faith in His perfect plan, knowing that He has already overcome the world and has accomplished ultimate victory (John 16:33). This is the line being drawn in the sand in this season, in this era. Will we say yes to the pertinent part we can possibly play, or will we give in to the gloom and give up our game? The eyes of the Lord are roaming the earth, looking for those whose hearts are fully committed to Him (2 Chron 16:9). He is looking for those who will say *'Here I am lord, send me!'* (Is 6:8). He is looking for those who are truly humble, meek, emptied, pure, living quiet, gentle lives, because He can trust and rely on those faithful ones. He is looking for His Esther's. His Mordecai's. He is looking for His Abraham's, His Moses', His Noah's, His Joseph's. He is looking for His Rahab's, His Ruth's, His Deborah's, His David's, His Elijah's, His Elisha's. He is looking for His Peter's, His Paul's, His John the Baptists. He is looking for *you*.

Just like Esther, and all these great witnesses, you have an opportunity in front of you - to give in to the despair around you or to give up to the God above you and within you. You can live a life of complacency and still scrape into heaven through His saving grace and the confession of your lips and belief of your heart that Jesus is the son of God who died for your sins and rose from the dead (Rom 10:9-13), or you can work out your faith with fear and trembling (Phil 2:12) and violently take by force the Kingdom of God (Matt 11:12), deliberately and actively bring heaven to earth each and every day (Matt 6:10), to force back the powers of darkness and ignite glorious, catastrophic, consuming fires of life and hope in Him. The former is safe and comfortable. The latter is scary, risky and unknown.

But…do it scared. Do it petrified. Who knows who are awaiting your 'yes'?

OVERCOME WITH FEAR - OR OVERCOME THE WORLD

When we reflect on the story of Esther we generally think of her as a bold and brave queen. But when we look to the scripture, it actually portrays the exact opposite. Verse 4 reveals that in the midst of this great and mighty moment, she was *'overcome with fear.'* OVERCOME with fear. Gripped, overwhelmed, overpowered, mastered, controlled, subdued, defeated…by fear. I find this so surprising, yet so reassuring. It's so easy to fall into the complacency of being too familiar with such famous stories. For some of us, we have heard them since we were infants or we've heard them preached again and again. We can get so caught up in the victory of the end of the story that we actually lose sight of tiny little details like this that change the dynamic so dramatically if we pay close attention. We easily rest in the comfort of knowing that God uses people like Esther and other great heroes of faith for His glory and victory, and rightly so, but let's not let our familiarity with the Word hold us back from digging deeper for revelation each time we read the same Scriptures over and over again. This is a single verse in the whole story but it is absolutely pivotal to not just the outcome, but the significance of the outcome and how it relates to us in our world today and in our own lives.

The reason Esther was brave and is considered courageous, is *because* she was scared. She was overcome with fear! Fear makes us brave. The greater the risk at hand the greater the act of bravery…when we push through, and do it scared. Does the current situation of the world, the state of culture and the future of our children grip you with fear? Do your circumstances, situations, grief, diagnosis, hopelessness make you overcome and overwhelmed by fear? This is the enemy's very plan of attack. We simply cannot look at our life, call and future through the lens of the worldly faithlessness, hopelessness and powerlessness, because it will only ever instigate fear. If I continue to view my circumstances as hopeless and base my future on *'what if…'* I will only ever end up riddled with fear, anxiety and worry. *'What if…'* has never created conquerers.

'But when…' Most certainly has.

But when my God comes through… *But when* His promises come to pass… *But when* He is faithful to His Word…What a world we would live in if we all lived according to His faithfulness, not our fear! My friend, we can only have faith because He is first faithful! (Heb 11:11).

Remember, Esther was still young. She wasn't this middle aged, mature woman, or even an experienced, elderly lady of life's wisdom. She was still in her youth, still learning, still growing and developing, *of course* she was overcome with fear! Look at what was at stake here! Not just the future of her people (or lack thereof), but even her very life itself. She had a choice in this moment. She could have rested on the position and promotion of the palace life that she had already received - she could have easily sat back in comfort of her blessings that she had been promoted to and that had been bestowed upon her. Although young, she was wise and faithful and had smartly surrounded herself with people of wisdom and discernment who she humbly submitted to. She knew there wasn't really an option here. Not when the entire future of her people was at stake. Her family. Her heritage. Her future. All of this was potentially about to be obliterated forever, and as Mordecai pointed out, don't for a minute think that she would escape. Her position did not protect her, it placed her on a platform to perform God's perfect plan. Where God has placed us, our call, anointing, prophetic words, giftings, promises, whatever, don't make us immune to the threat of the enemy's attacks. But they do provide parameters for us to partner with Him to believe for the impossible.

THE COST OF OBEDIENCE

> *"Mordecai also gave [Hathach] a copy of the written decree issued in Susa ordering their destruction, so that Hathach might show it to Esther, explain it to her, and command her to approach the king, implore his favour, and plead with him personally for her people. Hathach came and repeated Mordecai's response to Esther. Esther spoke to Hathach and commanded him to tell Mordecai, "All the royal officials and the people of the royal provinces know that one law applies to every man or woman who approaches the king in the inner courtyard and who has not been summoned - the death penalty - unless the king extends the gold sceptre, allowing that person to live. I have not been summoned to appear before the king for the last thirty days." Esther's response was reported to Mordecai."* **Esther 4:8-12**

I find this aspect of Esther's story so encouraging and inspiring because although we consider her the queen of boldness, bravery and victory, these verses show us that she didn't rise up straight away. After receiving Mordecai's command (yes - command. Not suggestion or snippet of information, but command that required her obedience) for her to approach the king, implore for his favour, personally plead with him for her people at the very risk of her own life, she didn't respond with immediate obedience. I don't know about you, but that kind of makes me feel a bit more human. Or, it makes Queen Esther more human in my eyes, because I do tend to hold her up with utmost esteem as the bold, brave queen we know she has gone down in history to be. But she didn't begin this way. And if she didn't begin this way, then maybe there is still hope for me, because I know for certain I have questioned the precepts God has place on my life. I know for certain I have counted the cost of what He has asked me to do. I know for certain I have calculated the risk and my own personal suffering for what He is calling me to and laying on the path before me.

But ultimately, I have had to eat my scroll. How could I not? Comfort and anything this world could possibly offer is no match for whatever assignment, mission, call God has for my life. I can't say no to my King. Even if my obedience has been slow, delayed, or I went in kicking and screaming, there is no greater joy than saying yes to *'whatever it takes.'* I have said yes to *'more of you and less of me.'* I have said yes to the Kingdom of God and relinquished my tight grip on the agenda's of my own heart, fleshly desires and worldly humanness.

And it's worth it. It is so worth it my friend. Do I think I am so important and strategic to His plans and purposes? Absolutely not! But do I stand in front of Him in total awe and fear and trembling of His glory and majesty and say yes to His call? ABSOLUTELY! What He has already paid for and purchased for me on the cross abundantly outweighs the risk of my own life and meaningless accusation, prejudice and suffering. Nothing could compare, nothing! Even if to the very point of death I know that it is all worth it. Every act of obedience to Him is worth every breath of my life. Because He is worth every breath, every heartbeat, every new morning, every pursuit, every desire of my heart. He is worth it all.

Let's take it back to our Esther. Up until this point, she has immediately obeyed everything Mordecai has instructed her to do. This was the first time she had come back to him with not just an excuse, but a calculated reason as to why this command of his was so serious. It's so easy to obey God when it doesn't really cost us anything. It's easy to obey when the blessing of such obedience is immediate gratification. And my friend, there is much immediate gratification for immediate obedience. Some things He requires of us are not just easy, but a joy to obey! Why would we choose anything else? It's so easy to obey God's path when He is leading us to become queen in the ruling palace of the world…but what about when we have already secured that great position and He asks us to obey in a way that will risk losing it all? Not just our position, but our very life itself? And not just our life, but the lives of our family - our people?

Our heart is truly tested and obedience genuinely revealed when He asks us to do something uncomfortable. Something that will cost us. Something that puts us at risk. Something that makes it all real. Our reputation. Our name. Our comfort. Our security. This is why the purging and purifying is so essential. We must be stripped of all of that, so that there is neither nothing to lose, nor gain.

There is always something valuable at stake when we are called to obey God. For Esther, this was her entire life. Not just the palace, not just her position as queen, not just the comforts of the blessings of her promotion, but her entire existence and her life on earth. She was facing potential death if she went ahead and did what Mordecai was requesting of her. In fact, there was a far greater chance she would be put to death than survive. Everything was at stake for her personally. But even more than that, if she didn't obey and rise to the occasion, even more was at stake for her people. Complete annihilation. Our brave and bold Esther didn't say yes to the call immediately - she entered into a dialogue with Mordecai - back and forth through Hathach. Folks, how often do we enter into dialogue with God when He has asked us to do something instead of acting in faithful, immediate obedience? We go back and forth, back and forth, reminding Him of what's at stake and what we are risking, when He is already 100% aware of it all. He knows more than we do! It's all in His hands, He knows the end from the beginning. Most importantly, He already holds the outcome, because He already has ultimate victory.

AN INVITATION TO PARTNER WITH THE KING

"For my thoughts are not your thoughts, neither are your ways my ways, saith the Lord. For as the heavens are higher than the earth, so are my ways higher than your ways, and my thoughts than your thoughts."
Isaiah 55:8-9

Here's the clincher…if we stall our obedience to God's call, we risk something else - we risk missing out on the invitation to partner with Him in His purpose. I remember almost two decades ago hearing a preacher tell the sobering story of how God had given him a dream to build a church building. In the dream He gave him the exact design, blueprints, plans, everything (a bit like Noah). I can't remember the reason why he said no to God, but that's what ultimately happened. Years and years later he came upon the very church building he had seen in his dream. When he questioned the pastor of the church about the design, he discovered God had shown this pastor the same dream that he had originally said no to. If we say no, someone else will say yes. God isn't dependent upon us alone to perform His will. In His love He invites us to co-labour with Him, but if we continually say no to the opportunity, and particularly if the moment is of urgency and pertinence, as it is in this era, He will find a willing and obedient heart elsewhere. Think that's not possible? Esther herself had the very opportunity… and very chance to miss that opportunity.

"Mordecai told the messenger to reply to Esther, "Don't think that you will escape the fate of all the Jews because you are in the king's palace. If you keep silent at this time, relief and deliverance will come to the Jewish people from another place, but you and your father's family will be destroyed."" **Esther 4:13-14a**

CHAPTER 7

POSITIONED FOR PURPOSE

GOD'S SOVEREIGNTY KISSES OUR FREE WILL

God is sovereign. His will is sovereign. God is not in any way, shape or form relying on us solely to execute His will here on earth. He doesn't need us, but He wants us. And He wants us because He loves us. What a great and glorious and gracious God we have! The very creator of the heavens and the earth who sits enthroned in the heavenly realm with the world as His footstool invites us, His children, to partner with Him in purpose to see His very plans come to pass!

He wasn't dependent on Esther. And He isn't dependent on us. This is the beauty of the intricate tapestry of God's sovereignty interwoven with His graceful invitation of co-labouring with Him. He doesn't need us, but He wants us. He has created us for union with Him and it is His joy to invite us into an intimate relationship with Him. He no longer calls us servants, but friends (John 15:15), we are adopted into His family, not as servants, but as children (1 Peter 1:4- 6).

If Esther had backed down in this opportunity, God would have used someone else and the deliverance of The Jews would have come from another place (Esther 4:14). His sovereign will was for the salvation of His people. He didn't need Esther any more than He needs us in whatever situation He has us in. She had a choice - free will if you may - to partner with Him or to pass on the baton to someone else. Either way, His will would come to pass, because His will is sovereign. But what a loving and gracious God who calls us to not only join us in partnership with Him as we co-labour, but to also co-reign and enjoy the abundance of blessing and inheritance that He has already paid the price for (1 Cor 3:9; Acts 20:32, 26:18; Col 1:5, 12)!

THE INVITATION REQUIRES ACTIVATION

I fully understand that there is a deep disappointment and discouragement within the hearts of many of God's people of not seeing His promises fulfilled in many of our lives…yet. There's a desperation to see the personal prophecies, words, dreams, visions given years and years ago come to pass in our situations and circumstances. How much longer Lord? When, Lord, when will your word be fulfilled? Did I not hear correctly? Was that not you speaking? We start to doubt ourselves and when we do that, we start to doubt His voice. The enemy loves this, because it gives him an open door and access point to sneak in and plant the seeds of his lies in our hearts and minds.

And of course, the religious spirit has a field day with unfulfilled prophecies. I have heard so many well-meaning believers accuse brothers and sisters of being false prophets because the very things they prophesied have either been delayed, remain unfulfilled, or the exact opposite has happened. People! Personal prophecy and promises are dependent upon our obedience and our stewardship! If not, then every single promise in the Bible would be completely fulfilled in every single believers life. As amazing as that would be, we all know that's unfortunately not the case. We can not scream *'false prophet'* when we sit idly back doing absolutely nothing to align with the word, agree with God's voice and activate the very thing He has spoken over us. Do we dare to declare God a 'false prophet' when His biblical promises don't come to pass in our life? The religious spirit is so quick to jump on what *doesn't* happen, when in reality, a mature believer who is sound in Scripture and has a New Testament teaching of the prophetic gifts of God can clearly reveal that the onus is most definitely on the recipient. Just look at Paul instructing young Timothy to fan into flame the gift that God gave him through the laying on (impartation) of hands (2 Tim 1:6). In 1 Timothy 4:14 Paul tells Timothy to not neglect the gift that was given to him through prophecy by the impartation of the elders. Why would Paul admonish and instruct Timothy to be so careful with his prophetic words and imparted gifts if it was inevitable that they would all flourish and come to pass?

Personal prophecy requires stewardship and management just like anything else God gives us in life. It requires us to partner, position, pursue and activate in obedience, the prophetic words spoken to us and every single promise in the Bible. We just have to look at the Old Testament and the history of Israel to see that not every prophetic word or promise delivered to God's chosen people came to pass. It was based on their alignment and obedience. Promises are given within the confines of covenant, and covenant is a two way street.

Most of God's promises to Israel were conditional. That is why most promises in the Old Testament sound something along the lines of *"If.... then..."* The 'if' is our responsibility. The 'then' is His. He will take care of His part when we take care of ours. Personal prophetic words aren't fortune telling, but invitations to partner with God's promises. Prophecies speak to our divine potential. As God's people we have the power to change, influence and redirect the course of history. God's will is sovereign, His plan will come to pass with or without us, but He lovingly offers us an intimate invitation to work with Him in His great purpose. Esther herself could have received all the prophetic words in the world about delivering her people, but if she didn't receive and accept the invitation and act upon it, it wouldn't have come to pass, and this Scripture clearly tells us that God would have raised up someone else to perform His will in this moment.

A PIVOTAL 'PERHAPS'

"Who knows, perhaps you have come into your royal position for such a time as this." **Esther 4:14**

Just like Esther, our position, realm of influence, gifts, talents or anointing don't guarantee our victory. Esther had no guarantees - death faced her either way, but so did divine opportunity. *'Who knows, perhaps'* definitely isn't a prophetic promise of security and certainty. We often quote the prominent line *for such a time as this,'* yet we forget the start of Mordecai's famous words. If Esther could risk it all based on a 'who knows, perhaps' proposition, then maybe we too can be willing to lay it all on the line, to risk everything we are and everything we may become, to draw the line in the sand and rise up to His call and step out in obedience…even if we are overwhelmed with fear. This humbling reminder from Mordecai was what encouraged her to rise up and say yes to the call.

IF YOU REMAIN SILENT

Sometimes not doing anything, is doing something. Sometimes not saying anything, is saying something. Sometimes being inactive, is taking action. Sometimes, our silence speaks louder than our words.

God is looking for all or nothing. Gone are the days of getting by with casual Christianity, slumbering souls, spiritual apathy, lukewarm lifestyles, convenient prayers and scraping into heaven. He is looking for Esther's. This is the era of Esther's arising. We have to put it all on the line and risk everything we are, everything we have and everything we can be. This is why the process of purging our reputation, our name, our ministry, our empire, our glory, our hidden idols, our vices, our security, our identity in anything other that Jesus, whatever it is, is so essential. If we try to keep our lives we will lose them, it is time to truly take up the cross as Christ's followers and co-labourers in this world.

The passive church is not going to prevail in this time. The complacent communities will not cut it. The tolerant and compliant pastors, leaders and believers who want to sit down, hide in the background, not stir the pot, not bring any attention to themselves or their ministries, will not make it over the line. There's another line in the sand moment given to us here in Esther, which is trumpeting loudly as a clarion call in the days we are now in… *"If you remain silent."* We are coming into times and seasons where we can no longer remain silent while calling ourselves God's people. We are entering this era where we have to pick a side and we have to loudly, boldly and valiantly declare - with our words, actions and lives - which side we are on. There is no in between. No fence sitting. No pew warmers anymore. There's no wishy-washy lukewarmness. It's hot or cold, in or out, up or down, good or evil, truth or lies, pick your side and make it loud.

Those who do attempt to remain silent in this time, whether individual believers, pastors, prophets, leaders, or entire churches, movements and denominations - will have their lamp stands snuffed out in the glorious days to come. Either out of fear, out of complacency or simply attempting to go under the radar and hoping we won't be noticed, we have to have more fear of God than we do fear of man in these days to come. We cannot for a minute think that we can remain silent on the issues of our day that God is so clearly declaring through His prophets and His intercessors who live in the secret place. It is undeniable that God's gavel of justice is coming down hard and fast on the ongoing issues and ideologies in this world and our western culture that His very Church has not just tolerated, but permitted - sometimes even deliberately and publicly partnered with - in the attempt to be accepted by the world, to be 'seeker sensitive,' to appear politically correct, to indicate our 'inclusiveness' so that we do not have to loudly or boldly stand up and say what scripture clearly declares that God says is *His* truth.

It is not a time to remain silent. Nor is it a time to preach a pretty message of 'peace, peace' that keeps everyone in their passivity and false comfort. I cannot emphasise any stronger - *mark my words* - this is an era of the end times Church awakening to her true authority, of the remnant army aligning in heavenly assignment, of warriors arising and being deployed to the battlefield, and a time of valiant warfare in the spiritual realm. We are *not* in a time of peace and passivity where we can sit back and expect the blessings of God to fall in our laps. The inheritance and promises will come, but not without a fight and first taking down the unclean giants who dare to mock our God. It is imperative we know the season we are in. This is a season of war in the spiritual realm, not of peace. But we are fighting *for* peace. We are fighting *for* the inheritance that He has promised us already. We are fighting *for* a legacy and future for our children and the generations to come. We must first be peacemakers before we can be peacekeepers. We must obtain the peace, before we can maintain the peace, and this requires fighting for it.

> *"They have healed the wound of my people lightly, saying ' Peace, peace,' when there is no peace."* **Jeremiah 8:11**

> *"Precisely because they have misled my people saying, 'Peace,' when there is no peace...the prophets of Israel who prophesied concerning Jerusalem and saw visions of peace for her..."* **Ezekiel 13:10, 16**

If we do cower away in fear, or if we partner with the plans of the enemy while slapping on the sticker of 'Jesus,' we will have to pay the price. God has given great warning about His impending glory, but His glory cannot reside with mixture or tainted, toxic impurity. If we want to see the justice we are praying for, if we want to see the exposing of truth that we are interceding for, then we have to be prepared for the glorious judgment of righteousness to comes against the evil in our world. Lamp stands are going to be snuffed out left, right and centre.

A RIGHTEOUS PRIESTHOOD

I believe we are in a time of the a prophetic picture of Ezekiel 44. In this chapter we see the priests who were worldly and compromised and became a stumbling block of sin to God's people because they went astray and did not keep God's holy charge, as instructed. They instead defiled both themselves, the temple and the Israelites. Ezekiel 34 tells us about these priests who neglected to feed the sheep in their care, but instead made themselves fat on the offerings. Even earlier in Ezekiel 8 we see that God takes Ezekiel in the spirit into the temple and shows him all the abominations and vile acts they are committing...*in God's house*. In Ezekiel 44 we see that these Levitical priests who compromised and brought in mixture, were allowed to continue to minister 'to the people' - taking care of the everyday tasks of the temple - yet they were unable to come into the presence of God any longer. They were banned from the Holy of Holies and from coming close to the alter, but became nothing more than caretakers and servicemen.

In comparison, the Sons of Zadok, remained pure when the rest of the Levitical priesthood went astray, and the glory and presence were with them, and they became the lineage of priests who were chosen to enter the sanctuary and minister to God, to come near to Him and stand before Him and perform the priestly duty to Him. If this reminder doesn't put the fear of God in us to remain holy, pure, undefiled and to stop tolerating the things of this world, to stop mixing the church with the cultural norms, agenda, ideologies and narratives, then we are going to see many churches, ministries and leaders in the coming days continue ministering to people, amongst the church, but the presence of God will have departed. The power, the glory, the authority, everything we need to remain close to Him and minister to Him shall tragically be removed, whether we realise it, notice it, discern it, or not.

This is a test of our hearts - what do we value more? Intimacy and being in His presence, looking at His face, hearing the beat of His heart? Or Platforms, positions, microphones, titles, numbers, views, followers? What we treasure most is where our heart will be found.

GOD HAS STRATEGIES AVAILABLE IF WE SEEK HIM

> *"Esther sent his reply to Mordecai: "Go and assemble all the Jews who can be found in Susa and fast for me. Don't eat or drink for three days, night or day. I and my female servants will also fast in the same way. After that, I will go to the king even if it is against the law. If I perish, I perish." So Mordecai went and did everything Esther had commanded him."* **Esther 4:15-17**

Esther didn't respond to the call with all guns blazing, running out all yippee-ki-yay, she didn't just fly on the seam of her pants (or royal queenly gown!), it wasn't an uncalculated risk that she leapt into with blind, naive faith. If she was going to risk her life for the sake of her people she knew she needed every heavenly resources in order to co-labour with God and to see His plans and purposes come to pass. Big assignments require bigger wisdom. When God calls us to do something He doesn't leave us stranded and empty handed. His calling comes with His equipping and empowering. He has given us every heavenly resource (1 Cor 3:21-22; Eph 1:3) to perform His will when He asks and the Helper to guide us. He doesn't require obedience based on our own limited ability, but based on His unlimited power. Even though He calls us to co-labour with Him, we aren't in a master-slave or employer-employee contract, we are in a Father-child covenant and Jesus calls us His friends, and everything He invites us into to perform and produce with Him, has a deeper purpose of drawing us closer to Him in love and dependence. He speaks to our soul and awakens our identity and as we learn to trust more and more in Him and His ability we are strengthened and matured to carry out the very purposes He has for His Kingdom. The relationship trumps the assignment. The end goal is internal transformation, not external transaction. He is more concerned with what He is doing within us than what He is doing through us. In fact, what He wants to do through us is determined first by what He does in us, hence the power of the purifying process.

The real reason Esther is renowned as our valiant queen is because she relied on God - not on her position, anointing or gifts. The purpose of the painful purging, purifying and polishing process is to establish us in our identity in Him, so that when the poignant appointment arises, we can act based on who He is, His Word, His promises, His Spirit - not what we have (possessions), where we are (positions), or what we do (performance). Esther didn't rely on her position as queen. She didn't rely on her gift of beauty. She didn't even rely on the obvious favour upon her life. She relied on God. We know this because we see that her response to the call was to first position herself in a place of humility and surrender to God - to seek, ask and pursue His plan, not hers. If we're willing to put ourselves out there and risk it all, we can't do anything based on our own abilities or agenda, we must pursue His wisdom, strategy and blueprints for the assignment through intercession.

Esther gathered her servants and told Mordecai to assemble all the Jews to fast and pray for three days. Strategies come when we seek God. Assignments of the enemy are broken when we fast and pray. God breaks through into our circumstances and the atmosphere around us when we position ourselves to purposely pursue Him and His methods. Turnaround and transformation takes place when we seek Him first. This long lost discipline is more than just a principle, it's a power. The western church is being re-awakened to the power of prayer, intercession, fasting and communion. The New Testament instructs us to live this lifestyle, yet how many believers are praying, interceding and fasting *as a lifestyle* these days? Instead of whinging and whining, complaining and crying about how bad the world is, we are called to position ourself in prayer and believe that our God can change, transform and conquer the very things that are so evil, destructive and horrible in this world. There is power in prayer and fasting, there is power in standing in the gap in intercession to seek God's solutions, there is power in taking communion as a form of spiritual warfare and decreeing and declaring the blood of Jesus and the finished work of the cross over our families, our homes, our children, this generation, our cities and our nations. As we rise up into this mandate we will see the potential it has to bring heaven to earth, to see His will come to pass. Things happen when we pray. Like...*really* pray. Intercession isn't for the little old ladies in the quiet closets of the church, it's for the bold and brave front line soldiers who are extending the borders of His Kingdom with violence. I believe in this era, the power of intercession is going to become prominent in and pertinent to the Church once again.

Imagine what our world could look like if the Body of Christ rose up and took hold of the tools Jesus gave us and instructed us to use - to pray, fast, intercede, speak to impossibilities. Imagine what strongholds in society would come crashing down? Imagine what laws of the lands could be transformed? Imagine what cultural norms could be changed? Imagine what geographical territories could be returned to God's rightful dominion? Imagine how marriages, families and households could be healed and made whole? Imagine what governmental mandates could come to pass? When Jesus' disciples failed to heal and deliver some people from demonic forces, Jesus' instruction to them of praying and fasting was not intended for that very moment - it was too late, it already hadn't worked (Mat 17:21). Instead, He was urging us to live a lifestyle of prayer and fasting, *before* we are faced with the stubborn situation, so that *when* that very thing arises, we already possess the faith, power and authority to command that circumstance to bow it's knee to Jesus. Prayer and fasting are powerful. We partner with His purposes when we pray and fast and intercede on behalf of those we are called to.

Intercession is powerful because it proves our authority and identity in Him. Prayer works! Intercession is an invitation to partner with Him in His purpose, to receive strategy and to perform His plan. Intercession isn't just about us talking to God, it's about hearing His voice, and in doing so, He reveals His heart for the matter and gives us His solutions, answers and blueprints to solve the problems and burdens He is calling us to conquer. We should do more listening and less talking when we pray!

The key to seeing answered prayers isn't just speaking the words, it's believing in faith for what we're asking for (James 1:6). It's about truly knowing our identity in Him and who we are and therefore what we have access to (1 Cor 3:21-22; Eph 1:3). It's about knowing our position in heaven and praying from that place, co-seated with Christ (Eph 2:6). It's about taking up the authority that has been given to us by Jesus and actually using it. Prayer isn't wishful thinking, or simply hoping, or begging God. He wants to see our prayers answered more than we do! He already has a plan, He already has the answers, but He cares more about the refining process of our hearts as we learn to trust and depend upon Him, His ability, His power, His authority, His love than He does about giving us everything we want instantly, even when it's in line with His heart and His will.

While we may be expecting a lightning flash from heaven or an all inclusive answer, as we position ourselves in intercession, He often provides the strategies that, when applied, are our invitation to co-partner with Him to see those very solutions come to pass. Of course He can fulfil every prayer instantly. But as a loving Father He would rather train us to fulfil our role of partnering with Him to see His sovereign will come to pass. It's funny how being invited into the process of partnering with Him actually makes us more dependent upon Him. As we see prayers answered we become more emptied of ourselves and our own ability and place more trust and faith in His ability. Prayer is so much more than just a duty or discipline, true intercession is a partnership, process and relationship

BE WILLING TO RISK IT ALL

that deepens our humility and maturity.

Esther fully comprehended the risk at hand. *"If I perish, I perish"* (4:16). Let's live this life with all that we've got. My greatest fear is getting to heaven only to realise that there was so much more I could have accomplished for the Kingdom. My fear is finding out that I actually had access to so much more of heaven here on earth, so much more of the Holy Spirit, so much more of Jesus and Father God, but I didn't realise it at the time. I don't want to miss out on a single thing! I'm so passionately determined to live every moment with eternity in mind, with His Kingdom at hand, with my ear so close to His chest that I hear the heartbeat of heaven and march to the cadences of His grace. I abandon all else and run with passion to win the victory prize! Everything that this world can offer me pales in comparison to the Kingdom of heaven. On that day when I am held accountable for every good work I have done and everything I have built (Rom 5:9; Rom 14:12; 1 Pet 1:17) when He weighs me up according to how I stewarded what He entrusted to me in this life (Matt 25:14-30; 1 Cor 3:8; 12-15), I want my reward and crown to be so ridiculously massive so that I can offer it to Him as my ultimate gift in worship of Him.

I am overwhelmed with joy at the thought of laying it at His feet, my beautiful Jesus, to give Him my greatest offering of all, that of my life and all I have lived for. It doesn't even come close to what He has given me, but I want to give everything I have, here and now, so I can give Him everything He gives me as the ultimate thank you, ultimate act of worship, ultimate gratitude, ultimate praise and honour for all eternity. I can't change that once I have crossed over into eternity, but right now I can store up riches in heaven that will be poured out to Him in devotion and adoration. I don't want to have a small reward to give back to Him, I want to receive the biggest gift to give back to the biggest Giver. We only have one chance at this, let's lay it all on the line and risk it all! If we perish in the process, then we perish! But oh what a glorious reward we will receive to bestow upon our glorious God! You have been positioned in the palace for a reason - it's not for your pleasure, but for His purpose. It's not for your personal gain, but for His people. You, my friend, are perfectly positioned for purpose.

CLOTHED FOR YOUR CALL

> *"As you yield freely and fully to the dynamic life and power of the Holy Spirit, you will abandon the cravings of your self-life. For your self-life craves the things that offend the Holy Spirit and hinder him from living free within you! And the Holy Spirit's intense cravings hinder your old self-life from dominating you! So then, the two incompatible and conflicting forces within you are your self-life of the flesh and the new creation life of the Spirit. But when you are brought into the full freedom of the Spirit of grace, you will no longer be living under the domination of the law, but soaring above it!"* **Galatians 5:17-18 (TPT)**

One thing in particular that the purifying and purging process really brings up and out of us as God reveals, deals and heals our hearts and lives in preparation for His purpose, is the awareness of worldly desires, agendas, values, motives, compromise and self-promotion - the impurities that are holding us back from holiness - to name a few. We may think we are ok in these areas, outstanding even, but when He begins to gently press on certain parts of our hearts, we quickly feel the pain of the open wounds that we may not have even realised were there. Suddenly we are aware of forces at work in our lives that shock us to the core - jealousy, envy, judgment, comparison, competitiveness, materialism, performance, pride, insecurity, idolatry. Don't for a minute think these things aren't within us as believers! Sometimes the very things we are idolising, envying, hungrily pursuing are beautiful and good things - family, ministry, the church, hospitality, our spouse, our call/assignment - but when we elevate them above our pursuit of God we have misplaced our worship of Him with things of this world. *Even good, beautiful, God-given things.*

You see, He needs to reveal our hearts to us so that we can recognise that it's not necessarily the 'things' themselves that are the problem, but it's our desires and our affection that need to be realigned back towards Him. To not seek Him for what's in His hands, or what He can do for us, but to seek Him for His face, His heart, His love, His embrace, His voice, His presence. When our hearts are set on Him, when He has established us in identity, security, sonship, daughterhood, it is then that He can bestow upon us the very things that once may have broken us because we weren't purified and fortified for the weight of the break-through or the fulfilment of the promise. It would have crushed us because we could not carry it without worshipping the gift instead of the Giver, without looking to the break-through instead of the Breaker and without praising the position, promise or prophecy instead of the Provider and the Promise Keeper.

God undoubtedly uses things of this world for His purpose and for His glory. God can and will use anything that He wants, however He wants, but our heart position must be humble, surrendered and emptied. And that's exactly what the purging process does in us. It empties us of the desires and security for the very things that God actually wants to bestow upon us, because once He has dealt with that stumbling block within us, He knows that He can then trust us with what He has for us, because we can be relied upon to steward responsibly what He has for His Kingdom and His glory, and no longer our own.

The religious spirit has caused many well-intentioned believers to vilify the very things that God intends to use. If we have the mindset that they are evil, worldly or unholy then we will miss the opportunity and invitation to be used by God. Hear this: God can and will use anything, however He wants, for whatever He wants, in whatever way He wants. Godliness is not denying a promotion, placement or position at the cost of your call, it's being emptied enough to give God all the glory when He elevates you to that very place. Humility is not living a life of poverty where you're unable to help anyone in need because you're barely scraping by yourself, it's stewarding and continually overflowing with the resources He blesses you with in generosity to others. Holiness is not saying no to the opportunity, it's saying yes knowing that He will build His Kingdom as He uses you in the position He has called you to. Purity is not denying ourselves of 'things,' it's ridding our hearts of the desires for them and valuing what He values over what the world does. Discipline is not self-flagellation, but self-control and putting to death the desires of the flesh. Maturity is not a head full of theology, but a life that lives the Word of God.

When we stop categorising things as either sacred or secular, and can see that God uses whatever He wants with excellence and purpose, then He can entrust those very things into our hands. When we are emptied of the fleshly desires, then He can flow through us more fully with the power of the Spirit who empowers us to live the humble, gentle and surrendered lives for His purpose.

In this chapter of the book of Esther we see these two opposing forces at work (Gal 5:16-18). Selfish ambition, pride and self-elevating, self-serving, self-promotion is at work in Haman, contradicted with the surrendered heart of Esther. Let's look at how God can use us in the world today, through the world, with the 'things' of the world and for the world around us, *for the purposes of His Kingdom.*

> *"On the third day, Esther dressed in her royal clothing and stood in the inner courtyard of the palace facing it. The king was sitting on his royal throne in the royal courtroom, facing its entrance. As soon as the king saw Queen Esther standing in the courtyard, she gained favour in his eyes. The king extended the gold sceptre in his hand toward Esther, and she approached and touched the tip of the sceptre."* **Esther 5:1-2**

CLOTHE YOURSELF

Esther's exact moment has arrived as the climax of the story commences. She is approaching the king, ready to act on behalf of her people. Right now she is facing impending death. Everything is at stake, everything is on the line, everything has gone into this. So how did she approach this situation? She prepared herself purposefully. She didn't casually approach the king and think to herself *'if it's God's will, then it will happen.'* Yes, if it's God's will it *will* happen, but for too long the religious church has lazily reclined back in the apathetic throwaway of 'if it's God's will' at the very cost of our call and commission. God had equipped and empowered her with everything she needed for this moment and He had perfectly positioned her for his purpose. She was wise and took hold of everything He had blessed her with and used what was at her disposal and what God had placed in her possession. She took the position and all its blessings and she used them as tools and resources. This is exactly what God had intended for her, and us, to do.

"*Dressed in her royal clothing.*" Not rocking up in her jeans and tee, or worse, pyjama pants or leisurewear, because, you know '*outward appearance doesn't matter, it's what's on the inside that counts.*' Remember the wedding guest in Matthew 22:11 who didn't *put on* the proper garments provided for him? This isn't about outward appearance, but with wisdom and humility Esther used what God had already provided for her, for His glory and purpose.

The prophetic implication of Esther dressing in royal clothing is that she stepped into the very mantle that was provided for her. In the Old Testament, a mantle was a cloak-like article of clothing, but spiritually it had far more significance than its practical purpose. Throughout the Bible, mantles represent an anointing - a call/gift/role/office, for example, the mantle of a prophet or an apostle - and the presence of the Holy Spirit working through that person, in that anointing. Mantles are also a covering - God's protection as we activate these gifts and walk in these God-ordained roles. God can have mantles for us, but if we don't step into them, don't clothe ourselves in them, don't walk in them, don't wear them or actually put them on, we can have the greatest call of God on our lives, but never partner with Him to walk in the anointing, presence and protection of the mantle He has for us.

Esther dressed in her royal clothes. Yes, this would have been the most exquisite, expensive and regal robes in her entire royal closet. Esther used what God had given her and put at her disposal and as she dressed in the physical robes - she stepped into her spiritual mantle - and was clothed in the anointing He had given her for this position and petition. It is imperative that we live walking in our mantles. Not other peoples mantles, not the wrong mantles, not the mantles the enemy tries to put on us, not exposed and vulnerable without any mantle, but the God-given, God-ordained, God-empowered mantle that He has for us. If Esther had not dressed appropriately for this occasion, both in the physical and in the spiritual, who knows if this story would have panned out differently?

POSITIONED FOR PURPOSE

ARISE AND TAKE ACTION

Although Esther would have been aware that she possessed great favour in the eyes of the king, she didn't rely on it. Again, with holy awe and fear of the Lord, she knew it wouldn't have helped her case to casually approach him for a matter so monumental. So, wielding everything in her possession, she then positioned herself where she knew she would be of the greatest potential.

> *"Esther dressed in her royal clothing and stood in the inner courtyard of the palace facing it. The king was sitting on his royal throne in the royal courtroom, facing its entrance."* **Esther 5:1**

If we want to be used for His purpose in this life, in this world, then it's required of us to partner with His call by stepping up, stepping out, taking action and positioning ourselves in obedience to where He can use us best. Esther stood in the inner courtyard of the royal palace, face to face with the ruling power at hand. If she had sat around in her beautiful harem waiting for the king to summon her, she could have been waiting a very long time and, I would imagine, miss the opportunity completely.

You have a call on your life. You have a purpose. You have an assignment. But God requires you to step up, step out and position yourself in the gateway of opportunity. You can have everything you could possibly need to do everything He has possibly called you to, but without action, your purpose will be nothing more than potential. His promises and prophecies require us to activate our faith and position ourselves in alignment with His plan. Only then will we discover if 'perhaps' we were created for such a time as this. To remain seated, remain stagnant, remain searching for a signal, sign or certainty will only ever see us slip further and further from the assignment we were created for as we waver in the waiting and relinquish our responsibility. Esther positioned herself in front of her very purpose. Face to face with the king. Face to face with the opportunity. Face to face with potential death. Face to face with her 'perhaps'. Face to face with all of God's promises. Face to face with her faith.

HE IS FAITHFUL WHEN WE STEP OUT IN FAITH

> *"As soon as the king saw Queen Esther standing in the courtyard, she gained favour in his eyes. The king extended the gold sceptre in his hand toward Esther, and she approached and touched the tip of the sceptre. "What is it, Queen Esther?" the king asked her. "Whatever you want, even to half the kingdom, will be given to you.""* **Esther 5:2-3**

God came through! She gained favour in the kings eyes, because she already had favour in *the* Kings eyes. We don't have the power to control the outcome, but we do have the power to partner with Him. We do have the power to position ourselves. We do have the power to step out in obedience. We have the power because when He instructs us to do something He empowers us with His very strength, grace, authority and power to do exactly what He is calling us to do. My friend, God will not call you without empowering you. But between the chasm of the calling and fulfilment of His promises, He requires us to trust in Him and step out. It's called faith.

CHAPTER 8

TESTING & TEMPTATION, REMEMBERING & REVERSING

TRIALS AND TEMPTATION

> "No temptation [regardless of its source] has overtaken or enticed you that is not common to human experience [nor is any temptation unusual or beyond human resistance]; but God is faithful [to His word—He is compassionate and trustworthy], and He will not let you be tempted beyond your ability [to resist], but along with the temptation He [has in the past and is now and] will [always] provide the way out as well, so that you will be able to endure it [without yielding, and will overcome temptation with joy]." **1 Corinthians 10:13 (AMP)**

> "Blessed is the man who remains steadfast under trial, for when he has stood the test he will receive the crown of life, which God has promised to those who love him. Let no one say when he is tempted, "I am being

> *tempted by God," for God cannot be tempted with evil, and he himself tempts no one. But each person is tempted when he is lured and enticed by his own desire. Then desire when it has conceived gives birth to sin, and sin when it is fully grown brings forth death."*
> **James 1:12-15 (ESV)**

When God has a purpose for you to perform His will on earth, He will fill you with His favour. And when the favour of God is upon you, you will have the favour of man that will open doors that no person can open, nor close. When favour is upon you there is nothing else you can do in and of yourself to try and strive to make things happen. His favour is the anointing and oil that enables you to slide seamlessly into situations that seem impossible. Having the favour of God upon you is the difference between slaving away striving to achieve something in the flesh by the works of your own hands verse resting in God's control, resting in your identity and resting in the call upon your life.

Favour is the oil of ease.

Esther had so much favour in fact, that before she even had a chance to put her request to the king, he promised to give her whatever she wanted…up to half his kingdom. What an offer! I mean, she was facing potential death, just to have her life spared would have been amazing, just to be heard by the king would have been enough, just to be able to ask would have been monumental, but the favour of God on her went beyond her wildest imagination and she was faced with a once in a life time opportunity that far superseded anything she could dream of.

Grand opportunities present us with two possible choices - to obey what God has already asked us to do, or to take the temptation for more. Imagine what Esther could have done with up to half the kingdom? Surely that could be used for God and His people? Imagine what good would come of such an offer? It may have been good, but it wasn't God. Esther had an opportunity to personally set herself up for all of the luxuries, leisure, lifestyle, wealth and wellbeing that half a kingdom could offer. She even had the opportunity to take more on behalf of the people and for the benefit of others. A noble pursuit, surely? She was tempted with the very worldly desires that we are tempted with. These moments of magnitude are exactly why God needs to purge our hearts first. Because when we pass His tests, He knows we will pass the tests of temptation to go beyond the borders of what He is requiring of us. Good intentions aren't obedience.

There will always be a temptation for more, a temptation for what *we* want, what we think is better or best, even what is 'good'. This is exactly why prior to being positioned, we are required to walk through the wilderness, the dry desolate desert, the dark night of the soul, in order to be strengthened and secured in the things that truly matter. To show that we are strong enough to withstand the temptations the world can and will offer us that come with positioning.

Esther wasn't the only one to be made such a grand offer. Before He entered His time of ministry, discipling and teaching where He performed His greatest miracles, healings, signs and wonders, Jesus was led by the Spirit into the same wilderness to be tested by the devil (Matt 4:1). The wilderness season of our lives isn't to be feared or avoided. It's crucial. It's not of the enemy, it's of the Spirit. It's not a place of weakness, but a place of strengthening. It's not our failure, it's our foundations. It is the very process we are required to walk through, just as Jesus did, so that when we are tempted in the same way that He was - with position, provision and power (Matt 4:1-11) - we too, can remain steadfast to the Word, will and way of God and not bow down to the lures and desires of this world. The wilderness strengthens us because we are tempted when we are weak and exhausted (Jesus hadn't eaten for 40 days). The wilderness fortifies us because we are tested when we are alone (Jesus was by Himself). But the wilderness process establishes us for what God can then build upon.

Another king was also given a similar offer of opportunity. King Solomon was asked by God Himself to name whatever his heart desired and it would be given to him (2 Chron 1:7). Just imagine the magnitude of what he could have taken possession of or achieved in his life! But I believe God posed this proposition to him because He had *already* tested his heart and He knew what was in there. The Father heart of God would not tempt him with anything that He knew he would fail in (James 1:13). When King Solomon chose something so selfless for the greater good of the people (wisdom to rule Israel - 1 Kings 3:5-14), God knew he could be trusted with much, much more, so went on to bless him with both wealth and power (the very two things he could have chosen, but didn't) to become the wealthiest king that ever existed in history. Everything in this world comes from God and belongs to God. They don't belong to the world, they belong to God himself and they are created to be used for His glory. However, the problem comes when the worth we put on them determines the affections of our hearts. The security we have in them determines our place of trust. Will our hearts be found to be fixed on Jesus, or the things of this world?

Esther proved worthy of this test of temptation, because her heart was already purged and purified and she was established, strong and secure in her identity. God knew she would make the right decision because she was consumed with His purpose and His plan, not her own desires and cravings. The process proves us so that the promotion doesn't consume us.

UP TO HALF THE KINGDOM

There were only two people in the Bible who were offered up to half the kingdom: one was Esther, the other was Herod's niece turned step-daughter:

> *"For it was Herod who had sent and seized John and bound him in prison for the sake of Herodias, his brother Philip's wife, because he had married her. For John had been saying to Herod, "It is not lawful for you to have your brother's wife." And Herodias had a grudge against him and wanted to put him to death. But she could not, for Herod feared John, knowing that he was a righteous and holy man, and he kept him safe. When he heard him, he was greatly perplexed, and yet he heard him gladly. But an opportunity came when Herod on his birthday gave a banquet for his nobles and military commanders and the leading men of Galilee. For when Herodias' daughter came in and danced, she pleased Herod and his guests. And the king said to the girl, "Ask me for whatever you wish, and I will give it to you." And he vowed to her,*

> *"Whatever you ask me, I will give you, up to half of my kingdom." And she went out and said to her mother, "For what should I ask?" And she said, "The head of John the Baptist." And she came in immediately with haste to the king and asked, saying, "I want you to give me at once the head of John the Baptist on a platter." And the king was exceedingly sorry, but because of his oaths and his guests he did not want to break his word to her. And immediately the king sent an executioner with orders to bring John's head. He went and beheaded him in the prison and brought his head on a platter and gave it to the girl, and the girl gave it to her mother. When his disciples heard of it, they came and took his body and laid it in a tomb."* **Mark 6:17-29 (ESV)**

Both Esther and Herodias' daughter were offered opportunities to ask for anything they wanted, up to half the kingdom of the rulers who were pleased with them. It's imperative that we as the Church awaken to what God wants to do and how He wants to do it - because for every Queen Esther who doesn't rise up to her divine opportunity there is a worldly spirit right behind her that wants the heads of all God's anointed to be cut off. If you don't emerge as the Esther you are called to be, to the assignment you are called to do, there is someone willing to usurp your position and that's why there are so many worldly people occupying the ground and the mountaintops that God intends for His people to reign in. Arts, entertainment, business, government, education, family, media, innovation, even within the Church.

We as God's people are the ones who are supposed to be standing in positions of authority, leading the world forward (just as we have seen in previous chapters - the mandate of Eden), but too many of us are not saying yes to the invitation - because it doesn't look how we expect. Don't be offended by where you're called to be positioned, don't let offence hold you back from the people God is calling you to (Acts 10), don't allow the spirit of religion to tell you you can't do that in the world, because while you are saying no, the spirit at work in the world is saying yes and occupying your rightful ground.

PREPARED WITH STRATEGY

> *"If it pleases the king,"* Esther replied, *"may the king and Haman come today to the banquet I have prepared for them."* **Esther 5:4**

The king offered her whatever she wanted. This was the moment to ask for her entire Jewish people to be spared. Yet…she asked for a party?

*Wow, another worldly, fleshly, carnal desire used for the personal enjoyment of herself and her friends to indulge and enjoy the luxuries of palace life. Do you know how much a banquet like this would cost? Hundreds of thousands of dollars! Can you imagine what better use that money could have? Think of all the starving people in this world, the homeless, the orphans, the unreached. That money would be far better off being used for God's purposes…*says the religious spirit. Sounds like a familiar bunch of Pharisaical fanatics, doesn't it?

But Esther wasn't led by that spirit. She had prayed and fasted and interceded for her people. She had surrounded herself with wise counsellors, more mature leaders who kept her accountable, experienced elders and teachers in the context of community. Hegai represents the Holy Spirit in this story, our ultimate gift Jesus gave us as a teacher, guide, comforter and counsellor. Listening to the wisdom of those around her, and being led by the Spirit through Hegai, she had a plan. And this plan had a purpose. The time of prayer and fasting had endowed her with heavenly strategy. She didn't starve herself to look holy, she didn't pray telling God what she thought best - she intercede on behalf of her people, she sought Him for His will, His ways and His plans. And He told her. Strategies are simply the actions we need to take in order to acquire our answers to prayer. They are the blueprints from heaven, the plans, the files, the recipes, the paths, the wisdom. How often are we moping around in misery thinking that God is not answering our prayers, when He is right there giving us the instructions and steps to do so!

"I have prepared…" Esther was strikingly strategic. She had a palpable plan. She didn't blow her chance the first opportunity she got, she had wisdom. She had sought God's leading and instruction and she used the very tools and

resources that God had already placed at her disposal, for His very purpose. She hadn't planned to host a party coming up soon, it was ready to go, waiting for them. This wasn't an invitation extended for next week, it was now. The table was already set, the food already cooked, the expenses already paid for. It was done, ready to go, simply awaiting their company.

This is stepping out in faith. She didn't wait for their RSVP to confirm all numbers and then go get everything ready. There was the very potential that the king would not just reject her invitation to the dinner table but reject her, herself. Yet she still prepared the feast. She still went ahead with the plan and was ready when the moment of opportunity came colliding together with the kings response. We too, must prepare in faith. What has God already told you to do that you can be doing now? Not waiting for the moment, not waiting for the divine crossroads, but something that will set you up so that *when* it happens you are fully equipped, empowered, prepared, positioned and ready to go with the flow of God's purpose? Often I believe we don't receive answers to prayers because we still haven't done what God has already asked us to do. If He gives you a strategy, implement it!

> *"Rejoice, childless one, who did not give birth; burst into song and shout, you who have not been in labor! For the children of the desolate one will be more than the children of the married woman," says the Lord. "Enlarge the site of your tent, and let your tent curtains be stretched out; do not hold back; lengthen your ropes, and drive your pegs deep. For you will spread out to the right and to the left, and your descendants will dispossess nations and inhabit the desolate cities."* **Isaiah 54:1-3**

HAMAN'S HUMANNESS

We take a little detour from our queen in verses 9-14, but what information this gives us about Haman gives us revelation as to why the purging process is so essential. Haman and Esther have very similar places of positions, power and prominence, yet Haman shows us what left to our own selfish, prideful, self-fulfilling, self-promoting devises we can become. While Esther shows us the purity, humility, holiness and maturity of a Spirit-led life.

> *"That day Haman left full of joy and in good spirits. But when Haman saw Mordecai at the King's Gate, and Mordecai didn't rise or tremble in fear at his presence, Haman was filled with rage toward Mordecai. Yet Haman controlled himself and went home. He sent for his friends and his wife Zeresh to join him. Then Haman described for them his glorious wealth and his many sons. He told them all how the king had honoured him and promoted him in rank over the other officials and the royal staff. "What's more," Haman added, "Queen Esther invited no one but me to join the king at the banquet she had prepared. I am invited again tomorrow to join her with the king. Still, none of this satisfies me since I see Mordecai the Jew sitting at the King's Gate all the time. His wife Zeresh and all his friends told him, "Have them build a gallows seventy-five feet tall. Ask the king in the morning to hang Mordecai on it. Then go to the banquet with the king and enjoy yourself." The advice pleased Haman, so he had the gallows constructed."*
> **Esther 5:9-14**

Both Esther and Haman were shown favour and given position. Esther humbly used what had been graciously bestowed upon her for the good of others, yet Haman took the exact same thing and pridefully boasted and used it for his own personal promotion. When we consume the blessings for ourselves it shows that we are caught up in the ways of the world and driven by fleshly desires. Just like Haman declares in verse 13, we will never be satisfied. When our hearts are set on anything that is not God (even good things!), and as we pursue pleasure, prestige, power and platform in this life for our own personal gratification, *we will never be satisfied.* But when we remember where we have come from, what has been freely given to us by grace, what we possess that we didn't earn or deserve, where we have been placed and positioned, when we know we are called to a greater purpose than merely our own lives - then we live from a place of gratitude, thanksgiving, worship, humility, contentment, surrender, joy, awe and deep fear of the Lord, because we know that we didn't earn any of this through our own strength or striving, and what the Lord has given us He can just as easily take away. Our security isn't in the position or possession, it's in God alone.

As long as we remain in this position of humility, surrender, purity and utterly emptied of ourselves, then God can continue to pour into us more of what we are humbly and faithfully stewarding for His good and His glory. The only way He will stop the flow is if we become a well of containment, instead of an overflowing fountain. When we attempt to keep what He blesses us with for ourselves, we will never be satisfied in life.

The preparation that Esther went through produced the character essential for her to handle the position. And not turning into a Haman. Do not despise the process. Do not fear the purging! Do not resent the purifying! Yes it is painful, yes it can be unbearable sometimes, but it is developing within you the greatest fortification to ensure you are established enough to endure all the glory and gain that the world can offer you and instead choose to use your life for His glory.

THE CRUCIALITY OF THE COMPANY WE KEEP

With his false sense of security based on his own delusional pride at being invited as a VIP with the king to Esther's intimate banquet, Haman's inability to feel joy and satisfaction led his family and friends to advise him to deal with his problems in a fleshly way. The world loves to tell us that if something doesn't make us feel good then get rid of it. If someone hurts or offends you, cut them out of your life. If something doesn't bring you happiness then dispose of it. Haman's inability to experience joy was based on his hatred towards Mordecai. Just because someone doesn't serve our needs doesn't mean they are not serving God's needs. Just because someone won't bow down to our beliefs and opinions doesn't mean they're not bowing down to God's. Just because someone hurts or offends us doesn't mean God is offended by them.

The problem is, when we live from a place of offence, hurt, pride, agenda, jealousy, envy, competitiveness, comparison, egotism, woundedness, bitterness or unforgiveness and are driven by desires of this world, we gradually and subliminally surround ourselves with people who tell us the advice we want to hear, instead of the wisdom of maturity. When we surround ourselves with people with hearts 'of' the world they will give us 'worldly' advice that appeals to our flesh. They will agree with our hurts and tell us we are rightfully wounded. They will instruct us to act in the ways of the world, according to the values of the world. Contrastingly, if we are mature believers, we will surround ourselves with both friends and leaders who tell us what we need to hear, *not what we want to hear*. If someone genuinely loves us, they will speak truth to us…even when the truth hurts.

> "Better is an open reprimand [of loving correction] than love that is hidden. Faithful are the wounds of a friend [who corrects out of love and concern], but the kisses of an enemy are deceitful [because they serve his hidden agenda]." **Proverbs 27:5-6 (AMP)**

The ways of the world are not the ways of God. God is graciously and gently cleansing the hearts of believers that are 'of' the world, but not 'in' the world. The truth hurts, but the truth also is the very thing that sets us free (John 8:32). For too long we have blocked our ears with our hands and stuck our heads in the sand when we hear a word of rebuke or reprimand that is given to purify us. We feel the conviction of the Spirit moving in our hearts, but because of our undealt with trauma, hurt, woundedness, unforgiveness and consequent baggage we are desperately holding onto, we filter that very conviction through guilt and shame and we call it condemnation. We label it as judgment.

How often have we rejected a sermon, a preacher, a pastor, a prophetic word, even a loving friend, because it touched on something so sensitive within us, that instead of leaning in to the safety of the Spirit and seeing what He may be trying to say to us, we rise up loudly, angrily and publicly against that very person. We shoot the messenger because we don't want to hear the message. We don't want to be confronted by our own sins, or failings, or wrongdoings, because that would mean we would have to take action. That would mean we would have to do something. That would mean we would have to do a 180 degree turn. That would mean we would have to...repent! We smack the sticker of 'condemnation' and 'judgment' and 'legalism' on anything and anyone that is calling us deeper into consecration, and we label it 'discernment,' when in reality, it is the conviction of Christ Himself, calling us into freedom.

"*This advice pleased Haman.*" Of course it did, it appealed to His flesh! It appealed to his ego. It appealed to his hurt, offence, anger, bitterness and unforgiveness that he was holding onto. When we hear what we want to hear, without a heart of purity, humility or maturity, it appeals to our fleshly, human, worldly desires. It justifies our thoughts, our pain, our anger. It causes us to kick into self-preservation mode and get all defensive. When we find ourselves here, our hunger for self-promotion has a foothold to build upon in our hearts and lives. It's in this place that, like Haman, we will do whatever it takes to get ahead, to get above, and to get in front of others no matter the cost. No mercy. No grace. No love. No Spirit

With this advice of those closest to him, he also did what Esther did and prepared. He had gallows constructed for Mordecai to be hung on, so that he would be free to enjoy and indulge in the bountiful banquet. My friend, the enemy is prepared. He has gallows for your ending already constructed, he has a plan for your destruction. He has a warrant with your name on it. He has a notice of assassination. He is prepared. You must be too. Not just prepared for your call and assignment that God has for you, but prepared for the attack upon that very call. He will do everything in his power to prevent you from taking your position, because he knows how powerful it will be. Like Haman, if he can't be happy, then no one will. If his desires can't be satisfied then he will bring everyone else down with him. But what the enemy has prepared for your harm, God will use for your good.

HE REMEMBERS

You may be reading through this book thinking, *"Yeah, but Nat, I don't have a position or platform like Esther. I'm not elevated to the level of influence of a queen.*

I'm just a little, everyday kind of person. I don't have the position you're talking about. I don't have the platform you're speaking of. I'm just little old me. I've had so many prophetic words over my life, so many promises from God when I read His Word. I used to believe, I used to dream with God, but somewhere along the way I gave up. The promises never manifested in my life, the prophetic words never came true. Disappointment, discouragement and even depression came flooding in. I gave up and what little faith I do still have left to believe that God could possibly use me in any way of significance, is slowly dwindling."

My friend, hear my words right now and let them sink deeply into your spirit and soul. You are perfectly positioned for purpose. I say that again…you are perfectly positioned for purpose. I decree over you in the name of Jesus, you are perfectly positioned for purpose. I prophesy over your dry bones and your weary heart, you are perfectly positioned for purpose.

God has not forgotten you. He has not made a mistake. He cannot lie. He is faithful and His Word is true. He will complete what He has started, His word will not return to Him void, He has chosen you, called you, prepared you and positioned you exactly where He wants you. You have a purpose in His plan, you have a call in His Kingdom, you have an assignment and a mission, you have a great invitation right now, right here. Partner with Him. Align your heart back to His. Fan into flame the faith that may be flailing. Decree His Word and His promises over your life again. Get out any old prophecies and prophesy them over your dry bones once more. Open the Word of God and speak forth His Scripture.

The Lord has seen it all my friend, every good deed done in seclusion, every tear poured out in the darkness of night. He has heard every prayer, every cry. He has seen your faith when there seemed to be no hope, He has seen you sow with your life, your love, your trust, your time, your generosity, your gifts, your servant-heart, and He will not be mocked - His promise to you is that you will reap what you sow (Gal 6:7-9; Ps 126:5-6). Our obedience to God and what we do and who we are behind closed doors - without a platform, without an audience, without followers or a 'like' button, without a public ministry, without a title, without a position - do not go unnoticed to God. Not only has He seen every single second of it, but He has stored it up and He knows even better

TESTING & TEMPTATION, REMEMBERING & REVERSING

than you do of the good that you have done, the faith you have held, and your heart set on Him. Everything may seem forgotten, everything may look lost, but God is putting disappointment to death in this season. Months, years, decades even, of what seems like unfulfilled promises, heavenly dreams that have never come to pass, visions that have not found the light of day, are being remembered, resurrected and restored to their full potential, in Him, and by Him.

You are not alone. You are not forgotten. You are not overlooked. You are perfectly positioned for His purpose in your life for His ultimate plan and glory.

THE GREAT UNVEILING

I believe we will see a great unveiling in both this life and in eternity. Eternity is going to blow our minds, not just because our simple, earthly imagination can't possibly comprehend its magnitude and majesty, but I believe we are going to be surprised and shocked by what earthly truths are finally revealed then. Who the saints really are, who gets the greater rewards, who is glorified the highest, who are Jesus' closest friends. It won't be who we expect it to be. It won't be who we look up to and admire here on earth. I'm not saying there's anything wrong with these amazing people of God, but what I'm really getting at is that we will be shocked at the little 'nobodies' who we have never heard of before, the truly humble who lived quiet, gentle lives, who don't have a following or big ministries, who don't have a public platform and who impact their world around them to an extent that none of us have ever heard about. Those who faithfully steward what God has put in their possession and are multiplying it one hundred fold, those who are obedient to His Word, those who have faith to see the impossible happen in their life and most of all, those who know Him so closely as their Father, their intimate lover and their friend. Those who have lived a life of intercession, hidden privately behind closed doors, for no eye to see. The secret agents of His Kingdom here on earth.

As God's children, adopted into His family, we won't be judged on our sins - Jesus has already paid for them on the cross and declared us innocent (John 3:17-18; John 5:24, Heb 10:10, 1 John 4:17-18), now our sins are forgotten, as far as the east is from the west (Ps 103:12; Col 1:22-23) and God looks at us as sees Jesus and declares us righteous (2 Cor 5:21). Our day of judgment is not for punishment, but for reward and our reward is determined by how we steward what He has entrusted to us in this life (1 Cor 3:7-15; 1 Pet 1:17; Heb 9:27-28). Let that sink in for a minute.

> *"Therefore do not pronounce judgment before the time, before the Lord comes, who will bring to light the things now hidden in darkness and will disclose the purposes of the heart. Then each one will receive his commendation from God."* **1 Corinthians 4:5 (ESV)**

One day, all will be revealed. Many Christians worry about what sins are going to be laid bare for everyone to see and they become paranoid about this day of judgment, even knowing they won't receive condemnation, they believe they will experience humiliation. But as believers we need to understand that this 'all' is not for our sins that have already been forgiven and forgotten. One day, *all* the good that we have done will be remembered, repaid and rewarded. In the footnote of this verse in the Passion Translation, Dr Brian Simmons explains that *"God will bring to light the secret motives of love, faithfulness, righteousness, kindness, etc. - the pure motives of believers. When the Lord judges His godly lovers, their secret devotion and sacrifices will be brought into the light and God will praise them for their faithful love. The reward of eternity will be that God affirms them. The word for 'praise' can actually be translated, 'thanks from God.' Can you imagine a day coming when God praises his faithful servants?"* [1] God sees and remembers each and every act, word, thought, feeling, intention, motive, desire and I can guarantee that His memory is far better than our own, He remembers everything. He hasn't forgotten, He holds it in His heart right now, waiting to reveal it to you so that even you can remember, every act, every word, every thought, every emotion that you have already sown. You may have forgotten most of it, but He hasn't. He knows, He sees and He is storing it up to bless you and reward you in eternity.

THE GREAT RECOMPENSE

But some of it is remembered, repaid and rewarded in this life on earth, this side of eternity, in the land of the living. God is a just God and He acts in justice here on earth because His judgment is righteous (Ps 94:15). He wouldn't be a holy God if He didn't act justly. You only have to read through the Psalms to know that the feeling of evil overpowering good, the sense of the wicked ruling over the righteous, the experience of the worldly oppressing the godly isn't anything new. We may look at the world around us and think *"How can you let this happen Lord? When will you come and save your people and rescue us from this evil that takes place all around us?"* We are called to trust in Him, to trust in His justice, to trust in His righteous judgment and to trust in His sovereignty, but most significantly, to trust in His love, despite what we experience. His godly lovers rejoice when His gavel of holy judgment comes crashing down into our circumstances! In this story of Esther we see a moment of this justice come to pass when the king is told how Mordecai prevented his very assassination.

> *"That night sleep escaped the king, so he ordered the book recording daily events to be brought and read to the king. They found the written report of how Mordecai had informed on Bigthana and Teresh, two of the king's eunuchs who guarded the entrance, when they planned to assassinate King Ahasuerus. The king inquired, "What honour and special recognition have been given to Mordecai for this act?" The king's personal attendants replied, "Nothing has been done for him."'*
> **Esther 6:1-3**

You would think that saving the king's life would have been a highly esteemed and celebrated act of service to the kingdom. You would think it would be noticed and attributed the accolades it deserved. Not only did this great deed of Mordecai go seemingly unnoticed, but this reveals to us how truly humble this man really was. He didn't sing his own praises, he didn't demand the reward due, he didn't seek glory or promotion. He just continued humbly going about his quiet, gentle life and serving his great God. His heart was fixed on the things that truly mattered, the things of eternity. And it was his humility that enabled him to be eventually elevated in great honour. We need to be so driven by one motive - our King and our King alone.

My friend, it may seem like everything is forgotten. It may feel like you have been overlooked. It may seem like God hasn't noticed all you have done for Him, or that 'nothing has been done for you' in return. But nothing could be further from the truth. He knows more than you do, He sees more than you do. God has a plan. Even if right now you can't see it, feel it, understand it, figure it out, even if circumstances seem the exact opposite to what He has spoken to you and declared over your life, He has a plan. A perfect plan. All this time He has been at work behind the scenes, ready for the curtain to be drawn open upon the magnificent production of His perfection. All this time He has been growing and strengthening those roots to go deep down into the soil of His love and deep foundations, ready for the first sprout to finally break through the surface and grow into a mighty oak. All this time He has been digging deep, deep down to the bedrock and establishing and fortifying a mighty and strong foundation from which He can build upon. You may not see it, but He is doing it. You may not believe it, but He is at work. You may not feel it, but He is coming. There will come a breaker moment when all is unveiled and revealed and you will look back and see how perfectly His plan has been at work in your life without you even realising it. You will look back and see how He has held you so closely in His hands this whole time. Some of it will be unveiled in eternity, some of it will be unveiled to you personally and some of it will be unveiled publicly to those around you. Hold on to hope with faith my friend, disappointment is being put to death in this hour!

THE GREAT REVERSAL

"Humble yourselves, therefore, under the mighty hand of God, so that he may exalt you at the proper time." **1 Peter 5:6**

TESTING & TEMPTATION, REMEMBERING & REVERSING

> *"Remember this: If you have a lofty opinion of yourself and seek to be honoured, you will be humbled. But if you have a modest opinion of yourself and choose to humble yourself, you will be honoured."*
> **Matthew 23:12 (TPT)**

> *"A person's pride will humble him, but a humble spirit will gain honour."* **Proverbs 29:23**

The pride of Haman in chapter six sets him up for the biggest downfall ever predicted. What I've been saying this entire time, and won't stop saying, is that God requires humble and holy hearts so that He can use us to the extent that He has planned. What He is doing in this new era is so powerful and pertinent that He is requiring a deeper level of humility than we have ever known before. And continually. God is about to flaunt Himself to the world. He will use His people to do His will, to exercise His healings, to manifest His miracles, but we are not the performers on the stage, we are the very platform from which He stands upon and is glorified through. The reason there's a deepening of humility and holiness is because there's a heightening of His power and glory. In order to use us, He needs to trust us, and the way He trusts us is when our hearts are emptied, purged and purified of pride, self-seeking glory, agenda, motives, jealousy, envy, comparison, competition, performance, ego and worldly desires.

While the pride and self-righteousness of Haman is blatantly obvious, there are still areas of our hearts that the Holy Spirit needs to illuminate His light upon in order to expose the darkness that is quietly lingering, deep down, unnoticed, unprovoked. We may think we're fairly ok, but there's always more and more layers to purity, maturity, humility and holiness. The process is painful, what comes to the surface may be shocking, but it is absolutely necessary and such a beautiful, beautiful thing when we embrace it. Haman's humiliating downfall began when he was ordered to give the very reward and celebration that he intended for himself over to Mordecai instead. If we wish to keep our life, we will only lose it (Matt 10:38-39; John 12:25), if we want to be the greatest we will be the least (Matt 18:1-5). We need to take on the nature of little children, with childlike hearts, who hang off every word of their Father, and who rest freely and tranquilly on His lap, embraced in His arms, and then God can use us for His great and mighty purpose - because we all know that children have the greatest faith, purest hearts and honest humility.

> *"I am humbled and quieted in your presence. Like a contented child who rests on its mother's lap, I'm your resting child and my soul is content in you. O people of God, your time has come to quietly trust, waiting upon the Lord now and forever."* **Psalm 131:2-3 (TPT)**

What the enemy has intended for your harm, God is turning it around and using it for your good. What the enemy has planned for your assassination, God already has a plan for your victory, triumph and restoration. The enemy's plans for you will be completely reversed and turned on him - just as Jesus' death on the cross and resurrection completely obliterated Satan and all of the powers of hell. The enemy thought he had won when Jesus breathed His last breath, but the greatest reversal of all had just taken place. The reversal of the fall, the reversal of the cosmic rebellion, the reversal of the power of death, the reversal of every curse, the reversal of the powers of darkness - Jesus trampled death under His feet, He crushed the serpents head!

Haman's friends and family realise the inevitable in verse 17, *"You have begun to fall before him (Mordecai), you won't overcome him, because your downfall is certain."* The enemy's downfall is already certain, it has already happened. Victory is already yours through Jesus. Satan knows he is defeated, he knows what destruction is destined for him, and he has determined to bring down as many souls with him as possible in the meantime. Through the cross and resurrection we can see the Great Reversal as God's plan all along. Everything in history, everything recorded in the Old Testament and up until Jesus death, every circumstance of Israel and their heritage, absolutely everything up until this point was for a purpose which we can now see so clearly because we live this side of the cross. You too, will see so clearly that everything in your history, every present situation and everything in your future, is being tied together for a magnificent purpose and woven into a beautiful testimony of His power, love and redemption.

God isn't just remembering every moment of your life and storing it up for His great unveiling, but He is also reversing every curse, every disappointment, every circumstance and situation and in front of the angelic realm and the heavenly cloud of witnesses you will be put on a chariot and celebrated for your faithfulness. All for His glory and all so you can lay your majestic crown at His feet in an act of eternal worship!

NOTES

1. Simmons, 2017, The Passion Translation: The New Testament with Psalms, Proverbs and Song of Songs, Broadstreet Publishing, p812

CHAPTER 9

ARISING IN IDENTITY & AUTHORITY

In this era, it is crucial that our heads are resting on Him, with our ears on His chest, hearing the heartbeat of heaven. It's imperative we walk in intimacy with Him as we live from a place of His presence so that we too can hear what the Father is saying in heaven and know how and when to act and what to do (John 5:19; 12:49-50). We need to know His will, but we also need to receive the 'yes' and the 'go' from the Holy Spirit so that we do His will at the right time and in the right moment. Discerning the times, the seasons and the atmosphere ensures we're going with Him in intricate partnership as He executes His will on earth in accordance with His plan. Not ours…as well intentioned as it may be. While He may have revealed His will to us, we can't be hasty, but must rest in His timing. Often this is the hardest part of receiving vision and promise.

> *"Hope deferred makes the heart sick, but a desire fulfilled is a tree of life."* **Proverbs 13:12 (ESV)**

Esther knew what she had to do. She had planned, prepared and positioned herself. She had already had plenty of moments of opportunity to ask the king her great request, yet here we find them all, two days into the party banquet and she still hasn't petitioned him on behalf of her people. What was she waiting for? This is a pivotal moment, stop feasting and start acting! Too often we hear the word from God and we plunge ourselves prematurely into the performance of trying to make it manifest. Yes, we heard correctly. But the timing just isn't right. We don't simply need to hear His voice, we need to sense His presence, His leading, His movement. We need to receive the 'go.' The 'now.' Our relationship with God has to be so close and connected that we walk in rhythm with His steps and what He is doing and when He is doing it, not running on up ahead nor lagging behind.

We constantly need to be living how Jesus lived, knowing what the Father wanted to do in each moment. Not relying on what has been done before or what God told us to do in previous situations, not what even worked before. Moses lost his opportunity to enter into the Promise Land because He relied upon an old word, rather than obeying what God told him to do in the moment (Num 20:2-12). If Moses can miss out on his promise fulfilled in this life, then how much more do we need to be so acutely aware of God's voice, God's presence and God's leading and not to act on our own good intentions?

HUMBLE, HOLY HEARTS

> *"Delight yourself in the Lord, and he will give you the desires of your heart. Commit your way to the Lord; trust in him, and he will act. He will bring forth your righteousness as the light, and your justice as the noonday."* **Psalm 37:4-6 (ESV)**

Esther's opportunity finally arrives. Here we are at the pinnacle of the story, everything we have been waiting for, her moment of opportunity, her day of destiny, all that she has been prepared and positioned for, the climax of her call, the 'perhaps' purpose of her entire existence. Everything rides on this request, not just her own life but the future and salvation of the entire Jewish people. The king has told her she can have whatever she wants and she now asks for the very thing she desires above all else.

> "*...spare my life; this is my request. And spare my people; this is my desire.*" **Esther 7:3**

This is her request. This is her desire. When our desires are in line with His will, we can request anything of the King and it will be done (John 14:13). When we grow in intimacy in relationship with God His heart becomes our heart, His desires become our desires, His passions become our passions, His values become our values. The purifying process is so essential to purge us of worldly and fleshly desires as it prunes and polishes us to align with His heart and to grow into the likeness of our beautiful Jesus. When our heart has become His heart and when our desires are His desires, we can ask anything and it will be done. Unanswered prayers may be nothing more than a request outside of His will or timing. He isn't going to align His will with our hearts, but He will align our hearts with His will.

Esther had an opportunity to ask for up to half the kingdom of the reigning empire of Persia. But she didn't ask for anything that she wanted, she asked for what God had instructed her to do. She obeyed. Our hearts intricately intertwine with Him the more time we spend with Him in the secret place where we get to know Him on a personal level and bask in His presence, rest in His arms and seek His face. Our wants, our passions, our desires grow into the shape of His heart, so that what we 'want' is exactly what He wants.

> "*And when he had removed him (King Saul), he (God) raised up David to be their king, of whom he (God) testified and said, 'I have found in David the son of Jesse a man after my heart, who will do all my will.'*"
> **Acts 13:22 (ESV, parentheses added)**

STEP INTO YOUR IDENTITY AND AUTHORITY

> "*Esther answered, "The adversary and enemy is this evil Haman." Haman stood terrified before the king and queen.*" **Esther 7:6**

After petitioning for her people the king questions how this could have even happened. Esther quickly points out who the culprit is. Haman stood terrified before the king and queen because he knew what fate awaited him. In the exact same way, the enemy stands terrified in front of the King and his Bride - you - because he knows the battle is already won, victory already belongs to Jesus and as you rise up into your God-given identity and wield the power and authority that has been handed to you by Jesus Himself and commanded of you to walk in (Matt 28:19, Eph 1:19-23), his plans are doomed and his fate is already destined. When we know our identity as sons and daughters of the King, when we walk in the authority we are called to live in, when we exercise the power of the God of heaven and earth, the enemy is terrified of us! This is exactly what the battle has been about in your life, this is the reason the enemy has been continually attacking you, beating you down, trying to get you to give up and relinquish the dream, the vision, the call the purpose that you know you are created for because of the promises of God. This is also the sole purpose of the spirit of religion - to prevent God's people from realising their divine identity and arising in their authority and power in God.

The Bride of Christ is rapidly rising into her royal identity in this time, because what God has in store for us requires us to be living like the rightful sons and daughters that we are, not with orphan mentalities. It requires us to be a royal priesthood, not slaves to religion. It requires us to activate the keys of authority that Jesus has already handed to us, not to passively sit by and watch, thinking that's not for us or worse, pointing the finger at others in judgment, accusing them of not performing to our mere interpretations and sheer opinions. It requires us to step out in faith knowing that the same power that rose Jesus from the dead lives in us (Rom 8:11). When we discover the depths of our identity in Him and rise up into our God-given royal position, when we arise in authority and stand with our King, in His presence, at His right hand, seated in heavenly places in union with Jesus, the enemy is terrified.

But do you know who the enemy is not terrified of? A child who does not know their sonship or a bride who is unaware of her betrothal. He is not intimidated by a soldier sitting on the sidelines who doesn't even wield his

ARISING IN IDENTITY AND AUTHORITY

weapons. He is not afraid of a cute little Christian who believes the power of God at work today has ceased to exist. Why would he? These people don't pose a threat to him.

Even Satan himself is more aware of the power, authority and identity we have in Christ than many believers warming church pews every Sunday. That's why he is terrified when you realise it too! Too many believers today do not know their position in heaven, their identity in Christ or their power and authority over the enemy's domain and that is why the world is getting worse, the days are getting darker, the times more evil. Don't get me wrong, biblically and prophetically the world itself is only getting worse - Scripture tells us this and we only have to look at the signs of the season to discern the times we are in. It is only ever going to grow darker...for the world. But for God's people - the holy, the righteous, the faithful, the chosen, the set apart, the consecrated, the remnant, those who have not compromised with mixture - we are promised protection and deliverance from the darkness and the powers at play, if we are in Him and Him in us. It is imperative that God's people wake up and arise in both our identity and authority, in Him.

We sit back and wonder why prayers aren't answered and it's because God has already given us the answers and the authority, He's just waiting on us to activate them in partnership with Him. The religious spirit strives to keep our true identity hidden under the filthy mud of guilt and shame and tells us we have no value or worth. It keeps us focused on our failures and flaws and busy under a heavy burden of straining to reach man-made requirements and tells us we have no power or authority. It ensures our eyes are always on ourselves and our human limitations, weaknesses, mistakes and shortcomings, instead of looking to the all-powerful God of the heavens and earth and discovering who we are in Him, because of Him and all He has done for us and will do through us, all because of His grace. The spirit of religion makes it all about us. But our identity can only be found in Him.

WHEN YOU TURN THE TIDE ON THE ENEMY...
YOU BECOME THE TARGET

In verse 6 Esther points out who the real enemy is. She names him by name and exposes the evil plans that he had prepared for the people of God. When our eyes are unveiled, then we too can finally see the plans of the enemy and his evil schemes, we too can then call him on it and point out his destructive plans to those around us. No wonder we have a target on our lives! Too many believers are walking around the palace thinking that 'Haman' is in the position of power, when the reality is that we are royalty, which means we have authority over him.

Please hear me out, this is not a witch hunt, we are not deliberately looking for demons behind every door. There is no need to focus on the enemy, but not acknowledging his existence or being ignorant of his ways is just as dangerous as giving him too much of our attention. We cannot be blind, we cannot be foolish, we cannot be unenlightened. The Holy Spirit will reveal the enemy's schemes as we ask, and as we seek Him He will give us the strategies to defeat the attacks in our life and the strongholds we are facing in our cities and nations. We are not fighting flesh and blood, but the powers, principalities and authorities of the spiritual realm (Eph 6:12). How can we defeat him if we don't even acknowledge him? How can we fight if we don't even recognise we're in a battle?

Just because we are saved and have Jesus on our side doesn't mean we are immune to the enemy. In fact, the more we wake up to who we are in Christ, as we work out our salvation, as we mature in our faith, when we know who we truly are, what authority, power, gifts and unlimited heavenly resources are available to us through Christ, it paints a big red target on our lives for the enemy to attack. Because *now* we *are* a threat. Passive, inactive, slumbering, casual believers who do not know their heavenly identity, who do not walk in the authority of Christ and who do not activate the power of God don't pose a threat to the enemy in this life. They also don't advance the Kingdom of God.

Just take a moment to selah that.

> *"From the days of John the Baptist until now, the kingdom of heaven has been suffering violence, and the violent have been seizing it by force."*
> **Matthew 11:12**

I believe in this era we are not just going to see the enemy's plans for us personally, but on a much grander scale, the eyes of many are going to be opened as the enemy's agenda that has been at work throughout the earth for thousands of years is going to be exposed. Evil that has been hidden for millennia is going to be seen for what it truly is. Empires, dynasties, kingdoms, nations, families and secret societies that have been controlling the world for centuries through the same spirit, are going to be caught red handed. The Babylonian systems of the world that we are financially, culturally and geo-politically enslaved to will be brought to light and come crumbling down. We are going to see such a large and deep unveiling of this evil that deception will fall from our eyes and minds and we will see the world for what it really is. This exposing is going to cause much pain and grief as many wrestle to process the very concept that we could have all been so deeply lied to and gone along with such an evil agenda, oblivious since birth, grown up in the systems and the indoctrination that we will soon find out is built on a foundation of pure evil, lies, deception and deliberately leading us away from not just love for God, but the entire notion of God and creation and our human design and purpose.

Even the modern church system, structure and establishment will be shaken from the inside out. Prepare your hearts now for what is about to come. Set yourself firmly in God, because what we see exposed from within the church and the religious establishment is going to shock us to the core and without a strong faith and foundation, many will be susceptible to abandoning the faith altogether. The level of sin that is going to be exposed, the prevalence of sexual immorality within high leadership, the depth of corruption with specific churches who are actually linchpins for some of the most horrendous crimes against humanity, is going to be unfathomable for us all. Perhaps the most shocking of all will be the unveiling of those serving Satan himself. Entire countries, cultures, systems and religions built on the worship of the gods with Lucifer at the very top. Watch this space.

This is going to be an era of awakening for many who surrender to truth and who's trust and security is in the Lord, no matter what shaking or exposing comes to this earth. It is so important to understand that this shaking is essential.

We must not be in fear while we watch the world as we know it collapse around us, but we must hold firm, knowing that this exposing is actually our liberation. This crumbling is our freedom. This destruction is our reformation. The level of truth and knowledge and freedom that will come from this exposing is going to catapult God's people into a lifestyle of such deep identity and authority in Him that we will see His Kingdom come, His will be done, on earth as it is in heaven in significant measure (Matt 6:10).

THE ENEMY'S EXECUTION

> *"The king arose in anger and went from where they were drinking wine to the palace garden. Haman remained to beg Queen Esther for his life because he realised the king was planning something terrible for him. Just as the king returned from the palace garden to the banquet hall, Haman was falling on the couch where Esther was reclining. The king exclaimed, "Would he actually violate the queen while I am in the house?" As soon as the statement left the king's mouth, they covered Haman's face."* **Esther 7:7-8**

The enemy recognises those who live in real relationship with the King. And a time is upon us where it will be blatantly obvious to everyone, those who know Jesus intimately, and those who simply know of Him. To be in relationship with God we need to dwell in the house of our King (Psalm 27:4) and we need to live from that place of His presence. We need to ascend the mountain of the Lord (Psalm 24) and we need to abide in Him as a lifestyle, not sporadic spiritual moments that are few and far between. Yes, the enemy's attacks are very real, but those who find shelter under the wings of God and take refuge in Him will always be safe and secure, protected from the forces of darkness (Psalm 91). It doesn't mean we will escape the suffering and persecution of this world, it means we can run to the refuge of our Father's residence and we can walk out our life and faith from this very realm. Then our Father and King can speak over our enemy *"Would you dare to violate my Bride while I am in the house?"* (Es 7:8)

You have been targeted by the enemy because you are a threat to him, and as you arise in your identity and authority into the royal position that is rightfully yours, you terrify him!

THE CURSE REVERSED

> *"Harbona, one of the king's eunuchs, said: "There is a gallows seventy-five feet tall at Haman's house that he made for Mordecai, who gave the report that saved the king." The king said, "Hang him on it." They hanged Haman on the gallows he had prepared for Mordecai. Then the king's anger subsided."* **Esther 7:9-10**

These verses paint a prophetic picture of a larger story at hand. All of the curses were reversed in the cross and resurrection. Everything in the history, present and future is held perfectly in the palm of His hand and His plan is sovereign and His purpose prevails. Everything that the enemy has intended for your harm God is turning for your good, He is tying together all the loose ends, He is pouring out His sovereignty over your life and He is using your designed and designated destiny for His divine plan and purpose to see His Kingdom come.

Today, rest in the reassurance that all curses against you have been reversed by the cross. He is recompensing you for all that has been stolen, resurrecting all that has been killed and restoring all that has been destroyed (John 10:10), He is reinstating you to your rightful, royal position in His palace and presence and He has a purpose for you to play in His perfect plan. Today, arise into your royal identity in Him. Today, align yourself with the power of God as His royal priesthood. Today, activate the authority of Jesus over your circumstances and situations.

> *"You prepare a table before me in the presence of my enemies. You anoint my head with oil; my cup overflows. Surely your goodness and love will follow me all the days of my life, and I will dwell in the house of the Lord forever."* **Psalm 23:5-6**

POSITIONED FOR PURPOSE

> *"Now to him who is able to do far more abundantly than all that we ask or think, according to the power at work within us, to him be glory in the church and in Christ Jesus throughout all generations, forever and ever. Amen."* **Ephesians 3:20-21 (ESV)**

SUPERABUNDANTLY MORE

Whatever darkness you have walked through, whatever disappointment or discouragement you hold deep down in your heart, whatever desolate dreams remain void, whatever promises unfulfilled, whatever circumstances you are experiencing right now, whatever impossible situations you are facing, please know that what the enemy intends for your downfall, God has a plan prepared for you for complete reversal of everything. The Kingdom principle of sowing and reaping goes both ways. While we reap the blessings for all the good we sow, so too will the enemy reap the due destruction that he deserves for his attempt and attack on your life. But what I love even more is that not only does the enemy get everything he deserves, not only are his curses on us reversed, but God goes even further and not just saves and sets us free from the evil schemes aimed at us, but He goes above and beyond to pour out undeserved blessing upon us for what we have endured.

He doesn't just recompense all that was stolen, He doesn't just reinstate us to the royal position we are rightfully in, He doesn't just restore what was broken, He doesn't just rebuild what was destroyed, He doesn't just revive all that was killed, He doesn't just renew our strength, He doesn't just rejuvenate life within us - He goes so much further than anything we could possibly deserve by His overflowing fountain of grace pouring into us, He gives us immeasurably more than we could ever ask, dream or imagine. He doesn't just bring us back to neutral so we can start again from scratch, He takes hold of us and places us in a position so far further than we would have ever been even if we had never endured the attack on our life and call.

Why? Because He loves us. Because we are His beloved children.

As a parent I love giving good gifts to my kids. If we know how to give to our children, how much more does the Father enjoy giving good things to those He loves (Matt 7:11). He goes above and beyond because His nature and character is good. He gives us superabundantly more than we want, more than we request, more than we need because He is a God of abundance, not a God of 'just enough.' He is a God of above and beyond, not 'just scrape over the line until you'll be ok.' He is a good, good God, He is a loving Father. He doesn't have to give us more than we need or ask, but He wants to. Because He loves us. Esther had one request, just one - for her people to be spared death. That's all she asked for, that's all she petitioned the king for, that was her single and only desire and request. Yet this chapter reveals to us just how superabundantly, over-the-top, ridiculously generous and overflowing in goodness God really is.

A BEAUTIFUL EXCHANGE

> *"That same day King Ahasuerus awarded Queen Esther the estate of Haman, the enemy of the Jews. Mordecai entered the king's presence because Esther had revealed her relationship to Mordecai. The king removed his signet ring he had recovered from Haman and gave it to Mordecai, and Esther put him in charge of Haman's estate."*
> **Esther 8:1-2**

Not only did Haman reap the punishment he deserved, on the very platform he had created to kill the godly, but all he possessed, every good thing he owned, everything he had built with his own hands, everything he had accumulated in life, everything he had stored up, everything he had worked, earned and strove for, every single gift and blessing he had received from the king - his entire legacy - was now handed over to Esther. Mordecai was elevated to the position that Haman previously possessed, because he had proven that he was worthy of such a place of power. He was given authority over the realm that Haman once ruled because he had faithfully stewarded in the secret and demonstrated his humility, purity and maturity with little, which validated him to rule over a lot. The godly prevailed over the wicked. Righteous justice poured out in judgment on evil.

In the very same way, everything that our enemy thought he possessed, everything he thought he had rule and power over, everything he held to use against us, Jesus reversed, repaid, reinstated, recompensed, restored and redeemed through His death and resurrection. Jesus gave us the keys of the Kingdom to bind and loose according to His will and His ways (Matt 18:18). As He ascended to the heavenlies He commissioned you and me to take those very keys and apply them to this life to rule over the spiritual realm in this world with His authority and power (Matt 28:19), in order to take ground for the Kingdom of God while we await His imminent second coming where this very Kingdom will be made manifest in its absolute fullness and He will reign with His faithful ones forever, just as Scripture prophesies. Everything the enemy came to steal, kill and destroy Jesus came to give life and life in abundance (John 10:10).

PROVEN WORTHY TO WORK IN HIS NAME

"Then Esther addressed the king again. She fell at his feet, wept, and begged him to revoke the evil of Haman the Agagite and his plot he had devised against the Jews. The king extended the gold sceptre toward Esther, so she got up and stood before the king. She said, "If it pleases the king and I have found favour before him, if the matter seems right to the king and I am pleasing in his eyes, let a royal edict be written. Let it revoke the documents the scheming Haman son of Hammedatha the Agagite wrote to destroy the Jews who are in all the king's provinces. For how could I bear to see the disaster that would come on my people? How could I bear to see the destruction of my relatives?" King Ahasuerus said to Esther the queen and to Mordecai the Jew, "Look, I have given Haman's estate to Esther, and he was hanged on the gallows because he attacked the Jews. Write in the king's name whatever pleases you concerning the Jews, and seal it with the royal signet ring. A document written in the king's name and sealed with the royal signet ring cannot be revoked."" **Esther 8:3-8**

ARISING IN IDENTITY AND AUTHORITY

Esther finally completed the task she was commissioned to do. She did the very thing she was called to. But not only did she obey, she did it with humility (fell at his feet), a pure and passionate heart of intercession (she was moved to tears on behalf of her people who God loved) and bold faith (addressed the king, *again*). When we obey the call and commission on our life with the same humility, passion, heart and boldness as Esther, we prove our purity and maturity to be used by God in even greater ways. When we steward the little He rewards us with more, because He knows we can be responsible.

He increases our favour because we have been faithful. Our King has given us His signet ring that carries the power and authority within His Kingdom, in this world and in the spiritual realms. When we understand what power we have in our possession because of the initials of the King of Kings on our hearts and lives, we realise that we can make a royal decree of whatever pleases us and seal it with the royal ring. God can fully trust us to ask whatever we please because we have proven our hearts are His heart, our desires are His desires, our will is His will (Acts 13:22).

> *"I will give you the keys of the kingdom of heaven, and whatever you bind on earth will have been bound in heaven, and whatever you loose on earth will have been loosed in heaven."* **Matthew 18:18**

EXCEEDINGLY MORE

> *"On the twenty-third day of the third month - that is, the month Sivan - the royal scribes were summoned. Everything was written exactly as Mordecai commanded for the Jews, to the satraps, the governors, and the officials of the 127 provinces from India to Cush. The edict was written for each province in its own script, for each ethnic group in its own language, and to the Jews in their own script and language. Mordecai wrote in King Ahasuerus' name and sealed the edicts with the royal signet ring. He sent the documents by mounted couriers, who rode fast horses bred in the royal stables. The king's edict gave the Jews*

> *in each and every city the right to assemble and defend themselves, to destroy, kill, and annihilate every ethnic and provincial army hostile to them, including women and children, and to take their possessions as spoils of war."* **Esther 8:9-11**

The petition for the people of God was for their preservation. Yet the king's edict offered them an even greater opportunity - to overcome and overpower their enemies and to triumphantly take possession of an abundance of spoils, plunder, booty, prize, loot. Wait a minute, this sounds really 'worldly' and 'fleshly' - a holy God wouldn't intend for us to steal materialistic possessions. Well actually, we're not stealing, we're taking back what was stolen. The Merriam-Webster Dictionary defines 'spoils' as *"Something taken from another by force or craft. More commonly, spoils applies to 'what belongs by right or custom to the victor in war or political contest.'"* [1] I love this definition. As God's people we have a right to forcibly take back that which rightfully belongs to us as victors. You are a victor. You have won this war. Whether you feel it or not, whether it looks like it or not, you have triumphed because He has triumphed over death and sin and the enemy is crushed under His heel in victory. So many believers have no idea what inheritance is rightfully theirs, they have no clue what belongs to them because of Him, they are oblivious to the amazing heavenly treasures and every spiritual resource open to the taking, to be used for the Kingdom.

The reason so many believers aren't walking in the promises of God that are blatantly in black and white in front of us in our Bible's is because we're not arising out of our comfortable seats and taking hold of what God has said is rightfully ours already. If every promise fulfilled was part and parcel of salvation then we would receive it in that very instant. But we haven't. And we don't. But it *is* there for the taking, if we violently take hold of the Kingdom of God as we are called to do - through both repentance and obedience. The Jews could have defended themselves and left it at that, but in God's goodness and grace He gave them an even greater opportunity to go a step further and to plunder their enemies. To take for themselves the spoils of war. And He has given us a smorgasbord of promises to take possession of, because He has fought for us and

He has triumphantly overpowered the enemy so that His people can possess the plunder!

THE 'JUST ENOUGH' MENTALITY

Esther asked for a little and she was given a lot. She obediently stewarded one opportunity and she was given an even one greater. Our faithful, humble obedience leads to greater opportunity as we prove our trustworthiness in the One who is faithful to fulfil whatever He asks of us to partner with Him in.

> *"For to everyone who has [and values his blessings and gifts from God, and uses them wisely], more will be given, and [he will be richly supplied so that] he will have an abundance; but from the one who does not have [because he has ignored or disregarded his blessings and gifts from God], even what little he does have will be taken away."*
> **Matthew 25:29 (AMP)**

I'm not referring to riches and treasures like finances and material possessions. Although I do believe that they are included as part of God's resources, which rightfully belong to Him and can be used for the Kingdom as tools. I'm talking about every key we need to be free, every power we need to see miracles on earth, to see healing take place, to be set free from every demonic force and stronghold in our hearts, minds, lives and bloodlines, every authority to overpower our circumstances and anything that comes up against God's Word and anything that currently prevails against God's promises. If it's not in line with His Word and what He has said, what He has spoken, then it's an opportunity for us to exercise the very spiritual tools, scriptural weapons and heavenly resources He has put in our possession.

Esther was given an opportunity for so much more than she ever imagined. She had but one simple request, yet here she was faced with a choice. She could have said no to the king's offer of so much more. After all, she had already denied up to half the kingdom. But I believe it was that very denial of worldly desires that would have served only herself, that positioned her for an even greater choice right now. Esther didn't need to say yes to the 'more.' She could have been a very good little Christian girl and responded with *"No no, I simply want my people free. You can keep all the goods. I don't need that, I don't want to take any more than I need. Thank you for your generous offer, but I humbly decline."*

The religious spirit loves to tell us to 'humbly' decline. The religious spirit loves to tell us that it's 'unholy' to receive more than we need. But the religious spirit doesn't know how to be generous. The religious spirit doesn't have the greater good of all those around us at heart. The religious spirit doesn't flow in the currency of generosity. The religious spirit doesn't allow us to understand the purpose of abundance. The religious spirit tells us to say no, because it understands the power of the overflow when we plunder the enemy's possessions and take more than we could ever need for ourselves alone.

A KAIROS MOMENT

Not only did Esther have the wisdom to say yes to an opportunity for the greater good of all, but she had the ability to discern the moment she was in. These are the very kairos moments the Bride is in, in this era. We must have discernment to know what to say yes to and know what to say no to. We must have discernment to not just know when to say yes or no, but to know when such a monumental, history-altering opportunity is in front of us that we so graciously have been given the invitation to partake in partnership with Him to see His will on earth be executed in excellence. Esther *carp diem*-ed every ounce of that opportunity! She took her 'who knows, 'perhaps'' moment and seized it for what it was worth. Every last morsel.

Esther could have used this moment for selfish gain and said yes to more for her personally, but her purged and purified heart had proven her humble and faithful. She could have been bound by the religious spirit and said no to the more, but her maturity and security in her identity, her obedience and discernment to the leading of God had proven her trustworthy. Instead, she used her very position and platform for the purpose she had been placed there for in His perfect plan. She seized the kairos moment she perceived.

ABOVE AND BEYOND

> *"Mordecai went from the king's presence clothed in royal purple and white, with a great gold crown and a purple robe of fine linen. The city of Susa shouted and rejoiced, and the Jews celebrated with gladness, joy, and honour. In every province and every city, wherever the king's command and his law reached, joy and rejoicing took place among the Jews. There was a celebration and a holiday. And many of the ethnic groups of the land professed themselves to be Jews because fear of the Jews had overcome them."* **Esther 8:15-17**

Salvation through Jesus doesn't just offer us a free ticket into heaven for eternity, it offers us a life of triumph, victory, power and authority over every opposition that we will face. It offers every resource in heaven to fulfil every need we will have. It offers peace and joy through every tribulation, persecution, hardship and circumstance we will have to endure. It offers supernatural grace and strength to empower us to walk through every trial we will come up against. It offers us freedom from the bondage that will try and chain us down. It offers relief, restoration, recompense, redemption from everything lost, stolen, given away, destroyed, broken and put to death in our life and calls us to take the hand of Jesus and receive His offer of not just life, but life in abundance.

> *"The thief comes only to steal, kill and destroy. I came that they may have life and have it abundantly."* **John 10:10 (ESV)**

We have been given a great commission and we have a great harvest at hand. It is imperative that the Church awakens to her true identity in Christ which includes the revelation of the unlimited heavenly resources that are not just available, but are intended for our application and activation to violently force back the powers of darkness as we extend the perimeters of the Kingdom of God in this world. It's time to plunder the enemy with force. Those souls do not belong to him, those lives are not his, those destinies will not be stolen, those hearts will not be held down any longer. That authority is not his, that power is not for his use, those weapons are not to be used against people but against the principalities and spirits of the unseen realm, those mountaintops of society are not his domain. All authority in heaven and on earth has been given to Jesus and He has commissioned us to go out of the four walls of our church buildings, to go out of our comfortable easy lives, to go out of our religious mindsets, to go out beyond our fear of what others may think, to go out beyond our doubts, disappointments and despair, to the ends of the earth and to PLUNDER THE ENEMY'S POSSESSIONS!

The harvest is ripe but the workers are few. Wake up, oh slumbering! Awaken to the time we are in, the moment around us, awaken to your destiny that was determined before the world was set into motion (Eph 2:10), awaken to the call you have been created for! You are not insignificant, you are pertinent to His plan! You are not hidden, you are perfectly positioned exactly where He wants you so that you would partner with Him to pursue the purpose He has prepared for you.

Awaken to your authority over the enemy! Hasten to the weight of the kairos moment and urgency upon us in this hour! Praise and rejoice and remain surrendered in a position of thanksgiving in faith before we even see the power, majesty and glory that God is about to unveil to the world in this era. This is how we fight our battles. Arise as warrior worshippers!

NOTES

1. Merriam-Webster. (n.d.) *Loot*. In *Merriam-Webster.com dictionary*. Retrieved October 18, 2019, from *https://www.merriam-webster.com/dictionary/loot*

CHAPTER 10

BREAKTHROUGH TO VICTORY

The Jews victorious breakthrough didn't come without a battle. They had been spared by the king, the edict was decreed, but they still had to fight for their freedom. Why? Because nothing of worth comes in this Kingdom without a battle from the enemy who wants the treasure, prize and possession too. The promises and fulfilment come at a price that we must be willing to pay, willing to sacrifice ourselves, our lives, our everything for. When we give our full yes to God we are also giving our yes to a lifetime of opposition. No, this life will not be easy, this life will not be comfortable, this life will not be without suffering, persecution or pain, and the victory won't come without a ferocious fight (John 16:33). Even the Israelites had to drive out the giants of the Promised Land, after they had already inherited it. It's in the battlefield where the real soldiers are proven and where those who's hearts are not truly willing will be revealed. The battlefield overtly displays those who are on board no matter what, from those who turn back to the comfortable, easy life when the going gets tough. But it's on this very battlefield where the Kingdom-builders are strengthened, solidified, fortified and established.

But we are not alone in this life, in this battle, in this warfare. His beautiful Bride has a bounty prize for her defeat - yet we have everything that we possibly need to overcome this and rise high with wings of an eagle. And we don't need to do a thing. We just need to turn to Him, look to Him, rest in Him, trust in Him, believe in Him, wait upon Him, and He will do every single thing that we cannot do. He will rescue us and redeem us, He will save us and restore it all.

Destiny alignments, kairos moments, stepping into your divine assignments, saying yes to the call, your obedience, most definitely puts you in a position with a big red target painted all over your life for the enemy to aim at. When we really step into the battle field, it really gets real. Whatever your heavenly assignments, whatever your position of purpose - whenever you approach that, whenever you are walking in it, whenever you are on the God-given path of your life, whenever you are entering into pivotal and crucial relational alignments, whenever lies of beliefs are being exposed and unveiled, I can guarantee it won't come easily or without a fight. I can guarantee every single thing around you will feel likes it's beginning to crumble. I can guarantee you will have to make a choice to serve this world or to serve God alone. I can guarantee He will purge you with depth-chargers that vomit up the most agonising truths from deep within you that are so ugly and horrendous for you to even acknowledge. But they are so beautiful, so essential, so imperative for you to walk through, so that He can use you. So that He can work through you. So that He can trust you. So that He can elevate and unveil you, in whatever capacity that may be.

On the day when the Jews enemies had hoped to overpower them, the exact opposite happened. The Jews overpowered all those who opposed and hated them! The very schemes and strategies that the devil has set up to sabotage you is being turned around from you and onto him. There is a royal edict over your life and a divine destiny set up for you by an omnipotent God. The cross and empty tomb are the very battlefield where your victory was already won and as you rise up and join forces with the heavenly army to create chaos and confusion in the enemy's camp, our Almighty Deliver is sweeping in to not just save you but to overpower everything that has come against you.

Passive, casual Christianity doesn't draw the attention of the attacker.

Slumbering believers don't feel the magnetic force of the fiery arrows upon their lives. Christians in bed with culture don't experience any warfare. But once we have been awakened to the very real atmosphere around us and once we have had our eyes opened by the unveiling revelation of the Holy Spirit, then this Kingdom call becomes real. It's not a walk in the park. It's a battle for the blessing. Yes, that very blessing, salvation and inheritance was redeemed for you in the resurrection, but you have to step up to the plate and take hold of what is rightfully yours.

WAGING WARFARE

How we fight is very different than we may imagine. Your greatest weapon is worship. Your strongest arsenal is intimacy. Your most protective shield is faith. Your most reliable dagger is the Word of God. Your battle cry is praise. Your banner is love. Your authority is the name of Jesus. Your strategy is prayer. Your assignment is intercession. Your power is the blood of the Lamb. Your victory is communion. Your equipping is the baptism of the Spirit. Your fortress is your identity in Him. Your position is a child of the living God. If you choose to step up to the front line of this Kingdom you can overpower your one and only enemy, because your Saviour has been given all authority in heaven and on earth and He has commissioned you to go forth and wield that authority and power over the darkness that surrounds you. Just like we see in verse 2 of chapter 9 of Esther, not a single scheme of the enemy can withstand you because he fears you when you exercise this authority and power that you have been commissioned to walk in and when you rise up in your identity as a child of the King of Kings.

Right now, the name of Jesus is being heralded throughout the world and His power is being made known. This is the era when the true fear of God will come upon many and we will be awakened to what is really going on in this life, what is really at stake, the real battle that unsurprisingly is not between one another but the powers of darkness over the hold upon this world, souls that are to be saved and eternities that are to be taken hold of. People throughout this Persian province quickly feared the name of Mordecai and his name became great, his fame spread and he became powerful (9:3). Throughout this world, the name of Jesus is spreading and He is taking His rightful position of power and influence. The Great Commission is coming to fruition and the harvest is here! God's Kingdom is quickly spreading to the ends of the earth, to every tribe and nation, to every people group. And you have been born into this end time generation, not out of coincidence or mistake, but with perfect divine intention.

The destruction of the enemy's domain throughout the world is taking place right now, as the children of God awake from their slumber and arise in their identity and authority. The battle is won through salvations, revelations, awakening, arising, unveiling of eyes and ears and hearts and setting the captives free. There is a great move of the Spirit right now sweeping the highest mountains of influence as well as the deepest valleys and depths of darkness throughout the world. Things that have been hidden are being exposed, things that have been prevailing are being served justice, things that have been slumbering are being awoken. We are in a moment where the King is asking us for whatever we desire - whatever we ask will be given, whatever we seek will be done. When we steward what we have already been given with faithful, humble and pure hearts, then we receive more opportunity to ask for whatever we want in His name, according to His will and He will do it. This is where God's people are at now at in this very moment of time. Increase of position, increase of favour, increase of opportunity, increase of authority, increase of power, increase of faith, increase of boldness, increase of resources. The enemy's kingdom is being overthrown through justice and judgment as God's people arise in the authority, call and obedience and seize the kairos moments and opportunities.

HAMAN THE AGAGITE

> *"The Jews struck all their enemies with the sword, killing and destroying them, and did as they pleased to those who hated them. In Susa the citadel itself the Jews killed and destroyed...the ten sons of Haman the son of Hammedatha, the enemy of the Jews, but they laid no hand on the plunder."* **Esther 9:5, 10**

Throughout the story of Esther we hear Haman referred to as an Agagite. This is no small detail! The Israelites were in exile in Persia, but they were of Hebrew heritage. Every time Haman is referred to as an Agagite, it's not just his nationally we're talking about, but something far more significant which both Esther, Mordecai, the exiled Jews and the Hebrew audience whose history this story was recorded for would have completely understood.

Haman was a descendant of Agag, an Amalekite. In 1 Samuel 15 we hear the Lord command Saul to 'devote to destruction' the Amalekites who were still possessing the Promised Land that the Israelites had inherited. The Hebrew word used for this command to devote to destruction is *charam* - which means to completely destroy and punish by extermination.[1] Charam was about purging defilement and impurity from the land and out of Israel. The Lord knew that Israel would be tempted to worship the foreign gods of the nations if they allowed the inhabitants to remain, but He wanted a holy, set apart nation for Himself. This is why He continually warned Israel against intermarrying with foreigners (because the wives would tempt them to worship their gods and create impurity) and why He continually commanded that all the high places, ashera poles (of Ashera worship on the mountain tops), all the alters, idols, statues to the gods of the nations be utterly destroyed. *Charam.* A command that the Israelites never fully obeyed, as we see later in Israel's history, it became the very fall of King Solomon who eventually led Israel into idol worship, far away from their one true God.

The Amalekites descended from Amalek, the grandson of Esau, born to his son Eliphaz and his concubine Timna (Gen 36:12). Timna was a Horite, named in Genesis 14 amongst the list of tribes of giants who possessed the land of Shinar. We know this to be the place where the tower of Babel was constructed (Gen 11:2), and later became known as Babylon. It's important to note that all through the Old Testament, Shinar is associated with the wicked worship of false gods, and in the end times, Babylon the Great is the centre of wickedness and demon worship (Rev 18:2-3). It's understood that Amalek most likely carried on the defiled bloodline of his Horite concubine mother, Timna, and that is why the Amalek were greatly feared in the land of Canaan, by everyone. The Amalekites certainly intimidated the Israelites as they were the first to attack them when they crossed into the Promised Land. Upon this attack, the Lord promised that He would utterly blot out the memory of the Amalek from under heaven (Ex 17:8-16).

Yahweh had actually already commanded the Israelites to charam all the inhabitants of the Promised Land when they entered, but here we are around 400 years later and we still find defiled, impure, demon worshipping, wicked, intimidating inhabitants of the land. Hence God's command to Saul, yet again, to charam the Amalekites, once and for all.

> *"Now, go strike the Amalek and devote to destruction all that they have. Do not spare them, but kill both man and woman, child and infant, ox and sheep, camel and donkey."* **1 Samuel 15:3**

These are very clear commands from the Lord. Yet we discover a few verses on that Saul didn't obey Yahweh in full. Sure, he devoted to destruction the Amalekites, but he spared Agag, their leader. He also spared the very best of the cattle and herds - 'all that was good, [he]would not utterly destroy them' (1 Sam 15:9). Saul's intentions may have appeared good (he wanted to offer them as sacrifices to Yahweh), but he did not obey the Lord.

> *"Has the Lord as great delight in burnt offerings and sacrifices, as in obeying the voice of the Lord? Behold, to obey is better than sacrifice, and to listen than the fat of rams. For rebellion is as the sin of divination, and presumption is as iniquity and idolatry. Because you have rejected the word of the Lord, he has also rejected you from being king."* **1 Samuel 15:22-23**

Stay with me while I tie this entire story of Saul, Agag and the charam of the Amalekites into our story of Esther and the exiled Israelites! Saul's disobedience to this one command of God caused him to lose his entire kingship. But it is so much deeper than that. Yes, God wants our obedience over our sacrifice (or our good intentions, or whatever we think is best), but the reason He wants us to obey is that there is so much more at stake than we realise, there is a much bigger picture at hand, that we often cannot see. His thoughts are higher than our thoughts, His ways are so much higher and bigger and broader than we could ever perceive. He is the Alpha and the Omega, He is the beginning and the end. We see but a glimpse of His plans and will, but our obedience must be so faithful to even the smallest detail, because He has a big picture plan at hand. Saul was supposed to fulfil the word of the Lord to blot out the Amalek from under heaven. Yet he spared Agag and the very best of the land.

Although the Israelites in Esther 8 were given permission to completely destroy, kill, and annihilate every ethnic and provincial army hostile to them, including women and children, and to take their possessions as spoils of war (Es 8:11), they *did* defend themselves and destroy their enemies, but they *did not* take the spoils of war for themselves (Es 9:10, 15, 16).

Why?

Because they were fulfilling the command that God gave to Saul! They destroyed the sons of Haman - the descendants of Agag, the Amalekite, who Saul spared, and it was under Mordecai's leadership. Guess what? Mordecai was a Benjaminite (Es 2:5), from the very same tribe of Israel as Saul. These details are incredible! They didn't lay a hand on the plunder for themselves like they were given permission to do, but instead, they fulfilled the original command of Yahweh to Saul, the Benjaminite. Can you see God's gracious and merciful goodness here toward His people? He is a God of second chances! Of third, fourth, fifth, as many as we need chances...but He does require obedience. Full and total obedience, even when we may not understand.

Isn't it fascinating how one man's disobedience to God's command resulted in him losing the kingdom, even though his excuse was that he wanted to use the plunder to worship Yahweh. Yet God didn't ask him for a sacrifice, He asked him to obey. But hundreds of years later, the same people group get a chance to reverse that curse, led by a Benjaminite, a descendant of Saul, to *charam* the descendant of Agag and his sons the Amalekite, and even though they could have kept it all for themselves, they didn't lay a hand on the plunder, therefore reversing and righting a wrong, all these generations later.

When Haman the Agagite eventually gets His due punishment, we see the final fulfilment of Israel's obedience and restoration to Saul's original disobedience, and it is so much more than simply Haman's own individual evil, but generational legacy of defilement, impurity, evil and defiance against Yahweh being righteously judged and vindicated.

DOUBLE FOR THE TROUBLE

> *"The king said to Queen Esther, "In the fortress of Susa the Jews have killed and destroyed five hundred men, including Haman's ten sons. What have they done in the rest of the royal provinces? Whatever you ask will be given to you. Whatever you seek will also be done." Esther answered, "If it pleases the king, may the Jews who are in Susa also have tomorrow to carry out today's law, and may the bodies of Haman's ten sons be hung on the gallows.""* **Esther 9:12-13**

In this story of Esther we see that the Jews in Susa - the fortress - represent those closest to the king. In the same way, those closest to God in friendship, daughter/sonship, who live in His presence will have a double portion, a double opportunity, double authority, double success for all that the enemy intended for harm against them. I also believe they were given this second day because the enemy doesn't give up so easily and he likes to make multiple assassination attempts. If the Jews had celebrated their victory prematurely, who is to say Haman and all those who hated them would not come the next day and slaughter them in the centre of their celebrations? We have to know the tactics of the enemy. He doesn't play fair. He doesn't play by the rules. He utterly hates every single person made in the image of God.

The Jews fought from a place of unity as they assembled together. We cannot fight the enemy alone and we certainly cannot fight him divided against one another. We as the church have to open our eyes to see just how much this division is costing the Kingdom. It isn't about who has the correct doctrine or denomination, who is right and who is wrong, it's about seeing the enemy's tactics for what they are and now joining together and turning on *him*. We must apostolically take back ground that we have allowed the darkness to rule over. We don't go looking for a fight, but we take up the chance to defend ourselves when we are attacked and we learns to live proactively on the offence, no longer in defence. When we do that we will finally gain some relief from our one and only enemy. My friend, you will have victory in your circumstances, you will enjoy a season of peace from your situations and sufferings, because Jesus has already paid the price and obtained your victory over the devil. Rise up and take hold of what is already yours! Victory is certain, the King has declared your freedom, but you must forcefully take what rightfully belongs to you because the enemy isn't going to hand you over without a fight.

THE PURPOSE OF PURIM

If you need a little help to stand and keep going then take a look back over your life. In fact, take a look back over history. The Jewish festival of Purim is still celebrated today all around the world, and this story of Esther is where it originated. Here we learn that Purim is a call to remember that which was birthed out of the victory from this very account. I love that there is an entire chapter dedicated to the instruction of remembering. The power of remembering is a key and tool that God has given us to use in our lives. It's not just celebrated in this annual festival, but it is all through Scripture. Remembering is a form of strengthening and encouraging ourselves in God. We are built up internally as we remember the goodness of God, remember the testimony of what He has done, remember the victories, remember His history, remember His faithfulness. There is power in remembering. We must remember what He has done for His people in the past and what He has done for us in our life. Because when we remember it gives us hope, it gives us faith and it gives us strength to face the situations and circumstances that we are currently battling. When we develop the discipline of remembering it reminds us of His faithfulness and how He has come through for us before. Remembering the victories of the past is what gives us a hope and confidence for the future.

OUR CALL TO REMEMBER

> *"...the Jews bound themselves, their descendants, and all who joined with them to a commitment that they would not fail to celebrate these two days each and every year according to the written instructions and according to the time appointed. These days are remembered and celebrated by every generation, family, province, and city, so that these days of Purim will not lose their significance in Jewish life and their memory will not fade from their descendants. Queen Esther, daughter of Abihail, along with Mordecai the Jew, wrote this second letter with full authority to confirm the letter about Purim. He sent letters with assurances of peace and security to all the Jews who were in the 127 provinces of the kingdom of Ahasuerus, in order to confirm these days of Purim at their proper time just as Mordecai the Jew and Esther the queen had established them and just as they had committed themselves and their descendants to the practices of fasting and lamentation."*
> **Esther 9:27-30**

The deliberate practice of remembering is an act of faithfulness and obedience. Remembering restores the fullness of joy into our lives.[2] Remembering is a method of strengthening ourselves in the Lord. Remembering is an often untapped and overlooked spiritual discipline that repositions our hearts and minds from current circumstances towards the goodness and faithfulness of God.[3] This is why the Israelite's were instructed to teach their children about all that God had done for them in the history of the nation. It is so important that we pass down from generation to generation all the powerful, magnificent, mighty, victorious, deliverance that God has done in our lives. Because when it comes time for my children to face their very own individual battles, they may not have anything personally to stand upon in remembrance, but they will certainly have everything that I have ever fought for to call upon and strengthen themselves in. And as I point them to the Word of God they will have an unending plethora of power to draw upon and equip themselves with. Some of my favourite childhood memories of my grandmother are when she would visit us and put me to bed at night. She would sing songs of worship like lullaby's and she would pray so powerfully over my life and future. But my favourite of all was when she would retell stories from her experiences of angelic encounters, supernatural happenings, miracles, healings of cancer and other deadly diseases, demonic forces she destroyed in an instant with the name of Jesus. Little did I know that one day I would be recounting those very testimonies later in my life in order to strengthen my faith and believe for the impossible situations that I was now facing myself. Talk about a generational inheritance!

Whatever battle you are walking through now my friend, I urge you to not only remember what God has already done for you in your past and in the history of the Kingdom of God, but the breakthrough you are about to encounter will become your strongest weapon in the future. The power of your testimony is being produced right now as you endure this current struggle. Your victory will be declared to the generations to come, and your descendants in both the natural and spiritual will call upon your story to strengthen themselves in their very own sufferings and situations.

Best of all, remembering what He has done gives us an assurance of peace and security of His faithfulness to His Word and promises (Esther 9:30). Saying yes to the call doesn't diminish the devils attacks in your life, it amplifies it. But do not fear, be brave, bold and courageous, for you have already overcome every fight you will face, for He has already overcome the world (John 16:33).

NOTES

1. Strong's Exhaustive Concordance of the Bible. (n.d). *Charam* #H2763. In biblehub.com. Retrieved November 1 2023, from *https://biblehub.com/hebrew/2763.htm*

2. Myers & Williams She Reads Truth Bible, Holman Bible Publishers, 2017 p767

3. Ibid

CHAPTER 11

ALL FOR HIS GLORY

Chapter 10 of the book of Esther is one of the shortest chapters in the entire Bible, with only three verses and 93 words (depending on translation). The grand finale to our story is suddenly summed up and brought to completion in such a quick and short manner. It may be one of the smallest chapters, but it holds one of the greatest keys to this entire story.

> *"King Ahasuerus imposed a tax throughout the land to the farthest shores. All of his powerful and magnificent accomplishments and the detailed account of Mordecai's great rank with which the king had honoured him, have they not been written in the Book of the Historical Events of the Kings of Media and Persia? Mordecai the Jew was second only to King Ahasuerus. He was famous among the Jews and highly esteemed by many of his relatives. He continued to pursue prosperity for his people and to speak for the well-being of all his descendants."*
> **Esther 10:1-3**

As we read through these three verses we notice that the book of Esther doesn't finish with proclaiming Esther's greatness, her victories, her ongoing purpose and position, not even her faithfulness and boldness. The heroin of our story receives no recognition whatsoever for the pinnacle role she just played in the saving of an entire people and nation. In fact, her name is never mentioned again! Instead, this entire closing chapter is all about the king's glory and Mordecai's fame. Her story finishes by listing *his* victories, *his* accomplishments, *his* honour, *his* achievements and describing how *his* name and fame spread throughout the province and kingdom. But wait…isn't this book about Queen Esther? Shouldn't she be the star of her own story? Shouldn't her name and her boldness and obedience be proclaimed, celebrated and remembered? While we're all so attached to our main character, we actually never find out anything more about Esther's reign as queen or anything else she went on to do with her life. We never hear any more about her as a person or how her own story wound up. But this story was never about Esther.

It was always about someone greater. And our story is not about us. Yes, it may be your life, you may be the leading lady/man, the title may even be your very own name, but ultimately, it's not about you. It's about someone far greater. Our story, our life, our purpose is all about Jesus. It's all about our King, our God. And our greatest achievement of all would be for our story to end with His name being glorified, with His fame reaching to the ends of the earth. Not ours. In a culture where the very opposite is the hunger, pursuit, ambition and drive of most people (and I'm not just looking at the world here, the Western Church is full to the brim of this worldly desire for name and fame), it just shows how vital it is to be surrendered, emptied, humbled, purified and mature in order to truly take part in the greatest story the world has ever seen.

It was never about us and it never will be about us. I thank you for journeying with me through this book that tells you you have a huge part to play in the perfect plan of God, but here's the pivotal clincher…

Your position is not about you.

Your purpose is not about you.
Your call is not about you.
Your favour is not about you.
Your anointing is not about you.
Your entire life, is not about you.

It is so much greater than you! It's about God's divine, sovereign plan and purpose. The story He wrote before the world began, that we are still actively invited into, to not just witness, but be used for His glory. It's all about His Kingdom, not our empire. It's all about His glory, not our name. It's all about His love, not our striving. It's about His grace, not our works. It's about His heart, not our good intentions. It's about His truth, not our opinions. It's all about His perspective, not our understanding. Everything you have been created for, chosen for, called for, destined for, prepared for, positioned for, anointed for, equipped for, empowered for, gifted for, is all for *His* glory, *His* purpose, *His* plan and *His* Kingdom!

FOR THE GREATER GOOD

Just as Esther used her promotion, position and platform for the good of others, so too are we called to use whatever God has given us, wherever God has planted us, however God has equipped us, for whoever He has placed around us. The realm of influence you have been given - however large or small, however far or wide - has been given to you because you have already stewarded faithfully and have been proven trustworthy. We see all through the book of Proverbs that as you grow in this stewardship you will increase in favour and influence. It's a biblical, Kingdom principle but it begins and ends in the heart. God is trusting you to make decisions that benefit those around you, not just yourself. He is trusting you to serve the needs of others, and sacrifice yourself. He is trusting you to put your needs, your wants, your agenda down and to take up the responsibility for the greater good of those He has called you to. He doesn't have to entrust you with these things, but He joyfully desires to, because He longs to work in personal partnership with you to see His purposes come to pass.

POSITIONED FOR PURPOSE

A beautiful Bride is awakening and arising now who's heart is so humbled that they can be elevated to platforms of governmental authority, into powerful positions of legislative law that affects nations and entire people groups. He is elevating to places of influence people in the media and creators in arts and entertainment to turn such a dark and destructive industry into something wholesome and pure. He is illuminating family units who carry strategies and solutions for thriving in healthy homes and moulding and shaping the generations to come. He is highlighting marriages that shine His design and carry testimonies of restoration and renewal. He is bringing answers and antidotes to medical afflictions, diseases and deformities with inspiration, ingenuity and ideas from His throne room. He is positioning His people high up in educational and intellectual institutions to not just remove the cultural ideologies of our days but to reform the entire system from the inside out. He is causing His business men and women to be marked and set apart amongst the monster of Mammon and the beast system that our society is so enslaved to, and using the ministry of the marketplace to bring His wisdom and ways to even the biggest companies and corporations. He is downloading strategies, blueprints, ideas, concepts from heaven into the minds of entrepreneurs and innovators, and He is removing both the religious and the contaminated from positions of power within the church and replacing them with His consecrated, purified, purged, proven people who will cultivate family, not hierarchy, intimacy, not idolatry. He is reforming every single area in this world and He is bringing it all back into alignment with His original design. He is restoring what has been stolen, killed and destroyed. He is redeeming what has been lost, given away or squandered. He is purifying what has been defiled, mixed and prostituted. He is recovering ALL and this is an era of reformation, not just of the Western Church, but of the entire earth.

Hear my heart - it is not about the position or the platform. The religious spirit causes many in the church to point fingers at this message, binding it in lies and accusation that 'it' is all about personal significance and individual achievement. No. It's the exact opposite of that. This is an era of Esther's everywhere over the earth arising to the call because God knows He can trust their hearts with such significant assignments. God wants to do something in this world but the very church itself is holding the chosen ones back, preventing His purpose and rendering His Bride impotent, all in the name of 'humility.' Funny. True humility is the very place where remarkable exaltation begins. God hasn't given us His light to hide under a bowl. He has given us His light to shine bright in the night to light the way to Him. How are we stewarding His light? Are we religiously, carelessly or selfishly hiding it under a bowl? Are we aiming it at ourselves like the dazzling spotlight that projects our own amazing life to all around us? Or are we standing on the highest hill we can find, being the very tool to hold it tall to shine for all around us to see, to illuminate the path, to be the lighthouse in the dark storm and point the way to the one true Light?

> *"But you are God's chosen treasure - priests who are kings, a spiritual "nation" set apart as God's devoted ones. He called you out of darkness to experience his marvellous light, and now he claims you as his very own. He did this so that you would broadcast his glorious wonders throughout the world."* **1 Peter 2:9 (TPT)**

The problem is that the spirit of religion takes biblical truths and filters them through worldly values and understanding. Being placed in positions of authority or on platforms of influence is scorned at because those people are viewing it through defiled hearts. But the ways of the Kingdom are not the ways of the world. The Kingdom reality is that positions of power are a responsibility to serve, not be served. And God can only elevate people high when their hearts are proven low. The spirit of religion loves to dress up in half-truths and make them appear holy, so that the full truth can never be actualised. There's always an element of truth to what it says, based in the Bible even, but it's not the whole truth.

Only the *whole* truth can set us free.

PURSUE PROSPERITY FOR ALL THE PEOPLE

We are called to prosper - in spirit, soul and body. Anything less is below the divine design that we were created for. We aren't called to live in lack, survival and poverty mindset under the label of false-humility and false-holiness. We aren't called to struggle and just get by. We aren't called to settle. We aren't called to live with torment, mental illness, or constant attack. We can do all these things for God but we won't be rewarded for settling for anything less than what He paid for on the cross and redeemed and restored in His resurrection. We can choose to remain under the power of the curse, or we can obtain and take hold of what is already in our heavenly account.

On the flip side, we're also not called to make idols of these very things and pursue them over the Healer, Deliverer, Protector, Provider. But when we find the point of truth within the Word and Spirit, we can begin living in complete contentment in all situations, because we have been purged of all fleshly desires, will, intentions and have been through the fiery flames that has burned away any worldly ways, any mixture, anything less than all He has for us. We desire, seek, pursue Jesus above it all, Jesus amongst it all, Jesus through it all. Yet we don't let our contentment become complacency. We never settle. We always seek all that He is.

I want to be so very clear, because the worldly church has most certainly made an idol of unbiblical prosperity and abused the gospel with deep deception, it's sickening. But the pendulum swings to the other extreme also, and the problem with the spirit of religion demonising prosperity is that it gets diminished to simply money and material possessions. That's part of it, for sure, because physical resources are a tool that God powerfully uses for His purpose and His Kingdom. But it's not about money. True wealth is so much more than financial or material gain. Prosperity is about every aspect and element of life. Biblical prosperity is spiritual, emotional, physical, mental, relational, material and so much more. It is about being victorious in every realm of life, it is about conquering and mastering each area, it's about reigning in life, thriving in every avenue. It's about walking in our original design of Eden that was restored to us through the cross. It's about living life so well because God is in us and working through us that everyone around us can't help but notice God on us and want God in them too. It's about returning to our call as His chosen people where all the nations around look and say *"Wow, they are blessed! Their God is good! Their God is real! Their God is powerful! Their God protects, defends, provides for them!"* Just have a look through the Old Testament and tell me what was the marker of God's chosen people when they loved and obeyed Him. Read through Proverbs and tell me how many verses give practical understanding, insight, wisdom and strategy to do with finances, from the wealthiest man who ever lived, and it was all given to him *by God*, because he proved faithful (1 Kings 3:13).

Does this mean we will never experience pain or suffering? No! It means *when* we experience pain and suffering we still prosper because we walk through the trials of life with the presence, peace, power, protection and provision of the God of heaven and earth. In fact, it's when we walk through suffering and hardship that our level of prosperity shines the brightest and the true worth of our spiritual wealth speaks the loudest. While we don't hear of Esther again, verse three tells us that Mordecai spent the rest of his reign pursuing prosperity for the people. This is exactly what position, promotions and platforms are given to be used for. It's to be used for the greater good of others and it's about bringing into possession of the world around us the purpose, intentions and design of God - the mandate of Eden.

Mordecai not only set up the kingdom for the benefit of everyone at the time, but he set it up for future generations to prosper, thrive, succeed, win, to live victoriously, triumphantly and life at their very best, for generations to come. This is true legacy. This is true inheritance. This is true Kingdom living. This is what Jesus did and this is the mandate He passed on to us! Jesus came to restore wholeness to every area of our life. We lack nothing in this life when we live in Him, because He lacks nothing. We can reign in life because He reigns over everything. This is the call upon the Church in this era - to arise into our God given position as the head and not the tail, as influencers and not influenced, as the leaders, developers, creators, not consumers. Awake! Arise! Go forth and multiply, create and cultivate in whatever realm He has called and positioned you to!

The heart and life that utilises prosperity for all other people is the very platform that God comes and proves Himself on. It's the very podium He flaunts

His power on. It's the stage He performs His miracles on. It's the canvas He paints His picture on for all to see. If we don't prosper in life then what is the purpose of living any longer than our moment of salvation? What did Jesus die for if we don't live any differently? If we don't transform? If we don't overcome? If we don't mature? If we don't get set free, if we don't take ground, if we don't transform neighbourhoods, cities, nations? What is the power of the resurrection if it's never put to use again? What are we here for if we're not making a mark, leaving a dent, doing damage to the darkness, extending the Kingdom, making a difference, instigating change, affecting the world around us, conquering the corrupt, overturning injustices, taking back what has been stolen, aligning our environment with the intention of God, overpowering our atmosphere with the power of the Almighty, bringing heaven to earth and achieving His will and purpose here in this world?

Prosperity is for a purpose and it's only when we understand the pertinence and power of this that we will be entrusted to steward it for His Kingdom.

REIGNING IN LIFE

Reigning in life means learning to live in God's original design and purpose for humankind. We were commissioned to govern (take responsibility and authority) over the world around us. This isn't about control, it's about stewardship. This doesn't mean over people, this means over our life, our environment, our atmosphere, the spiritual realm. We are called to rule over our circumstances, not allow them to rule over us, to rule over our resources, not let our resources (or lack of) rule over us. In Genesis 1:28 Adam and Eve were commanded to take dominion. Notice it doesn't say they were automatically granted dominion, but they had to take it. They had to dominate it and subdue it and overpower it for themselves. The fall made this commission much more difficult when sin brought curse upon the man and the woman, but Christ broke every curse on the cross and we now have the ability through His power and authority, through our identity as children of the King and through our inheritance in Him to reign in life once again. If Adam and Eve had to step out and take it *even before the fall,* then so too do we have to step up to the smorgasbord and load up our plate with everything redeemed for us. We can't passively sit back in our comfortable chairs waiting for the feast to be placed in front of us. We certainly can't expect to be spoon-fed. I'm afraid there's no table service here.

God handed the Promised Land over to the Israelites, but they still had to fight for it. They had to go in and take possession. They had to slay the giants, they had to go to literal battle, they had to slaughter the cities and take what God had already given them - their inheritance. I honestly believe this is one of the biggest revelations the western church needs to awaken to and receive. Yes, absolutely everything was done and paid for on the cross. There is nothing left for God to do, and it is not us mere humans who can do anything. But He does call us to step into it. He requires us to take possession of it. We are saved by grace through faith, but this doesn't end at salvation. We must walk every single day in His grace, living by faith. It is all Him, none of us, but by faith we step forward and face every battle, just like the Israelites did, both in the Promised Land, and here in Persia as exiles battling for their very freedom that had already been handed over to them. It was DONE. But they still had to fight for it. IT IS DONE! But we still need to step up, step out and take possession of all that He has paid for us on the cross.

AUTHORITY TO GOVERN

For so long I have been seeing the number 12 everywhere. 12:12 on the clock, 1212 in random places when I'm out and about, 12 or 1212 everywhere I look! I am definitely not into numerology or new age ideology, nor am I condoning it in any way, but I absolutely believe in the biblical significance of numbers all throughout Scripture and their Hebraic meanings and I believe God speaks powerfully even today through these. In Jewish tradition 12 is the number of government, leadership and ruling authority. I believe in this era the Bride is stepping into her position of authority to govern and lead for the good of all people. For some of us that may mean governing and leading our families. For some of us that will mean governing large businesses, organisations. For others it will be any form of leadership within the seven mountains of influence in society and culture. Whatever realm and extent we are positioned in, we are all called to govern and reign in life. This doesn't mean we rule over people or places, but it means we are appointed and anointed for positions of influence where we can make a change, turn a ship around, take back the power and create culture that benefits the good of the people and glorifies God, because it's in accordance with His design, plan and purpose.

For some of us it will begin by learning to govern ourselves and our own life first. Any dominion over the atmosphere and environment around us begins by reigning first within us. It means ruling over our own life - in our mind (thoughts), spirit (being led by and surrendered to the Holy Spirit, not fleshly desires or canal passions), soul (emotions and feelings), body (disciplines, physical health and wholeness) and then further into our marriage, family, home, friendships, relationships, workplaces, neighbourhoods, communities, cities, nations and onto our larger realms of influence. It begins by stewarding what He has already entrusted to us. Faithfully steward over the little and we will be granted to govern over a lot more.

As far as my own personal journey is concerned, God graciously showed me that I wasn't reigning in certain areas of life because I had to take back my authority. I had partnered with the lies of the enemy for too long and that alignment had stolen years of my life and caused me great torment and my family unnecessary pain. The only way the enemy can have authority in our life is if we give it to him. All authority in heaven and earth was given to Jesus and upon His ascension to heaven He commissioned us to take it and use it to extend His Kingdom. Satan has no power. Satan has no authority. So he has to take it from those who possess it. When we believe his lies and partner in agreement with him we are opening up an access point, an open door, providing him with a foothold and handing over the very key that was given to us.

To begin reigning in my own life and over my own circumstances I had to first reign over my thoughts and break agreement with every lie that the Lord revealed to me I had partnered with. I had to repent of, renounce and break every curse the Spirit showed was spoken over me or thought towards me, even from myself. I had to be delivered from strongholds and set free from bloodlines. I had to take back my authority and the keys to rule once again. As simple as that sounds, it was not instantaneous, but yet another process. And it's an ongoing process as we are daily transformed by the renewing of our minds, as we are daily awoken to more and more of the love of God, as we are daily awoken to our identity and worth, as we are daily awoken to His truth and promises by His Spirit. It won't happen overnight, but it will happen.

In this era there is an extra grace being poured out that I am seeing in so many lives, all over the world - grace for a quickening. There is an acceleration of natural processes that would normally take time that are happening swifter and smoother, healing and wholeness processes are that occurring instantaneously and with increased speed. I personally believe that the reason for this acceleration of our internal processes is because of the urgency of this hour upon us where He is requiring His people healed, whole, mature and pure, set free and delivered, established and fortified so that we can join together in unity to embark on the exciting task ahead. I also believe there is a window of time closing - quickly - but in His grace, He is accelerating the internal processes of repentance and refinement because there is swiftly coming a moment where He is going to close the ark door, and if we are not dwelling in that refuge with Him, we will have to suffer the consequences of ignoring His messengers and clarion call to obey. This is serious stuff. May the fear of the Lord return to us. TODAY is the day of grace, act now!

The amazing thing is that as I began governing and stewarding my own life, the very areas of breakthrough I had experience in personally, I began to move in corporately. As I was healed I was able to be used by Him to exercise His healing. As my mind was set free I was able to release His freedom to others. As I was unbound in areas of torment and trauma in my life I began ministering in deliverance in the same areas in others lives. Over the years, I have seen the authority of Jesus increase within me and through me as I surrender to Him more and more. This isn't our authority, this isn't our power, it is all His and we are simply the humble emptied vessels and tools that allow His Spirit to flow through us as we obey His leading, lean on His strength and learn to listen to His voice.

USED TO CREATE HISTORY

Just because we don't hear again of Esther does not mean she was used for her purpose and then thrown away. God never uses people like a replaceable commodity. We weren't created to be used, as the spirit of religion does, but to be joined in intimate union with our Creator and given an invitation to be useful to Him, with Him, for Him and through Him. Just as He did with Esther, so too does He invite us to join with Him in creating history and unveiling His story here on earth, because He so desperately loves us.

He is a Father. He has a Father's love. He offers His children a heavenly invitation to play a part in His plan. He has significant purpose for your life, you have a special and specific part to play and He has chosen you and called you for this very role because He wants you. And He wants you because He loves you. God could easily achieve everything on His own. He doesn't need us mere humans to accomplish His will. But He is a God of love, a Creator of love, a Father of love, a Saviour of love, a Friend of love. He is the Author of covenant and family and it is in this context in which life is to be done, not just with one another, but with Him. The trinity is the perfect example, no - definition, origin - of relationship, and when He created us it wasn't because He was lonely, nor wanted to be served or worshipped. We were birthed out of relationship, out of His love and we find our fulfilment in relationship and in His love. He desires to be close to us above anything else and for us to know Him truly, deeply, intimately, uniquely and to live from and dwell continually in His presence, beholding His heart, eye to eye, looking upon the magnificence of His face. His heart isn't about the mission, His heart is about the person. The mission is only important because of the goal - the person...you. Your heart. Your affection. Your love in return. This Kingdom mission is about taking possession of the greatest treasure to Him - the lives of His created. The unique, individual beings. His highest priority, pursuit and purpose is for you, me and us as people. For everyone to discover and be drenched in His love, to be touched and transformed by His love, and to walk in and overflow in His love. It's all about intimacy with Him, because He is love itself.

SHARING IN HIS GLORY

The paradox of our story not being about us - but all about Jesus and for His glory - is that He actually promises throughout His Word that we will experience His glory, encounter His glory, share in His glory for all eternity (John 17:22,24; Rom 8:17). Even Jesus Himself is living proof of this message, that everything is for the greater good of others. I mean, it doesn't get any more real than laying your life down for all of humanity by enduring an excruciating death so that the due penalty of sin would be paid for on behalf of all who call upon His name. Jesus has given us the perfect example of what it means to be emptied, selfless and serving, and the complete picture of love. Yet the reality of this all is that those spending their life, energy, time and resources on pursuing their own glory will end up with nothing. And those who are willing to make themselves low, to serve others, to go last, to be the least, will be the very ones who end up sharing in and enjoying His glory for all eternity. He is such a good, good God. It's all for His glory, but in His goodness and love for us He invites us to share it all with Him, if we too are willing to take up our cross and pay the price, joining in union with both His suffering and death. The price is costly, but the reward of eternity with Him is so worthy of our life here on earth.

CHAPTER 12

FOR SUCH A TIME AS THIS

"Truly, truly I say to you, whoever believes in me will also do the works that I do; and greater works than these will he do, because I am going to the Father. Whatever you ask in my name, this I will do, that the Father may be glorified in the Son. If you ask me anything in my name, I will do it." **John 14:12-14 (ESV)**

ENTERING THIS ERA

As I draw this message to an end I really want to emphasise the times we are in - the pertinence of this new era and beyond that we have entered and the urgency that is upon us like never before. Not so that we worry or get flustered or fearful, but so that we can see with clarity the weight of what is being poured out upon the Bride in this era. If we understand the value of the gift, then we will treat the gift accordingly, and the Giver with awe and reverence. Biblical prophecies are being fulfilled left, right and centre. The times of the Matt 28:18 great commission are increasing in both activity and acceleration. He has saved

His best wine for last and He is pouring Himself out in abundance. The heavenly atmospheres are colliding in opposition over this very moment because even the realms of darkness can sense what is taking place and the momentum brewing. God is unveiling Himself, His power and His glory in greater ways in the days ahead. He is the same yesterday, today and tomorrow, but this world is about to see the God of love, truth and justice that He sincerely is - His true character and nature revealed and displayed. Jesus is being unveiled in these days. The concept of 'revelation' is the act of God unveiling our eyes to see deeper truth and with more clarity, and the Book of Revelation is exactly that - Jesus being revealed. Jesus being unveiled to all - first to those who know Him intimately and then to the entire world to see that He truly is the God of heaven and earth.

Jesus' ministry gave us the example and prototype of what it looks like to live a lifestyle of power and authority to see the impossibilities of everyday life made possible in a real and tangible way. He gave us the very blueprint and framework from which we are to live from and then build upon. He empowered us with His Spirit and He instructed us with His Word. The two go hand in hand. The apostles and early Church carried on His command to continue these distinct acts of faith and it doesn't take much to discover through the Scriptural mandates, Biblical examples, Church history, testimonies from the persecuted church (the fastest growing church in the world!), the underground church, and from many other cultures around the world today (we, the Western Church, seem to forget that we aren't THE Church, just a small part of it), that they have never ceased. His power has been at work through His faithful people, empowered with the Spirit, fixed on His Word, for more than two thousand years. It is real and it's becoming even more real.

But what we have seen, even what Jesus did, is nothing in comparison to what He has in store. We've barely even seen the same miracles as Jesus yet, let alone the greater things that He prophesied, empowered and commissioned us to do (John 14:12-14). His Word says that the fruit, evidence and proof of preaching, teaching, speaking and living the full truth of the gospel will be that His power follows (Mark 16:17-20; Acts 14:3; Rom 15:17-19; 1 Cor 2:4-5; Heb 2:3-4). For too long a powerless gospel has been preached from the pulpits, but in this era the message of Christ will go forth with miracle working power as it did with Jesus, the disciples and the early Church, and as He commanded and commissioned us to also carry on.

I believe the Word of God over my extremely limited experiences. If I don't witness and encounter His power at work in miraculous signs and wonders of healing, deliverance, freedom and breakthrough then I can only assume I haven't preached the full gospel. If my everyday life and circumstances don't overflow with God's heavenly answers, miracles and supernatural strategies then I guess I'm not living to the full potential of the Spirit within me. I don't say this from a place of pessimism or to condemn, but to inspire, encourage, equip and empower all His saints to continue to ask, seek and knock until He opens the door and His heart, grace and power cascades into our lives and world, transforming every situation and circumstance! I will keep preaching the truth and pursuing His heart and obeying His Word until His power floods in and encompasses us in seeing the impossible manifest before our very eyes. I can hear the religious spirit now stirring up in legalistic attack, *we shouldn't pursue signs and wonders* - and that's exactly right. Scripture says *they will pursue us*, so we don't need to concern ourselves with that, except to believe, have faith and expect them to follow the proclamation of Jesus and the truth of the full gospel. We don't pursue signs and wonders, we pursue Jesus. And as we take His Word for what it is, He will endow us with the baptism of power that equips us to be the vessel through which He performs His miracles to this world. As we seek Him alone, above all else, He will drench our hearts in His unfailing, unending, incomprehensible love and will transform us by the renewing of our minds.

A REVELATION OF INTIMACY

In this era God is being made known to the lost and unbelieving world by His intimacy. But in order for that to happen His people first have to encounter His love, experience His love, be transformed by His love, have secure identities in His love, pursue nothing but His love so that we can overflow with love in truth. The Church must awaken to intimacy. We can only overflow with what we are filled up with. In this day, miracles will flow from love, healing will flow from love, the impossible happening before our very eyes will flow from love. Families will transform because of love. Heavenly ideas, creativity, concepts, strategies, answers, blueprints, inventions, cures will flow from love. Transformations of entire cities, nations, cultures and people groups will flow from love. Historical injustices will be overturned by love. Corrupt and evil governments and leadership will be brought down because of love. Everything in this world that is against God's perfect design and creation can be completely consumed by His amazing love.

> *"Teacher, which is the great commandment in the Law?" And he said to him, "You shall love the Lord your God with all your heart and with all your soul and with all your mind. This is the great and first commandment. And a second is like it: You shall love your neighbour as yourself."* **Matthew 22:36-39 (ESV)**

Jesus summarised all the Old Testament commandments into two succinct mandates for us to obey as New Covenant believers. When a religious scholar came and asked Him what was the most important precept to live by, Jesus' response was so simple yet so powerful: to love. To first love God in passionate pursuit with every fibre of our entire being, and then to love those around us. To overflow in love in all of its forms. In this coming time, God's people will be known by God's true love, not by a counterfeit gospel of tolerance. We will be known by our unity and oneness, not our division. We will be known for our encouragement and edification towards one another, not our criticism, comparison, judgment and jealousy. We will be known for our joy, not our torment, our wholeness, not brokenness, our identity, not insecurity, our power not impotence, our holiness, not worldliness, our purity, not mixture. Our light will shine the brightest in the darkest times of this world because His light is love. The Scriptures will be fulfilled when it says that the world will see God in us because of our love for one another (John 17:20-21). And when they see our love for one another they will see our love for them, and when they experience our love for them they will encounter God's love that completely transforms. But this great revelation and transformation of love begins within our own hearts before it permeates within the Church towards our own brothers and sisters, and then overflowing to the world around us.

Our God is finally going to be seen and known for who He really is, not who we have made Him out to be for centuries on end. And when the world truly sees Him they will be drawn to Him, because His love woos, His love heals, His love transforms, His love is the answer, His love has power, His love is everything and the only thing that every single soul is searching for in this life. It is all about true love.

NEW WINESKINS

> *"Remember not the former things, nor consider the things of old. Behold, I am doing a new thing; now it springs forth, do you not perceive it?"*
> **Isaiah 43:18-19a (ESV)**

The only way we can embrace what this era holds is to ask for new wineskins to hold His new wine that He is abundantly pouring out. Embracing the new paradigm is critical because the level of offence that is going to rise up within the church and within the hearts of believers as God does unexpected, unconventional, never before seen, incomprehensible, shocking things is going to be what separates those who are able to perceive the truth and those whose hearts can't handle the new and whose minds remain locked onto the old. As God's people, if we're unable to accept simple and basic things like hearing God's voice, healing and deliverance, then what chance do we have of embracing the miracles and powers that are going to overturn complete cities, nations and cultures? If closed minds can't comprehend that God could use the very least and lowly of this world for His purpose, plan, Kingdom and glory, then what power are we rending Him redundant of? If we believe the powers of darkness in the world are greater than His power at work in us, then we're going to miss out on this move and all He has in store as He unveils Himself in these times. God is sovereign. God's will prevails. I suggest we don't get in His path while He is on this beautifully holy rampage of reformation and justice because we will be the very ones thrown to the side if we dare to come up against His adamant, resolute plan and purpose for this time.

    If our minds are set on anything else, then we are elevating our opinions and agendas above His power and ability. We might be doing it 'in the name of God' but sadly, and tragically, God Himself is not on it. We might use Scripture to try and justify ourselves, but it contradicts the 'whole counsel' of God (Acts 20:27). If we don't have the ability to discern good and evil, which the Bible says is spiritual maturity (Heb 5:13-14), then we won't be able to perceive what He is breathing on, where He is going and what He is doing. I don't know about you but I certainly don't want to miss it. And I don't want to spend my life slaving away for religion or the world, only to discover in eternity that I had it wrong all along and wasted my days exerting my energy into the very things that were going against what God was actually doing. All because I couldn't accept something outside of my human paradigm and limited lifelong experience. All because I was too stubborn to admit that my long-held beliefs and opinions were possibly incorrect and humbly adjust myself to the actual truth.

> *"'For my thoughts are not your thoughts, neither are your ways my ways,' declares the Lord. 'For as the heavens are higher than the earth, so are my ways higher than your ways and my thoughts than your thoughts.'"*
> **Isaiah 55:8-9 (ESV)**

If we want to move with the fresh flow of the Holy Spirit wherever He blows, then we have to be prepared to get shocked, perplexed, triggered and offended in order to be transformed by the renewing of our minds, because it's about to get real offensive. However, this is a good thing! A much needed thing! When we recognise offence within ourselves we can pinpoint what areas of our heart and mind aren't properly purged. The Holy Spirit reveals where religion has a hold of us, or when we are too conformed to the culture around us, and when the truth is exposed it can then be dealt with. In His grace, whatever He reveals He also heals and deals with, as we surrender to His process. Offence handled correctly, submitted to God, frees us from old wineskins if we recognise it for what it is and open our minds, heart and spirit to whatever God wants to do however He wants to do it. If it can fit into our own paradigm then it's too small and not the God of the impossible. We must be open to the radical realignment and recalibration through His gracious correction in our hearts and minds.

THE SUPERNATURAL PRODUCES BOTH FAITH AND RAGE

When faced with the impossible and never before seen, done or heard (to us!), we will be overtaken. But this can go one of two ways. We can be overtaken with great faith as we face the impossible and witness the supernatural glory of God or we will be overtaken with violent rage and block our ears to what we think is blasphemy and drown out the voice of truth with our screams of offence.

> *"Why would you be so stubborn as to close your hearts and your ears to me? You are always opposing the Holy Spirit, just like your forefathers!... When they heard these things, they were overtaken with violent rage filling their souls, and they gnashed their teeth at him. But Stephen, overtaken with great faith, was full of the Holy Spirit. He fixed his gaze into the heavenly realm and saw the glory and splendour of God—and Jesus, who stood up at the right hand of God. "Look!" Stephen said. "I can see the heavens opening and the Son of Man standing at the right hand of God to welcome me home!" His accusers covered their ears with their hands and screamed at the top of their lungs to drown out his voice."* **Acts 7:51, 54-57 (TPT)**

I know that I don't want to be found on the side of doubt, disbelief or most disturbingly, disapproval of God's very doings in these days. I certainly do not want to be found with even an ounce of mixture, tolerance of the evil agenda of this world, or impurity because I valued fleshly ways over the holy call of consecration. Offence creates the foundation for deception to overpower and completely detour our hearts and minds. Offence is both the doorway to, and the stronghold of, deceit. If we don't want to be deceived then we must face the offence in our hearts, deal with the core issues that it is bringing up (what is *really* our problem with whatever is happening/being said? *Why* is it triggering us?), pull the roots out once and for all and let go of the comfort of control that we are unwillingly clinging to so that we can truly embrace what God is doing. An offended heart is a brick wall built up around us preventing the truth of God from permeating into us. It is the blindfold over our eyes that we filter everything through. It holds us down and keeps us deceived, thinking we are the ones enlightened, only to one day discover that we were the ones who had it so very, very wrong.

> *"So be very careful that what the prophets warned about does not happen to you: 'Be amazed and in agony, you scoffers! For in your day I will do something so wonderful that when I perform mighty deeds among you, you won't even believe that it was I who did it!'"*
> **Acts 13:40-41 (TPT)**

THE SEASON OF SAUL'S TO PAUL'S

We cannot have an ounce of pride in 'the new' (that is actually the old, ancient ways we are coming back to), that we prevent others from entering by the leading of the Spirit. We are not spiritual gatekeepers. We can never think that this is about 'us and them' as we have for so long in Church history. We do not own the new thing He is doing in our time. We do not own the new wine or the new wineskin. God does! Remember, we too were once under bondage of the old wineskin, we too were once blind to what the Spirit was doing. We are not called to create a castle for the Kingdom, we are called to build a bridge from the old to the new. In this transition season of reformation we have to be so humble, so open to who God chooses to use from the world and transform from the most unexpected lifestyles to His positions of purpose in this era. So too do we have to be open to who God converts from within the religious and legalistic church who will be suddenly moving powerfully in His Spirit (Acts 9:26). Recently as I was reading through the book of Acts I heard the Spirit speak to me *"These are the days of many Saul to Paul conversions. My people will be shocked and surprised to see who* turns to Me. Those who are known for 'persecuting' and publicly coming against My chosen ones and the moves that I am instigating will suddenly join in and be a part of what they once persecuted and condemned. Be open to who repents and who turns to Me in Spirit and in truth because of My miracle working power."

As I sat with Him asking so many questions He revealed to me that many in the Church who are renowned for being overtly religious and legalistic, those within His Bride who publicly mock, judge, accuse, point fingers, condemn and teach against His Spirit at work within His people who live from faith and take His Word for what it is, will have instant and immediate conversions through their own personal experiences of not just His power, but encounters of His deep, deep love, His manifest presence and have their spiritual eyes and ears opened to hear His voice and see His face. Many will meet Jesus for the first time ever, despite preaching His name for years, some decades even. They will come face to face with the God of their Bible, whom they have so much knowledge of, but have never truly encountered in relationship or affection. Jesus will go from being their Saviour, to being their Lord. He will go from being their God to being their Father. From being their teacher to being their Friend. They will go from covering, to covenant. These Saul to Paul conversions within the Church will see many people who think they are doing God's will, suddenly realise that they are the very ones persecuting the Spirit Himself and the remnant of God.

> "And immediately something like scales fell from his eyes, and he regained his sight. Then he rose and was baptised; and taking food, he was strengthened. For some days he was with the disciples at Damascus. And immediately he proclaimed Jesus in the synagogues, saying, "He is the Son of God." And all who heard him were amazed and said, "Is not this the man who made havoc in Jerusalem of those who called upon this name? And has he not come here for this purpose, to bring them before the chief priests?" But Saul increased all the more in strength, and confounded the Jews who lived in Damascus by proving that Jesus was the Christ." **Acts 9:18-22 (ESV)**

POSITIONED FOR PURPOSE

But God warned me that we must have open hearts and willing spirits, just like Ananias and the apostles did, to welcome these brothers and sisters with wide open arms. It is our duty to embrace these ones in great love and to take their conversion seriously. We are not to hold them at a distance out of scepticism, we must be prepared for and believe that it is a very genuine and authentic turnaround, because God showed me that as we love and embrace these Saul to Paul conversions, doors of opportunity will open up within the Body of Christ to hardened hearts and places that have no Spirit flowing. These people will be the very key that unlocks the religious church. These people will overflow to their personal realms of influence and extend the surge of His glory, grace and mighty power to those bound by religion who have been kicking against the goads their entire lives. It is imperative we embrace these significant religious converts, because their obvious humility and excited repentance will be the sign of their true transformation and they will require us to accept, love and embrace them in unity to see His Kingdom extended in truth. Their testimony will carry the same level of power that Paul's testimony did:

> *"In this connection I journeyed to Damascus with the authority and commission of the chief priests. At midday, O king, I saw on the way a light from heaven, brighter than the sun, that shone around me and those who journeyed with me. And when we had all fallen to the ground, I heard a voice saying to me in the Hebrew language, 'Saul, Saul, why are you persecuting me? It is hard for you to kick against the goads.' And I said, 'Who are you, Lord?' And the Lord said, 'I am Jesus whom you are persecuting. But rise and stand upon your feet, for I have appeared to you for this purpose, to appoint you as a servant and witness to the things in which you have seen me and to those in which I will appear to you, delivering you from your people and from the Gentiles— to whom I am sending you to open their eyes, so that they may turn from darkness to light and from the power of Satan to God, that they may receive forgiveness of sins and a place among those who are sanctified by faith in me.'"* **Acts 26:12-18 (ESV)**

The Holy Spirit is falling in greater measure within the Church today as He did in Acts 10 and 11. Just like Peter and all the Jewish believers needed new wineskins, so too do we have to have open hearts and open arms to say *'Who are we to stand in the way of God?'* (Acts 11:17).

POWER FROM ON HIGH

In order to achieve all that God has purposed us to do to see His great commission come to pass, God gifted us with the only thing we will ever need to live for Him, through Him and by Him - the Holy Spirit.

> *"But when the Helper comes, whom I will send to you from the Father, the Spirit of truth, who proceeds from the Father, he will bear witness about me. And you also will bear witness, because you have been with me from the beginning."* **John 15:26-27 (ESV)**

The Holy Spirit is named the Spirit of Truth because He reveals truth to us as we submit to Him. One way He reveals truth is by exposing lies. Jesus illuminated this when He said in the preceding verse *"If I had not performed miracles in their presence like no one else has done, they would not feel the guilt of their sins." (John 15:24).* The presence of the Holy Spirit brings awareness to the darkness, deceit and death. He awakens it to consciousness because it has something to compare it to. Without comparison we remain ignorant to the truth. Jesus' miracles revealed the truth that He was the Son of God because they were blatant evidence and proof of His identity, power and authority. In the same way today, with the commission of Jesus, the power of God at work reveals the truth to the unbelieving hearts because it gives a comparison that exposes lies and brings them to light. It is evidence. Proof. Immediately after encouraging them about this great gift of the Spirit of Truth He then told them they would also be rejected by religion and be persecuted by people thinking they were doing God's will.

> *"I have said all these things to you to keep you from falling away. They will put you out of the synagogues. Indeed, the hour is coming when whoever kills you will think he is offering service to God. And they will do these things because they have not known the Father, nor me."*
>
> **John 16:1-3 (ESV)**

We cannot be double minded about the power, purpose and presence of the Holy Spirit at work today. We cannot be confused or in doubt wondering whether or not His power is still relevant or if He still performs miracles, healings, deliverance, signs and wonders. The Western Church can no longer simply dabble in the supernatural when, or if, it suits us. It's time to plunge deep down and abandon ourselves to God's Kingdom and surrender to His ways and will. He has given us the Holy Spirit not just to strengthen and encourage us on the inside, walking with us as a friend through life, but He has offered us the chance to be empowered with the very power that rose Jesus Christ from the dead to work in and through us to see His Kingdom prevail. This is serious stuff! The baptism of power is not to be taken lightly. Either we're in or we're out. The line is drawn in the sand, which side will we stand on? If we're in, then let's be ALL IN!

SURRENDER TO THE SPIRIT

In the same way that Jesus stirred up the spirit of religion in His day, so too is the power of the Holy Spirit at work stirring up religion in the Church today. The purpose of the stirring is for purging and purifying. Exposing lies and unveiling deception. The key is knowing Jesus and the Father intimately. Many are feeling the conviction of the Spirit through the preaching and prophesying of truth in this day, but we are avoiding the consecration it then requires because we're calling it condemnation. Many are pointing fingers at pure prophets who are calling us all higher and deeper in purity and holiness, and labelling them as legalistic, judgmental, emotional, passionate, opinionated, hateful, sometimes even blatantly wrong, because to receive their words of holiness, we have to repent of our worldly and lukewarm ways.

So instead of stepping lower into humility and submitting to the holy conviction of the Spirit at work, we label the messengers harsh and judgmental and reject the message entirely. This is dangerous ground. In God's great grace He has given all His people - leaders especially - an open window of opportunity to repent and receive, to humble ourselves and rid our lives of all the compromise, to realign with His will and His ways as He prepares to completely reform the Church in this day and reinstate it back to His original design, ready for His glorious return for a mature, pure and spotless Bride.

If we want to know what the Father is doing and saying in this time then we have to know the Father Himself and have a two way relationship with Him. We can know the Father through the Son, and we can know the will of the Father through the Holy Spirit revealing to us what is spoken in heaven as we develop and deepen our relationship with Him. Further on in John 16:7, Jesus tells them that it is to their advantage that He goes away and that the Holy Spirit is sent. These guys have just spent the last three years with Him and not only had the relational love and friendship but they had seen all He had done and heard all He had taught. Can you imagine the new wineskin mindsets they needed to even comprehend this idea that they would be better off without Jesus? Whoever this Divine Encourager is has some pretty big boots to fill! Yet, while Jesus was with them He was all they had. But when The Holy Spirit was given to them it was the very Spirit of Jesus Himself (Acts 16:7). It was for their best because when we have the Holy Spirit we have the very Spirit of Jesus that was at work when He walked the earth.

Can you imagine what traditions, rituals, rights and religion of thousands of years heritage they had to rid themselves of in order to embrace the new wineskin Kingdom values and principles that were upon them? Can you fathom the paradigms they had to shift to expect that suddenly they were supposed to be showered in power from on high? This is why Paul and the apostles and the early Church were so heavily persecuted, not by the world, but by the religious - because miracles prove God's power, and His power at work to deliver people from the impossible proves His love, His sacrificial love proves His grace, and grace proves that we do not have to spend our time striving to save ourselves, and resting in His ability proves that it is the Holy Spirit Himself who pours His power into us to see His will come to pass. Of course the spirit of religion was enraged at losing control! And so too in this day the message of grace, love, unity, purity, humility, holiness and consecration is bringing forth a battle with both the religious and worldly churches. But the battle is already won by the Spirit of Truth as those with hungry hearts fully yield to Him.

IT IS TIME

> *"And so, dear brothers and sisters, you are now made holy, and each of you is invited to the feast of your heavenly calling. So fasten your thoughts fully onto Jesus, whom we embrace as our Apostle and King-Priest."* **Hebrews 3:1 (TPT)**

My friend…my brother, my sister. I don't know your circumstances. I don't know your story. I don't know your past. I don't know your suffering, your torment, your struggles, your weaknesses. I don't know your pain or your aching heart. I don't know your wounds, your hurt or your betrayal. I don't know your dreams and desires. I don't know your personal promises and prophecies. But I do know one thing about you. You have an assignment and divine role to play in the Kingdom of God that all of heaven is waiting for you to rise up into. Whatever situation you find yourself in right now, whatever your life looks like, wherever you live, whatever you have achieved, whatever you haven't achieved, whatever you possess or whatever you lack, I know you are perfectly positioned for purpose. You are the Esther in your life and your world. And your great King is waiting to be glorified by you laying down your life, at whatever cost, for His Kingdom cause.

It is time to awaken, arise and take your place for Him to come and do what only He can do. You have been chosen, called, anointed, commissioned, commanded, purged, pruned, purified, proven, prepared and positioned for such a time as this. Who knows, perhaps…? God knows. All of heaven knows. The great cloud of witnesses know and they are watching, waiting and cheering you on. Your brothers and sisters across the earth know and we are binding together in unity and oneness, with humble and pure hearts to strengthen and encourage one another as we prepare for the greatest outpouring of His power and glory of all time. The Spirit knows as He empowers and equips you for what only you can do. Jesus knows as He sits in His heavenly authority at the right hand of God holding onto your inheritance He purchased for you. Even the kingdom of darkness knows and has been doing everything possible to prevent you from realising and activating your God given assignment, identity and authority.

And I know. I know you are called for such a time as this. I know you are positioned. I know you are in the perfect place, no matter how imperfect it may appear. Do not miss your opportunity, do not live in complacency, do not allow your assignment to be passed on to someone more willing. God doesn't need you, but He is wooing you, asking you, wanting you and inviting you to partner with Him. Say yes! Say yes to partake in the greatest story of all time! You are called to a significant purpose and part to play in His plan, but it's an invitation that you are required to respond to. And silence isn't neutral, it's a very clear answer - a definitive decline.

It's imperative we fasten our thoughts on Jesus so that we can remain faithful to our calling and not miss out on the victors prize (1 Cor 9:24-27), because I can guarantee it will get tough. It will be difficult. It is not going to be a walk in the park. There will be opposition, attack, persecution and suffering for saying yes to Him. There will be a costly price you will be required to pay. We are never promised that this life with Jesus will be easy, but there are countless promises to say that it will be joyful, powerful, extraordinary, and completely worth every second. When you step into eternity you will have no regrets for saying yes to the King of Kings, but you will have every regret for saying no, or not even realising what was at stake.

It is time to say yes to the call. It's time to ask the Spirit to unveil your eyes, to purchase eye salve and to be able to see in truth the hour we are in. It is time to open your spiritual eyes and ears - maybe for the first time ever, maybe to tune in even finer. It is time to not just know your identity as a child of the King but to arise and activate, to take up possession of what is rightfully yours, to walk in the power and authority of the name of Jesus and to live in the security of your identity in Him. It is time to surrender to the purging and purifying process - perhaps for the first time or to ask for a deeper illumination of the depths of your heart for Him to prune, purge, purify and polish.

It's time to let go of offence, bitterness, hurt, pain, woundedness and unforgiveness and to ask Him to heal those deepest places of your heart. This is not your identity, you are not a victim and it is not your story. It's time to unite together, with one heart, one mind, one purpose, in one accord. It's time to move onward and upward from not just forgiveness, but to love - a whole other level of obedience and action that is required of us. It's time to love one another and show the world who our God really is, as He loves through us.

It's time to live consecrated and separated for a holy cause. It's time to let go of complacent, casual Christianity that conforms to the culture around us and compromises God's holy call. It's time to draw a line in the sand and decide once and for all which side we're going to stand on. It's time to say no to the things that grieve God and His Spirit, it's time to get rid of lifestyles that don't glorify Him. It's time to obey His Word, at its very word.

It's time to overthrow the enemy in our lives. It's time to take back the power and authority over our very selves. It is time to overflow to all around us with all that God has given us. It is time to stop living for ourselves and our own pleasures, agendas, image and empires and live for His values, His heart, His desires and His will.

It's time to develop, pursue, seek and hunger after the lifestyle of intimacy - living from His presence, abiding in Him. It's time to live the ascended life - those with clean hands and a pure heart are invited to ascend the holy mountain (Ps 24). Let Him wash you clean as the Bride makes herself ready. It's time to live from our position of authority - seated in the heavenlies in Him. Our greatest pursuit in this life must be His heart, His face, His presence, His love, His truth. Him! Everything will flow from this as His deep love cascades over us, into us, through us and from us, transforming everything it crashes into.

It's time to overthrow the powers and principalities of the unseen realm. It's time to take on - with divine, strategic, spiritual intelligence - the strongholds over our cities, regions, lands and nations. It's time to conquer the ancient spirits and strongholds who we as the Church have given legal access and authority to remain in our land, because of our mixture, tolerance and union with the very powers we think we're attacking. It's time to tear down the alters, smash down the pillars, destroy the idols and remove all other gods from the midst of our congregations, gatherings, denominations and movements. It's time to come out of her - Babylon - for she is being judged as God's justice and righteousness is administered, and if we are found *in* her, we too will be caught up in her great fall. It's time for the Church to be truly set apart from the world around us, with no mixture or union with her abominations. It's time to finally engage - as a mighty end days Bride - the battle in the heavens, through wisdom, discernment and walking completely in step with the Spirit as we arise in our authority and live as the true sons and daughters of the living God, seated as kings *in* Him, reigning as priests of the royal priesthood and walking in truth, justice, boldness and fear of the Lord through the voices of the pure prophets.

It's time to recognise that we have entered the era where we will see His power and glory displayed to the world like never before and the great awakening and reviving of our hearts and homes to host the harvest will come through the humility, purity, maturity and unity of God's remnant people as His Bride makes herself ready for His imminent return. It's time to believe that He has called you, chosen you, equipped you, empowered you and He is inviting you to arise into your position as His child and partner with His plan and purpose.

Beautiful Bride of Christ...it is time! Awake! Arise! Esther's emerge! You are perfectly positioned for purpose, *for such a time as this*. Say yes to the King of Kings for the mighty call of this era!

Forever your fervent sister in Christ,

Nat xxx

MOUNT OF OLIVES PUBLISHING

This book is also available as an ebook through Amazon, on Kindle, and an audio book on Audible. If you have enjoyed reading or listening to this book, we would love your support by writing a review on Amazon.

Mount of Olives Publishing offers an exciting new publishing option that releases Kingdom voices - *Scribes of the New Era* - who have a powerful story, testimony or message to share, and particularly those who carry a prophetic and/or reformational anointing. We provide many advantages of traditional publishing, yet take away the hassle, stress, and technical skills required by self-publishing which can be overwhelming and daunting for a creative author. Have your book shared across the earth, *for such a time as this.*

For more information or to submit a manuscript, you can find us on mountofolivespublishing.com

ABOUT NATALIE FULLER

Natalie is a passionate and intimate lover of Jesus Christ, a pursuer of the heart of the Father and seeker of the presence and friendship of the Holy Spirit. As a prophetic voice she is called to encourage, exhort, empower and equip the Body of Christ through teaching and preaching and to draw all people to the intimate love of God. She longs to see people healed and liberated into wholeness, strengthened and established in faith and set free into their identity and authority of God. Natalie writes, preaches, teaches and ministers with the prophetic edge of a reformer and a great faith for the future of the Kingdom of God.

Natalie is a mother of five young children - Hugo, Everly, Fleur, Ophelia & Séraphine - and a wife of 20 years to Gavin. Together they have church planted and pastored churches and creative communities in Sydney, Australia, which led to their various ventures of collaborations with multiple remnant ministries across the earth today.

Natalie is studied and qualified in counselling and psychology as well as ministry and theology. She is a passionate preacher, speaker, teacher and prophetic voice and loves to write and share His heart throughout the Kingdom and across the earth.

To contact Natalie for any enquiries or bookings please email nat@nataliefuller.co
To follow her on social media, you can find her on Instagram: @nataliefuller.co

Made in the USA
Columbia, SC
02 May 2025

57477737R00124